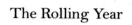

The Rolling Year

THE ROLLING YEAR

Listening to the Seasons with Vivaldi

HANNAH FRENCH

faber

First published in 2025
by Faber & Faber Limited
The Bindery, 51 Hatton Garden
London EC1N 8HN

Typeset by Typo•glyphix, Burton-on-Trent, DE14 3HE
Printed and bound in the UK by CPI Group (UK) Ltd, Croydon, CR0 4YY

A CIP record for this book
is available from the British Library

ISBN 978–0–571–39199–8

Printed and bound in the UK on FSC® certified paper in line with our continuing
commitment to ethical business practices, sustainability and the environment.
For further information see faber.co.uk/environmental-policy

Our authorised representative in the EU for product safety is
Easy Access System Europe, Mustamäe tee 50, 10621 Tallinn, Estonia
gpsr.requests@easproject.com

2 4 6 8 10 9 7 5 3 1

for Thomasina

'. . . there are remarkable things all the time, right in front of us, but our eyes have like the clouds over the sun and our lives are paler and poorer if we do not see them for what they are.'

Jon McGregor, *If Nobody Speaks of Remarkable Things*
(London: Bloomsbury, 2002)

'These, as they change, Almighty Father, these
Are but the varied God. The rolling year
Is full of thee.'

James Thomson, *The Seasons*
(London: John Millan, 1730)

Contents

PART FOUR: WINTER

Prelude

'Hang on, you're heading *home* at nine this morning?' The taxi driver had barely drawn breath in the twenty minutes since we'd left BBC Broadcasting House and, stopping at the lights, it was as if he had suddenly realised the time. It's the lot of a Radio 3 Breakfast presenter, I tell him. Quick as a flash, he replies: 'Radio 3 – the classical one?' I nod. 'Oh, *I* know classical music,' he says, and bursts into the opening of Vivaldi's *Four Seasons* before adding: '*Proper* classics, those are.'

The lights change. Pedal to the metal, and I'm pinned to the back of the seat. Not bad for 300 years old either, I muse out loud as we skid to a halt again. 'No – 300? Well, they've done all right.' I ask him if classical music is his bag. 'Don't know really, but I like *The Four Seasons* – Vivaldi, and Frankie Valli.'

Antonio Vivaldi's *The Four Seasons* has long been a gateway into classical music. There's a power in the work's attention-grabbing melodies, toe-tapping motor-rhythms and rich harmonies that gets into the bones. My daughter had an interactive story book when she was little, a journey through the seasons that we'd read every day. She'd haul the heavy hard-backed book onto the sofa so we could curl up and trace our fingers around the beautiful illustrations, tracking the changing scenes through spring flowers, summer sun, autumn leaves and winter snow. There were buttons to press and snippets of Vivaldi's music would strike up, prompting her to leap to her feet and dance. She'd march, lips pouting and arms swinging, then twirl with reckless abandon around the living room. At what point do we stop doing this? When does our dancing to classical music become confined to the privacy of a kitchen or a shower, if anywhere at all? This music was always supposed to make us move.

While dancing may not be on the cards, crowds continue to step out for *The Four Seasons* – especially when candlelit performances are promised. But for all their richly deserved popularity, the worldwide fame of these four violin concertos has made them victims of their own success. They're the stuff of on-hold music, the strains to which you roll your eyes, before inevitably humming along as you wait for a GP receptionist, airline company or bank. They are tasked with powers of jollity in any number of patience-sapping scenarios.

If you're new to classical music, Vivaldi's *The Four Seasons* is a perfect way in. It's music that has drama, tension, great tunes and an impressive soloist – exactly what you might imagine classical music ought to deliver.

If you're not new to classical music, *The Four Seasons* remains a set of four concertos that you think you know, or you might even consider you've heard one too many times. However, I'd wager that if you sit down and give the work a close listen, you'll realise you don't actually know these four concertos as well as you thought you did. It turns out that there's far more to this work than first meets the ear – stories to be told and secrets to be unlocked, which help explain how it has stood the test of time.

Back to my cabbie, and there's been minimal progress getting home. London's rush hour spills on into the morning and as we inch along the Holloway Road, he's moved on to another bit of *The Four Seasons*. The singing has also evolved into whistling and, having been up since 4 a.m., I'm not wild about this development. He swings an impromptu right turn and we take off down a rat-run littered with excruciatingly bouncy speed bumps. Our conversation about classical music wanders freely, in the way that new companions jabber on about half-baked ideas and personal experience. Then it strikes me how, in certain situations, a companion is all you need to give you the confidence to explore.

In the depths of the pandemic, a listener wrote to me: 'I've not left the house for days, but I've had you on the radio, so I've not really been on my own.' Radio presenters across the country were overwhelmed with messages like that; the radio was the companionable, friendly voice in dark and lonely days. Ironically, the process of making radio can be pretty solitary. Preparation and production may be a team sport, but when you're presenting live, everyone else is on the other side of a soundproofed glass window. Yes, you can wave at them, and discuss and adapt the show while the music plays out, but when your mic is live, you're on your own. To counter this, I often imagine an eclectic bunch of friends in my car, or around my kitchen table – that way I can tell each of them different things about the music that might interest them.

Arriving home, I flop onto the sofa, open my notebook and scribble down: *The Four Seasons, a Companion*. My taxi driver had well and truly proven that *The Four Seasons* is still a way into classical music, and that there are plenty of people who just need a geeky friend like me to lead them past the on-hold music to Vivaldi's world beyond. That's where we find that these seasonal violin concertos have the power to ground us in our own experience of marking, observing and celebrating the rolling year.

Introduction

Nestled between the likes of Beethoven's 'Ode to Joy' and Puccini's 'Nessun dorma', Vivaldi's *Le quattro stagioni* (*The Four Seasons*) is consistently found in the top-ten charts of popular classical music. Countless concert programmes, more than one hundred film soundtracks and any number of TV and radio adverts have ingrained these concertos into the classical music of our cultural consciousness. But what do we truly know about this iconic music? The short and rather surprising answer is: not a lot.

Vivaldi's original manuscript is lost, and with it all the information we'd usually garner to work out the origins of the composition and its first performances. It's one of the many black holes in the history of music. A fair amount of detail about Vivaldi's life is lost, too. That's less surprising, perhaps: few musicians of the age kept a diary and employment records were famously patchy, but in this case it's led to some pretty wild theories. For example, we know that he was a priest; however, there has been speculation from some quarters that he could have also been a spy. While this is highly unlikely, he was certainly an extraordinary man with an extraordinary musical mind, and one of the most important composers of his age.

The Four Seasons has survived and thrived because it was published as part of a collection of twelve violin concertos by Vivaldi in Amsterdam in 1725. This is not where its story begins, but it's the first point of certainty in its origin. It confirms that Vivaldi himself ascribed the individual titles *La primavera, L'estate, L'autunno* and *L'inverno* (*Spring, Summer, Autumn* and *Winter*), and included corresponding sonnets, likely of his own creation. He very deliberately and comprehensively tapped into the ultimate shared human experience: the seasons of the year.

Across art, literature, architecture and fashion the idea of the turning – and returning – four seasons is universal. They offer a neat and tidy view of the year, a concept as popular in naming hotels and restaurants as it is in inspiring artistic tableaux – although perhaps their most famous representation is in the pizza. The four distinct toppings of a *Quattro stagioni* resonate with Vivaldi's compact concertos in that there's little time to be bored by a single flavour. Perhaps it's the rapid pace at which Vivaldi's musical ideas form and evolve that makes them, like the pizzas, so instantly appealing and artistically nutritious.

There are plenty of fresh, dramatic concertos from eighteenth-century Italy, but very few have such memorable subject matter. Seasons, when they are not explicitly linked to months, allow for a universality of understanding, and their simple titles transcend any language barrier. You certainly don't need to be aware that Vivaldi put poetry alongside *The Four Seasons* to appreciate these concertos – in fact, many people who've known the work for years remain blissfully unaware of the sonnets. In their wordless form, the concertos are untethered to time and place and remain relevant in every age.

Time marches, but the years roll – season to season. It's a neat analogy for someone like me, who currently uses a wheelchair. The roll is constant and waits for no one, whether progressing smoothly and predictably, or cartwheeling chaotically. But without that constant circularity of the turning year, we wouldn't experience the yearning for the *return* of a particular season. Knowingly or not, we ache for the seasons to turn, longing for the cyclic moments that bring happiness and contentment, whether lighter evenings or festival celebrations. It's not just the big stuff either, but the little wins of life: stretching our toes wide in sandals or reaching for a winter coat only to rediscover lost gloves and a favourite lip balm.

Our seasonal experiences are bound up in memory. For me, spring sparks renewed outrage at the injustice of being allergic to pollen yet adoring the smell of freshly cut grass. Thoughts of summer drift to my honeymoon: a route plotted across Tuscan towns according to gelaterias as much as the sights, and long evenings dreaming up plans while swallows soared the pink skies. In my mind's eye, autumn is the sight of my toddler jumping for joy in the golden leaves that carpet Ontario's woodlands, her discovery of long shadows and her wide-eyed reaction to her first taste of warm apple cider (the Canadian, non-alcoholic variety). And finally, winter evokes the visceral memory of riding hairy ponies across Yorkshire moors in the bitter cold, teenage hands blue on the reins as we raced the fading light to get home. I know that you will have your own equivalent memories inexorably attached to each season.

Is Vivaldi's *Four Seasons* a musical postcard of memories from eighteenth-century northern Italy? The vibrant port of Venice and the more rural setting of Mantua perhaps go some way to explaining these four concertos' alchemy of lyricism, scenery and poetry. Are they a keepsake of events from the composer's own life, a musical equivalent of his photobook of annual events? Vivaldi's seasons are certainly a clear-cut, equal quartering of the year, characterised by distinctive key colours, and textures. While never sugar-coating the brutality of each season, they remain the epitome of the year's dependable pattern. If that's the reassurance we seek – consciously or not – in our fragile, fractious lives, then they continue to deliver in spades, and it only adds to their popularity. Yet increasingly, those neatly compartmentalised seasons are not our shared twenty-first-century experience. Thanks to air conditioning, central heating, ease of travel and the availability of food from around the world, we can live our lives *in spite of* the seasons. Add into this mix the widespread and devastating impact of climate change, which is wreaking havoc with seasonal weather, and no wonder our body clocks are out of whack.

A poster takes pride of place in our kitchen, 'A Seasonal Guide to British Fruit and Vegetables', and we vaguely attempt to live by it. My husband is militant about asparagus. It's been singled out for special attention, and we eat it by the lorryload, but only from mid-April until the end of June. It's off the menu when it's flown in from Peru. I approve of that, though I miss it the rest of the year and am loath to highlight the short season of aubergines . . . The calendar is aspirational, and as tidy as Vivaldi's four quarterings, but in reality we know the year is messy. Harvest times vary with unseasonable weather, and at best the seasons blur at the edges rather than cadencing at the end of a concerto. Their durations and characteristics are now changing so fast that there may well come a time when Vivaldi's seasons carry keener nostalgia for their defining qualities and segmented vision of the year.

Change may feel inevitable, far from our control, but the rhythm of the seasons can still serve to counter the accelerating pace of life if we're prepared to embrace it. Take the recent trends in field-to-fork cookery: the move to living according to the bounty of seasonal produce is a way to help us treasure the resonances and qualities of the year. There's a healthiness and power to be found in observing seasonal change, which can in turn generate a grounding effect in our lives, particularly when we spend so much of them online. Can music play a part in this?

There's rarely any mysticism in the way you listen to classical music: you might put it on as you cook, clean or work, and if I say that's listening 'passively', it's not to suggest you're not listening properly; rather, that we frequently appreciate music while doing something else. To stop and listen more consciously demands your time – yet it offers rewards in abundance: experiences that catch you staring into the middle distance, or staying put in your car in order to hear to the end of a piece. Your day is altered because of it; you stopped, and it stays with you. Think of this as active listening, something you commit to as if you'd decided to attend a live performance.

Why don't you try it now, for fifteen minutes or so? Perhaps with *Winter* from *The Four Seasons*. No one is watching you; no one is judging you. It's an experience in which you choose who you want to be; in my musical mind palace I often walk around, something I certainly can't do in reality. Closing your eyes might help, or sipping a drink, or doodling on the back of an envelope to stop your mind wandering to work, a to-do list or any area of potential stress. There are no rules, no correct or incorrect reactions. You don't need to know the names of the musicians playing, where they're from, how old they are, how good their techniques are. Instead, you might marvel at textures in the music, as if they emerge like fabrics. Your ear might be drawn to the top-line tune, or to the bass or the inner parts, perceiving the layers of music as if Vivaldi was coating a canvas with paint.

Stopping for just fifteen minutes is enough to make a world of difference to your day – and longer term, too, if it becomes a habit. You probably took deeper breaths while listening, your mind whisked away from the moment – not necessarily completely calmed, but distracted, distanced from day-to-day stresses. The fact is, for that short time you were part of a creative process. Vivaldi's musical designs always involved you – he wasn't writing for himself; he intended you to be caught up in the world he created and to feel you belonged there. You could say that listening in this way is escapism, but perhaps it's better described as a grounding.

A way to expand this listening experiment is to listen to each of *The Four Seasons* in its specific season. If you do, you'll hear more immediate resonances with the natural world around you; there is purpose and meaning to be found in listening to music according to the season it was intended for. Many years ago, when I was lecturing at the Royal Academy of Music, I gave my class of students the task of listening to Johann Sebastian Bach's *Christmas Oratorio* over the Christmas holiday. Pretty heavenly homework, by all accounts, but there was a catch. I didn't want them to just bung it on when they were getting glammed up for a Christmas party, or while they were distractedly checking for updates on social media. I especially didn't want them to listen to it all in one go the day before term started again. You see, contrary to the suggestion made by its title, the *Christmas Oratorio* is not one work, but six cantatas written for church services over six feast days of the festive period. The dates and themes are as follows:

25 December (Christmas Day) – the birth of Jesus

26 December – the announcement to the shepherds

27 December – the adoration of the shepherds

1 January (New Year's Day) – the circumcision and naming of Jesus

The first Sunday in the New Year – the journey of the Magi

6 January (Epiphany) – the adoration of the Magi

The longest cantata is about twenty-seven minutes and the shortest is around twenty-two minutes, so I asked my students to set aside a maximum of half an hour on each day to do their listening. I sent them an email on each specific date, with a link to a recording – all they were required to do was check their emails, click on through and listen. It was up to them *how* they wanted to listen – on their own or not, with a score or not, with a translation of the words if they wanted. They could make notes if they felt the urge to, but I didn't need to see them; I just wanted to talk about their experiences in the first class of the new term. The point was that they made time for a cantata on each of the set days. Here is some of the feedback they gave:

I liked that we were all listening to the same things
each day even though we were in different places
across the world.
It's a cool way to listen to a really long piece.
It feels like I've had a Bach-style Christmas experience.
The music stayed with me through the day.
I missed listening on the quiet days between the feast
days.

These comments summarised, to my mind, the essence
of seasonal listening. The *Christmas Oratorio* experiment
captured the sounds of a very particular time and place,
and in the hyper-individualised modern day made a
musical experience feel more communal, more connected.
Each year I listen to it in this way; it makes me part of a
continuum of people experiencing the passing year and
expressing it in music.

That is the impetus for this book: a companion for
exploring one of the most famous pieces of music in the
world and with it, entry into a world of seasonal listening. Read it any way you wish, cover to cover or dipping
into a season; perhaps enjoy listening to each seasonal
concerto before or as you read about it.

Until the fall of the Republic of Venice in May 1797,
the city eschewed our familiar Gregorian calendar, and
followed the ancient Roman custom of beginning the
year on 1 March. I'm therefore mirroring Vivaldi's
musical year in the structure of this book, with a life

cycle of the seasons starting, as he did, in spring. Spending a year with these four concertos offers us the chance to unlock their secrets, and the potential to answer the questions of where, when, why and for whom they were written. I've divided each season into three chapters, corresponding with the three movements of each concerto and their accompanying sonnets, which are newly translated here by poet Kate Wakeling. Through each chapter, possibilities open up for us to hear afresh the sounds Vivaldi heard, imagine the air he breathed, taste the harvest and glimpse the effects of severe meteorological events on his landscapes. Even though this music has such a strong narrative, it prompts wildly subjective interpretations and so, in addition to the views of myriad musicians, I seek out the perspectives of cooks, ornithologists, architects, art historians, wine experts and medics in order to gain a broader understanding of Vivaldi's world. When time and action slow in the middle movements, there's an opportunity to glimpse Vivaldi as he progresses through the seasons of his own life, and between each concerto we see the development of the *Four Seasons* themselves. Using the analogy of nature, we can track the concertos' life cycle – from seeds of ideas and innovations to their long legacy far beyond Vivaldi's Italy. We find their roots and shoots in early eighteenth-century performances and witness them branching out through publication in 1725 before gathering the fruits and flowers of recordings and sowing new seeds through the many re-imagined, re-composed versions of the concertos over the last century.

My aim is not to demystify *The Four Seasons* – the work's aura is far too strong for that; rather, this is an invitation to give time to these concertos, to be surprised by them – however well you think you might know them – and see where they might take you. Whether we engage with seasonal music on the go or with new-found focus and curiosity, listening habits can ground us in the year, providing a sense of stability and change, and a reminder that messages of hope and comfort are always there if we stop to look for them.

The Inspiration of *The Four Seasons*

Antonio Vivaldi's name may be synonymous with *The Four Seasons*, but he was far from the first Baroque composer to be inspired by the subject of the rolling year; seeds of the seasons can be found scattered all over Europe.

In the mid-seventeenth century, Christopher Simpson (*c.*1605–69), a distinguished viol player, composer and one of the most important English writers on music of his age, composed *The Seasons*, a set of four suites for viol consort (forerunners of today's string instruments). Each begins with a Fantasia, or Fancy, and is followed up by two elaborate, embellished dance movements: an Ayre, or Almain, and a Galliard. Simpson leaves no further instructions, nor descriptions of the seasons, but your mind's eye might take you to his family seat up on the North York Moors to conjure migratory birds soaring the big skies, shadows playing on Yorkshire stone, and the vast landscape of heather and gorse either baked by the summer sun or frozen solid in midwinter.

If you stay on these shores, but head to the end of the seventeenth century, you'll find Henry Purcell (1659–95) inspired by the seasons in his semi-opera *The Fairy Queen*, dubbed the most lavish and expensive show of the decade.

In Act IV, Oberon announces the end of winter, wakes Titania and commands a 'Masque of the Seasons' to celebrate their reconciliation. A springtime soprano bids 'all your sweets before him lay / Then round his altar, sing and play', while a high tenor keeps the mood buoyant for summer with flowers for all who are 'smiling, wanton, fresh and fair'. The voice parts get lower with each season, and the tempo slows too; and so by autumn, a melancholy baritone offers 'many-colour'd fields and loaded trees', and winter's bass sings of a season that's 'pale, meagre, and old / First trembling with age, / And then quiv'ring with cold.' As the music is numbed by frosts and snow, the bass singer prays to Phoebus to restore the seasons and roll them back round to sprightly spring. It's a vision of the seasons associated with music, and not only the weather, but also age and activity.

Over in France, Henry Purcell's near contemporaries, the composers Jean-Baptiste Lully (1632–87) and Pascal Collasse (1649–1709), hit upon the idea of the four seasons for their *Ballet des saisons*. A spectacle for the grounds of the Château de Fontainebleau, it was an event that held up a mirror to current power play at court. To give a taste, meet three aptly cast main characters. First, King Louis XIV in the role of 'Spring', setting forth his plans for France – to renew hope and vigour among his subjects. This seems proper and predictable; however, opposite him is 'Diana, Goddess of Light and Queen of the Open Sky', played not by his pregnant queen but by the wife of the king's brother Philippe. 'Madame, la duchesse d'Orléans', known not by her given name of Henrietta, but simply as 'Madame', was rumoured to be having an affair with Louis at the time – and as the pair often met outdoors, 'Queen of the Open Sky' was particularly fitting. Lest he should forget his situation, Philippe was very deliberately cast as a lowly grape harvester in melancholy autumn. Symbols and allegories lived long in the memory when it came to courtly entertainment, and the *Ballet des saisons* was an ideal vehicle for sending messages to spectators.

When Collasse added extra music to the ballet in 1695, he introduced four pairs of lovers, each to be tested by the quarters of the year. The flighty young Zephyr and Flora appeal to the pleasures in 'Spring'; the doubting Pomona and her changeable love Vertumnus eventually unite in 'Summer'; a wine-fuelled Bacchus and Ariadne extol marriage in 'Autumn'; and 'Winter' tells the icy tale of Boreas and Orithyia overcoming all jealousy. In the conclusion, Apollo appears and congratulates the seasons on banishing discord, inviting everyone to enjoy games and pleasures.

If you sensed a little seasonal competition there, it's made explicit in the popular Baroque opera *Pomona*. Its most famous setting was made in 1702 by the leading German opera composer Reinhard Keiser, and the plot sees seasonal deities take part in a superiority contest. Among a cast of gods and goddesses familiar from

Collasse's ballet, Pomona – goddess of fruit-bearing trees and gardens and this time assigned to autumn – spells out the idea of the seasons as life's stations, but spats break out on stage as the gods insist on the relative merits of each. Finally, the ruler of the gods, Jupiter, arrives to resolve matters and for inspiration looks to the patron of the production: the King of Denmark. Equating King Frederick IV and Queen Louise with the divine autumnal pair Pomona and Vertumnus, Jupiter decides in favour of marriage, and so Pomona receives the crown of victory – and the title of the opera.

This sample of Baroque operas and suites paints a picture of the four seasons as a familiar trope for seventeenth- and eighteenth-century audiences. The associations with particular deities, stages of human life and visions of the weather and landscape were deep-rooted, represented in illuminations, tapestries, paintings and poetry.

Enter Antonio Vivaldi and some new ideas. His first innovation in *The Four Seasons* is in the detailed narrative of the music – his decision both to publish accompanying sonnets and to label the music to show exactly what is being depicted and where. As a result, he is often credited with writing the first 'programme music', not that he knew or used the phrase himself. It was the piano virtuoso and composer Franz Liszt, who articulated the concept a century later, describing 'a programme' as 'a preface added to a piece of instrumental music, by means of which the composer intends to guard the listener against a wrong poetical interpretation, and to direct his attention to the poetical idea of the whole or to a particular part of it.'[1] Liszt admitted that composers had been doing this for years, whenever a descriptive title was added to a piece of instrumental music. It had been commonplace in keyboard pieces: for example, William Byrd's fifteen-movement suite *The Battell,* which he completed in 1591 and to which he added subtitles including 'The Marche to the Fight', 'The Retraite' (The Retreat) and 'The Burying of the Dead'. In *The Four Seasons* Vivaldi not only adds titles and introduces sonnets, but also, in contrast to his predecessors, describes extra effects directly in the performers' printed parts. He fully intended to make the seasonal scenes explicit in the music, giving the musicians the poetic directions that previously would have been the preserve of singers in the texts of songs.

The second of Vivaldi's major innovations in *The Four Seasons* was the decision to express a seasonal narrative through violin concertos. A virtuosic piece for soloist and band of string players may seem a natural choice for a talented violinist like Vivaldi, and the concerto as a genre was currently very much in fashion. However, it was a fixed form principally defined by solo sections and a ritornello. Literally the 'little return', the ritornello was an instrumental chorus that the ensemble players would come back to after each virtuosic display from the violin soloist. The form quickly became standard, but Vivaldi proved that it could be far more flexible. A concerto could follow the narrative through delaying or altering the ritornello, and in doing so toy with audience expectations. In *The Four Seasons*, this plays into the gradual revelation of the shifting fortunes of various characters throughout the year.

Vivaldi didn't stop there, either. Rather than portraying the allegorical visions of the year, as favoured by previous composers, he introduced the modern concerns of the eighteenth century. You can still find plenty of mythological elements – his north Italian musicians would have known the names of the winds, or spotted the Arcadian themes – but it's the psychological responses to nature that define his account of the rolling year. For Vivaldi, the priority is not to portray a bucolic idyll but to engage emotionally with the fears and joys prompted by the realities of each season. This had been done before in isolated operatic storm scenes, or depictions in songs of individual seasons, but to reassemble the complete year in this way points to a new philosophy and way of portraying the world in music.

You can see this immediately in an overview of Vivaldi's choice of musical keys for each concerto, a decision keenly relevant in an age that placed increasing emphasis on the power of different keys to draw specific emotional responses. *Spring* begins in E major, not a key Vivaldi often used, but one that the eighteenth-century French composer Jean-Philippe Rameau maintained carried associations with tenderness, grandeur and magnificence – a natural choice for the feelings of new life in spring. *Summer* is in G minor, a key that for early eighteenth-century composers signified anxiety or threat. It's the key Vivaldi uses for many of the fast movements in his concertos depicting storms – his musical palette for violence in nature, and human discomfort. *Autumn* breaks out in the key of F major, the natural key of hunting horns and, in the ears of German theorist Johann Mattheson, a key of generosity, which makes it ideal for the harvest. Finally, *Winter* slips into F minor, which Mattheson notes is 'mild and relaxed, yet at the same time profound and heavy with despair and fatal anxiety', a contradiction perhaps, but so is winter weather.[2]

These keys, from the four sharps of *Spring* to the four flats of *Winter*, describe the musical plan of *The Four Seasons* on the broadest scale – the overall characteristics rather than nuances of movements or specific episodes within them – but they show that Vivaldi chose keys with deep-rooted musical and emotional associations. He opted for major keys for temperate spring and autumn, in which nature is idealised and benign, and minor keys for the extreme temperatures of summer and winter, in which it is rampantly malign and where the focus is on suffering. Taking the long view of the year, this brings balance; a very eighteenth-century way of viewing life, whether in the body, the weather, the world or the universe.

PART ONE
Spring

I: Allegro

Spring has come again.

Hear how the birds sing glad greetings,
how the streams chuckle and murmur
at the warm touch of the breeze.

The sky is cloaked in darkness
(spring will bring her storms)
but soon the bellow of thunder passes.
Peace breathes across the blue
and the birds begin once more
their clear, bright song.[1]

A warm spring breeze flutters through Venice in March. As it wends its way from the leafy boulevards on the eastern island of Sant'Elena to the waterfront promenades of Zattere and the secret palace courtyards in Santa Croce, the city springs alive. Coffee machines hiss to the clatter of crockery, as tourists return to the cafes around St Mark's Square and the already humid city emerges from the cold grip of winter. Just round the corner from where crowds throng the Basilica, the light plays across the trellises of a tiny secluded garden behind the Pietà Church and falls on a terracotta bust of Antonio

Vivaldi. This is a place where he once sat, and if you stop for a moment, look up to the rooflines of the oldest buildings – and maybe squint a little – the centuries fall away. This is Vivaldi's Venice.

His depiction of the season of hope and renewal bursts into our ears with the brightest, most optimistic music of the age and rightly so: spring is the season of sound. Of the five senses, hearing is the one that eighteenth-century audiences would associate specifically with this time of the year. The soundscape of *Spring* is an eternally uplifting combination of courtly dance and birdsong. When we dance, endorphins are released, and when birds sing, there's promise of life – it's a marriage of fresh starts, which features in pretty much every culture. As the music of this brisk, lively opening Allegro unfurls, Vivaldi creates a vision of nature in perfect harmony.

Spring also signifies the first stage in a creative process, in the genesis of a work of art. Violinist Adrian Chandler points out that this concerto is extremely unusual in that Vivaldi chooses not to repeat the opening musical idea. The first six bars are only heard once, and it is the second melody that Vivaldi treats as the ritornello. Perhaps in this way these opening bars instil in us the reality that you can only have a true beginning once. As art often mirrors life, we may find inspiration for this first concerto of *The Four Seasons* in the activities back in the springtime of Vivaldi's own life: his performances, teaching and early operatic ventures. Late seventeenth-century

Venice was not, however, an idyllic setting of dancing and birdsong; rather, it was the gloaming of a golden age. The city's financial fortunes were in decline, and it no longer enjoyed its former status as a world economic or political powerhouse. This dynamic trading post had lost its monopoly on links to modern-day China as other European states expanded their colonies; the Ottoman Empire had taken its lands in the eastern Mediterranean; and, come the new century, old alliances with countries like Austria would collapse in Venice's ongoing wars against the Turks. In short, the merchants and shipping tycoons who had ruled the city needed to diversify, turning into financiers and venture capitalists in the pursuit of transforming Venice from a trading crossroads into a cultural destination. Antonio Vivaldi entered the stage at a moment in which chances could be taken and opportunities seized, although not without risk, and with more than a whiff of financial jeopardy.

Spring brings its own degree of jeopardy, too, as we find in this opening Allegro: dark clouds gather, and thunder threatens. 'March comes in like a lion and goes out like a lamb', goes the old saying, as the temperatures at the beginning of spring are still cold, and in Europe the variability of very localised weather keeps everyone on their toes. Willing temperatures to rise and watching for sudden downpours is a national obsession, not only for Venetians, or Italians, but for Europeans in general. In rural communities − the landscape of Vivaldi's concertos – the threat of bad weather is at the forefront of everyone's mind, since spring is the season of planting, and the rest of the year depends on it.

'Spring is in the air', we gleefully declare at the first opportunity, and it's a phrase that carries both literal and symbolic truths, because the season's ancient corresponding element is air. It's initially represented by Vivaldi through the zephyrs, the warm breezes that promise good weather to come. But air is a volatile element. Aristotle reported its hot and wet properties, which make the air we breathe and the weather that defines the season so changeable. A heated dialogue between the cascading downpour of the band and the frenetic thunder and lightning of the soloist brings a brief early storm to proceedings. That Vivaldi throws in a storm immediately after introducing us to *Spring*'s birds and brook is symptomatic not only of the unpredictability of springtime weather, but also of the idea that the planting of seeds in any new phase, cycle or project will be accompanied by doubts, fears and hazards. However, there's another old saying, 'If it thunders on All Fools' Day, it brings good crops of corn and hay', so this storm heralding spring isn't necessarily ominous. Thunderstorms occur when warm air rises rapidly to charge cumulonimbus clouds, and for the ground to be warm enough for thunderstorms at this time of year suggests an early start to a good growing season. Happily, this appears to be the case in this concerto – a storm in a teacup, the rumble and dramatic flash of a mere twelve bars of turbulence is just enough to ruffle the feathers and promise a year of good crops. The fact that birds have already returned by the end of the movement reminds us that hope springs eternal – and that Vivaldi is a master of birdsong.

—

Wherever the location, spring, the season of sound, opens our ears to the everyday joys of nature. There's nothing out of the ordinary in the babble of a stream, or even the roar of thunder; they are part of the annual waking of the world to new life. However, birds are conspicuous throughout each of Vivaldi's *Four Seasons*, either by their presence or their absence, and so I seek the expert advice of a fellow presenter and keen ornithologist at BBC Radio 3, Tom McKinney, on its cast of feathered characters. In *Summer*, the birds are named in the score, and Tom promises to take me out to find them in situ, but here in *Spring* their songs are sung by a generic flock that takes centre-stage after a brief introduction. That these birds are not named specifically suggests a memory, a deeply ingrained soundscape that Vivaldi and his contemporaries would have associated with the start of the season.

We know nothing of Vivaldi's pursuits as a child or young man, but it's unlikely he was an outdoorsy type. His pale skin would have quickly burnt, but more significantly, a childhood respiratory condition would certainly have limited his physical activities. The birds he and his contemporaries heard in spring were no doubt indicative of the Northern Italian skies in general, with distinctive calls that people didn't have to travel to the countryside to hear, but would have recognised from outside their own windows. These were the sounds that would have cut through the babble of life, a life without today's roar of traffic and planes to distract the ear, and remind people that a new season had begun.

Tom and I pore over the score and agree that, based on the different figures or motifs that Vivaldi writes, there are at least three types of bird here. This creates a depth of sound, which Tom points out is a little like sitting in a hide where you can hear layers of birdsong. The soloist and first violin begin with a duet on one type of call: an accelerating repeated note that turns into a flourish. Tom instantly identifies this as the nightingale, the repeated note entirely characteristic of its call. Having wintered in West Africa, the songbird would reappear in Europe by mid-April at the latest and its call was a universal signal of spring's arrival.

Unintentionally, and yet aptly, Tom and I meet on the centenary of the BBC broadcasting a historic live duet from a wood in Surrey between cellist Beatrice Harrison and a nightingale – a feat of early on-location recording that resonates with Vivaldi capturing the birdsong of the eighteenth century. Nightingales are bountifully represented in music – they intrigue us with their elusive nocturnal song and spring's symbolic link with coming of age, and their call has inspired composers for as long as anyone can remember. They appear in traditional songs like 'One Morning in May'; they are the topic of madrigals by the likes of the Renaissance composers William Byrd and Thomas Weelkes or the Dutch Golden Age composer Jacob van Eyck; depictions of their song abound in pieces such as Clément Janequin's *Le Rossignol,* and Baroque compositions such as Heinrich Biber's *Sonata Representativa* for violin, George Frideric Handel's aria 'Sweet Bird' from *L'Allegro, il Penseroso ed il Moderato* (The Cheerful Man, the Thoughtful Man and the Moderate Man), or his organ concerto *The Cuckoo and the Nightingale.* Vivaldi had all manner of precedents, to say nothing of a specific handbook resource in Athanasius Kircher's 1650 *Musurgia Universalis.* A vast treaty on the workings of music, documenting everything from the mysteries of harmony to the history of instruments and the science of acoustics, it was Kircher's most celebrated work. Among its pages is a much-referenced catalogue of musical birdsong – one that was widely referenced by the likes of Biber, Bach, and Beethoven.[2]

Fig. 1: 'De reliquarum volucrium vocibus' (On the voices of other birds) in Athanasius Kircher's *Musurgia Universalis*.

While the images of the birds may be far from realistic (Tom explains that many would be drawn from dead birds, which accounts for the somewhat lifeless depictions), their notated calls are fascinatingly accurate. The song of the nightingale is the most extensive, with six staves of written-out examples. Here we see a direct correlation with Vivaldi's springtime birdsong: the repeated notes that halve in length as the call grows in intensity, the bird's oscillating calls and the dotted rhythms. There was no need for Vivaldi to spell out the nightingale's identity in the score; like Tom, his audiences would have immediately recognised its song.

But what of the identity of the other birds? The second violin part brings a punctuating flourish, trills, little descending phrases and a dotted, swung rhythm that turns into a trill. Tom spends a while over this one, but decides a contender would be the blackcap: a tiny bird with a big voice, whose song includes a downward sweep and short punctuated chirrups.

A third violin joins in to form a trio for the next call – a fast, leaping song and a series of independent trills. Skylarks would be a good fit for this, Tom reckons. They are exactly the type of bird to be perpetually on the move; and, having been silent throughout the winter, would have arrived in early spring to sing again in northern Italy.

Vittore Carpaccio (c.1465–1525) was considered a definitive painter of Venice, and so we consult an online catalogue of his landscapes for long-standing clues to back up these ideas. *Hunting on the Lagoon* hangs in the J. Paul Getty Museum in Los Angeles and is a prime example of Carpaccio's meticulous attention to the details of the city and its activities. Seven flat-bottomed vessels are featured across the full canvas, propelled by standing oarsmen or gondoliers. They carry hunters and fishers across a rural stretch of lagoon – a stark contrast to the usual view of Venice's gondoliers ferrying tourists across the Grand Canal. The fishing takes place with the help of cormorants, trained to dive and bring fish to the boat; the hunters also shoot with bows and arrows in the shallow waters and drape large silver fish over the bows of the boats. There are reed fences across the water, possibly to corral the fish for their sport, and poles stuck deep into the mud to attract mussels. But could these hunters be after birds, too?

Tom and I zoom in on the background, past the V formation of swans and a solitary crane in flight, to the unmistakable landscape of reedbeds. A scene like this strengthens the idea of the birds that herald the return of spring in Vivaldi's concerto being early-arriving migrating warblers like nightingales, larks and other songbirds, who might make a stop, or even a nest, amid the reeds and mud flats of Venice. We travel to wildlife sanctuaries to catch sight of these birds today, but before the advent of complex road systems and urban sprawl they were far less confined to the reedbeds; these were calls Vivaldi would have heard across the city.

We think of Venice as a city of seafood, but fowl caught by hunters in scenes such as Carpaccio's were a key part of the local diet. Menus or recipes may give further clues to the avian sounds of springtime, Tom suggests, and I turn to a legendary historical Italian cookbook from 1570, a huge tome by Bartolomeo Scappi called *L'arte et prudenza d'un maestro cuoco* (The Art and Craft of a Master Cook). Scappi was arguably the most famous chef of the Italian Renaissance, overseeing meals served to cardinals and acting as personal cook to two popes. At the height of this career, he recorded more than a thousand recipes along with numerous menus that reflected medieval customs and the food fashions of the day, and anticipated upcoming trends. His book was the accepted authority on cooking for some two hundred years, and he dedicates the second of his six chapters to fowl. The first thing to strike me from the latest translation of these recipes is the sheer variety of birds eaten, ranging from familiar ducks, chickens and geese to the types of birds that Vivaldi might have eaten inland in Mantua: pheasant, partridge, quail and grouse. There are recipes for birds as big as turkeys, cranes (crane lasagne anyone?) and peacocks (a major culinary undertaking), but significantly, it seems the Italians, like the Romans before them, had a particular fondness for small game birds. These include songbirds such as larks, thrushes, turtle doves and sparrows, along with waterfowl such as small coots and teal ducks, and many more generic small birds, which we can assume included nightingales.

These recipes linger in detail over care in preparation, including the differences when cooking a young, old, male or female bird. Recipe No. 135 seems most relevant to Vivaldi's *Spring*:[3]

> To spit-roast sparrows, robins, and other small birds, and to do them up.
>
> In the spring when sparrows, robins and other small birds are young, when they are plucked dry immediately after being killed, and without being drawn, they can be roasted on a spit with slices of pork fat between them. In winter though, old birds can be cooked in a larded broth.

Scappi suggests the broth should be made with slices of prosciutto and pork jowl, common spices, prunes and dry visciola cherries, sage tips, must syrup or sugar, and common or muscatel raisins. Admittedly, there is a propensity throughout history for chucking sugar and juices at dishes in order to either preserve or disguise the taste, but the flavour here is much more linked with seasonality. When a bird was in season it would be plucked immediately without fear of the meat being bitter, so the taste of the meat did not need masking with as many fruits. These were lives lived much more by the turning of the year than ours today, and when a bird or any other produce came into season, people clearly adopted a beak-to-claw attitude to reducing waste, with recipes giving ideas as to what to do with gizzards, livers and so on. As a result, delicacies sprang up, such as the bird tongues beloved of the Venetians, the best of which were imported from Cyprus, and which were preserved in fennel flower and then added to fricassees and pottages, parboiled and fried in rendered fat, or, if fresh, cooked on the coals with a little salt. Some of the recipes are not for the faint-hearted, but they show the diversity of diet and bring another aspect to the festive nature of spring – returning songs signal that new dishes will be on the menu. The modern Italian dessert *polenta e osei*, a sponge cake made with hazelnut cream, coated with marzipan and topped with apricot jam and chocolate birds, has memorialised one old savoury recipe that featured polenta topped with quails – or whatever other birds were available.

Back to Vivaldi's first movement of *Spring*: when the birds return after the storm, we only hear one, the repeated call of the nightingale. I'm not suggesting that all the others have been eaten, but it's not out of the question. On the repeat, the nightingale is the only bird required to reinforce the idea of spring, and it signals good weather is on the way. Tom confirms that small songbirds can die of hypothermia if they get rain-soaked, so they hunker down until bad weather passes, and the male birds sing when the rain stops. Shy nightingales keep a low profile at the best of times, so Vivaldi is unlikely to have seen them – and perhaps that's the reason for them being unnamed in *Spring*. But he undoubtedly heard them; their song was truly a common touchstone sound of the season in his time. It's one we should now treasure, as their numbers are falling dramatically – a drop of 90 per cent in the last fifty years is thought to be the result of climate change affecting habitats in Africa, and evolving farming practices across Europe leaving their favourite fallow ground hard to find.

Not long after Vivaldi wrote *The Four Seasons*, he travelled to Rome, where he wrote a number of sacred motets. Among them is *Canta in prato, ride in monte* (Sing in the meadow, smile in the mountain), an alternately joyful and doleful number for soprano that is infused with the same sort of birdsong as we hear in the first movement of *Spring*. The first aria of the motet evokes the nightingale – styled in classical fashion as Philomela – who from the opening bars repeats the characteristic call of the songbird that we hear in *Spring*. Vivaldi would develop birdsong of all kinds in various concertos, sometimes making the birds' identities explicit through titles such as 'The Goldfinch' or 'The Cuckoo'. In this Roman motet we can hear the birds from *Spring* are still on his mind. The soprano who performed it was likely to have been one of the principal singers from his opera productions, as the part demands an excellent voice, and she, like the nightingale itself, would migrate with ease, in her case between theatre stage and church choir. It's further evidence, lest we need it, of how Vivaldi's mind could also move with ease between different musical contexts, and how they met in his seasonal concertos.

II: Largo e pianissimo sempre

The meadow is flushed with blooms.
Leaves whisper on the trees.
Laid soft on the ground
and deep in his dreams,
the goat-herd sleeps,
his dog curled warm at his side.[1]

After the upbeat, refreshing atmosphere of the opening movement of *Spring*, we arrive at an episode of understated drama. To achieve this effect, the music begins in the key of C sharp minor and, technicalities aside, you can immediately hear how this introduces an edgy vibe. Vivaldi's sonnet paints an idyllic picture of flowers across a meadow, one he insists is pleasant and flushed with blooms, but his music creates an uneasiness through undulating waves of sound. Mere moments ago, the opening movement evoked the innocent idea of murmuring streams, but now the whispering leaves create a slightly creepy atmosphere, emphasised by the complete disappearance of the bass line. The action hovers above the ground as a result, and the eerie effect is compounded by the proximity of notes across the ensemble. It plays with our idea of time and space; part of you feels it could go on forever, and another wishes that it would stop. At the centre of it all we find the violin soloist in the role of the sleeping goat-herd, the music suggesting theirs cannot be an entirely peaceful slumber, more a fitful and often-interrupted rest. The texture that really sticks out is the viola. It plays the part of a trusty dog lying beside its master, but it's no calm pooch. It barks. All the way through. Marked 'sempre molto forte e strappato' (always very loud and with 'wrenched' bow), it's the lowest sound we hear, as the cellos and continuo instruments are resting. Without the viola, the high strings would sound far more otherworldly in their sepia vision of the meadow, but the dog is the persistent anchor of the music. Perhaps the barking is repetitive enough that, at a stretch, the goat-herd *can* sleep though it? Maybe it's even a reassuring sound – offering comfort that goats are protected, as the dog scans the horizon. While his bark remains consistently the same, it allows everyone else to get what rest they can. The dog also highlights the strong bond between animals and humans noted around this time by the Scottish philosopher David Hume, who observed that an animal's happiness or misery will 'affect us, when brought near to us, and represented in lively colours'.[2]

—

The middle movements of each of Vivaldi's *Four Seasons* often seem quite removed from the rest of the action, offering a pause for perspective, and so while our violin-playing goat-herd sleeps in the flower-strewn meadow, we'll take our leave of him so that we can glimpse Vivaldi in the springtime of his life. He was a spring baby, born on 4 March 1678, yet on his arrival, little Antonio didn't look or sound too healthy. Breathing difficulties most likely prompted the provisional baptism he was given by the midwife, encouraged no doubt by his mother, whose firstborn, Gabriela Antonia, suffered from 'spasms'. Unbeknown to the young mother, when Antonio was born, two-year-old Gabriela had only three months left to live. Experiences like this make a mother all the more resolute to protect her children – a feeling that transcends time.

Little Gabriela had been the reason for Vivaldi's parents' hasty marriage, not in either of their own parish churches of San Martino Vescovo and San Giovanni in Bràgora, but with bump-on-show at the Church of San Giovanni della Zuecca on the Venetian island of Giudecca. Antonio survived his sister to see his official springtime baptism on 6 May at San Giovanni in Bràgora and to become older brother to five siblings: Bonaventura Tomaso, Margarita Gabriela, Cecilia Maria, Francesco Gaetano and Zanetta Anna.

Antonio's father, Giovanni Battista Vivaldi, hailed from the Venetian-ruled city of Brescia. He had a reputation as something of a hothead and had spent six months in prison for beating up the son of a priest. The Vivaldi family had moved to Venice in 1665, where Giovanni Battista initially plied his trade as a barber, before turning to music. In April 1685, when little Antonio was just seven, Vivaldi Senior assumed the name Giovanni Battista Rossi (on account of his red hair) and took up two prestigious posts: violinist at St Mark's Basilica and *maestro di strumenti* (director of instrumentalists) at the Ospedale di San Lazzaro e dei Mendicanti, one of the city's four charitable institutions. Venice was a city of opportunity for musicians like Giovanni Battista. It was not only her distinctive waterways, currency, army, dialect and seagoing culture of trade that set her apart from the other Italian city states, but also the fact that she was a republic. 'La Serenissima', or 'The Serene One', as Venice was known, had no emperor, royal court or pope, but instead an elected doge, who oversaw the well-established governing systems. Self-preservation was Venice's priority, maintained by a highly developed and arguably somewhat threatening culture of surveillance, but, freed from the constraints of either church or court, she also promoted a world of commercial prospects. While old Venetian families such as the Grimanis and Trons still controlled the commercial interests of the city, a musician of any rank could make a living in the many theatres and churches. Giovanni co-founded the Sovvegno dei musicisti di Santa Cecilia, the Venetian Musicians' Benefit Society, in 1685, and appointed Giovanni Legrenzi, music director of St Mark's Basilica, as its president. Young Antonio was possibly taught by them

42

both, and through them had access to the rich musical traditions of St Mark's.[3]

There was no doubt that young Antonio – who had inherited the family flame-red hair – possessed natural talent, a real flair for the violin and an innate ability to move the emotions of an audience. From an early age he could be found playing alongside his father around Venice, in nearby Padua and in Turin. Giovanni Battista was at one time thought to be one of the best violinists Venice could boast, and received a special mention in the 1700 edition of the visitors' handbook, *Guida de' forestieri* (Guide for Foreigners).[4] Such was the renown of both father and son that they became an essential sight and sound on the itinerary of any aristocratic young man's eighteenth-century Grand Tour of Europe. It seems they enjoyed a harmonious relationship, very much a duo in the limelight, and when Antonio's star rose higher, Giovanni Battista stepped into the shadows to become his son's silent support system.

The distinctive Vivaldi ginger barnet earned Antonio the moniker of 'the Red Priest'. As the oldest son of the family, embarking on the path to priesthood in 1693 was – aside from any spiritual calling – a strategic fast-track to raising the family's social status. The cloth was also deemed a suitable vocation on account of Vivaldi's lifelong respiratory condition, one he described as *strettezza di petto* (a 'tightness of the chest'), which affected him both physically and mentally. As young Antonio trained for the priesthood, he lived at home with his family in the parish of San Marino, serving the local churches of San Geminiano and San Giovanni in Oleo. He was granted a springtime ordination on 23 March 1703; however, two years later his priestly calling all but ended in practical terms. It was no secret that music was his first priority, yet he retained the image of an eccentric cleric for the rest of his life.

Antonio Vivaldi's youthful success as a performer was thoroughly endorsed by local Venetians, who, thanks to the city's wealth of virtuoso violinists, were connoisseurs of great performances. Vivaldi completed a notorious quartet of characters who were the talk of the town. Francesco Maria Veracini, Pietro Locatelli, Giuseppe Tartini and Antonio Vivaldi were a foursome who waged a battle of bows with their sonatas and concertos; musical fencing masters who sparred with one another both on and off stage. It's said that Vivaldi described Tartini as a bad violinist and he retorted that Vivaldi's style was superficial; meanwhile Veracini, known for his habit of quarrelling, even threw himself out of a window after a musical argument − fortunately, he survived. Vivaldi's theatrical, virtuosic violin solos dazzled, and inspired pyrotechnic compositions from the other three, even if they weren't shy to accuse him of trickery − of knowing how to lead imaginations to carry the effects of his technical wizardry even further than his ability to play the instrument.[5]

—

Back to the Red Priest's music, and I'm heading to see violinist Rachel Podger. When the wisteria blooms on the terraced town houses in Camden, you know spring has arrived; that, and when my itching eyes necessitate a dive into the glovebox stash of antihistamines. Driving into Regent's Park, I'm struck by a seemingly sudden change in colour scheme: the pink cherry blossoms that lined the roads only a few weeks ago have given way to lilacs in every shade of purple, and deep-blue ceanothus. London wears spring well. My destination today happily involves drinking tea, the leaves of which were first brought to Britain in the early seventeenth century by the East India Company. Catherine of Braganza, the wife of Charles II, led the tea-drinking charge in the English royal court, and from there the aristocracy took it to their hearts and drawing rooms. The lady of the house was responsible for the ritual, a ceremony of brewing and serving before locking up the expensive product. With the eighteenth century came the import of a greater variety of teas, different grades and price points making the drink accessible to the middle and lower classes, too. In 1717, just as Vivaldi was dreaming up his *Four Seasons*, a certain Thomas Twining opened the first tea shop in London. It was expressly for ladies: the menfolk had their coffee houses in which to gossip and plot, and this was a place for women to do the same. Rachel Podger and I sit down to do exactly that, to talk about the *Spring* concerto and Vivaldi the violinist, and to drink tea.

Dubbed 'the unsurpassed British glory of the Baroque violin', Rachel is one of the great Vivaldi interpreters of our age.[6] Her recording of *The Four Seasons* has won almost every prize going – and don't just take my word for it: the *Financial Times* admired its 'freedom and buoyancy', *Gramophone* magazine hailed its 'serene virtuosity', and its 'myriad subtleties' captivated the reviewer in *The Times*.[7] Rachel and her group, Brecon Baroque, play with great finesse on period instruments: instruments that are either the real thing, or imitations of the instruments of Vivaldi's day. Rachel is one of the few violinists to transcend the personal tastes of fellow musicians, whatever their stylistic preferences when it comes to performing Vivaldi – and string playing in general.

Thinking of springtime, and the seeds of greatness, I wonder where it all began for her. As if holding a mirror up to Vivaldi's life, she beams and says: 'Oh, my father.' It transpires he is a singer and a priest, and that years ago he put together a band of players for a young Rachel to perform with as soloist in the *Spring* concerto. 'Dad spoke to the audience so naturally,' she says, 'he brought it to life.' This has stuck with her. 'When I perform the *Four Seasons*, I always like to read out the sonnets,' she notes, 'or get someone from the ensemble to do it – the audience love it, and it's great when you have an Italian player in the group who can read the original too.' Rachel says that first experience as soloist helped shape her interpretation of the work today. 'They're not easy to play,' she admits. 'You've got to give everything all the time, it's a bit like doing a monologue; even though it's an effort with everyone, ultimately you're telling the story as a soloist.'

Finding and developing her voice as that storyteller led Rachel to playing period instruments, whose sounds prompted Vivaldi to write the effects we find in *The Four Seasons*. 'He was clearly fiery, and I imagine full of energy,' Rachel says with a glint in her eye. 'I reckon he was constantly inventive, no cup of coffee or Prosecco for him in the intervals of his operas; he'd be up there improvising for the crowd.' What, then, makes the violins of Vivaldi's day so special for her?

First, the strings. The experience of playing on the type of strings Vivaldi used – made from twisted sheep intestines – versus modern metal ones is so completely different for Rachel that comparisons are futile, but she finds the key to unlocking the sounds of them in patterns of speech, especially in a programmatic piece like this. 'Naked gut is porous,' she explains, 'so the actual contact point with a gut string is rough and it asks you to relax into it if you want to make a beautiful, warm singing sound – a resonant sound. It's a little bit like letting the voice resonate in your head.' Then there's the bow, which in the eighteenth century had a very different shape to a modern one: shorter, lighter, and more like a Robin Hood bow. Rachel dubs it the 'speech *tool*'. 'You need to be very in touch with what you're doing with your bow,' she counsels, 'it's your intonation when you ask a question; your voice when you're implying a double meaning or telling a joke.' Bring those two things together and the sounds that emerge from Rachel's Baroque violin really do make sense – physical features create meaning in shaping the lines. 'You have parts of the bow or a particular string that you really love,' she reveals, 'and muscle memory will kind of do the job for you, but if in the moment you think "Ah, that sounds good", then "What if I relax that bit of my upper arm?" and it releases the resonance *again*, then you are uncovering the best of the sound.' This is the essence of bringing meaning to the music from the inside, from the very physical shapes of the lines, and it's all part of her interpretation: 'It's how I'll shape the message, the emotion, or whatever it is I'm after, in order to portray the mood of a particular movement.'

And so that is what we experience in this middle movement of *Spring*. Are you the goat-herd, in this moment, I ask, or are you painting a picture of them? 'Oh, it's me,' Rachel shoots back without hesitation, 'and that's what I love about playing the seasons, it's as close to being an actor as you'll get, really stepping into the character, *being* the character.' Go on then, I challenge: set up your scene for this middle movement of *Spring*. 'Well, I'm asleep,' she says, 'I'm enjoying being part of the scenery, and I'll say to the viola player, "You're the dog, you're calling the shots, and you can do with it whatever you like because that's what dogs do", then to the other strings: "You're the murmuring of the leaves, active but gentle in that lovely, balmy breeze that you get in spring – not a cold spring, a warm one."'

For Rachel, there's an intangible, unconscious power to this, and the other middle movements of *The Four Seasons*, something that comes with years spent getting to know the inside of Vivaldi's musical mind, but also with knowing what works in concert, how you might pace yourself through an evening. 'It's the things that you do with your breath, for instance,' she goes on, 'how you prepare for what you know is coming up next without giving anything away, you need this moment just to hold it together, to gather yourself, before daring yourself: "Come on. Do it. Do it!"' It's the first-hand experience of Vivaldi the violinist knowing how to pace a concerto, but especially with *The Four Seasons* in which so much information, imagery and invention is concentrated into mere minutes. As Rachel concludes: 'There is really no figurative hot air.'

Hot tea, meanwhile, flows aplenty and our conversation turns to the rest of Rachel's cast of characters in her group Brecon Baroque; she may be the storyteller, but her ensemble is vital to the success of the production. It turns out that her very first experience of *The Four Seasons* wasn't in fact the time she was soloist in her father's church, but an occasion when she was principal violinist in a children's orchestra performance of *Spring*. She had heard the music before but never *seen* it, and the score shocked her. 'I hadn't realised the extent to which I'd be involved in the principal material, and thought,

"Oh I get to do the birdies for *that* long!"' She laughs at the memory. 'It was exciting and quite a revelation.' Next came the experience of playing it with *single* string instruments, i.e. one player on each part rather than a whole team of violinists, viola players, cellists, etc. It is a completely different experience: chamber music rather than orchestral music. 'There's just much more flexibility,' she says, 'and responsibility to carry your own line; and players rise to it because it's so much fun, responding, reacting together.'

Rachel checks her teapot and gives it a swirl, releasing more aromas in my direction. That's what I love about your recording with Brecon Baroque, I say, the way it smells. She glances my way. I reassure her it's a compliment – the musical smell of blossom on the breeze, or of petrichor (rain on hot dry ground). These are intangible things from a technical, musical perspective, but they are the effects you experience in a top performance, things that are created in the chemistry of an ensemble. I wonder how that dynamic works with her players. 'I'm a player-director,' she says 'so I'm one of them. I don't believe in announcing how it should go because then people will try and do the *right* thing, be "correct", and I don't think that's very interesting. You want to hear the individual voices and inspire players to take risks.' This is the infectious enthusiasm that Rachel gives off, and which makes sense of how she keeps her performances of *The Four Seasons* so fresh, because that is the ultimate challenge for both musicians and audiences. 'These days everyone knows them so well,' she readily admits. 'My taxi driver from the station asked what I was up to and when I asked if he knew *The Four Seasons* he gave me an indignant "*Of course* I know them."' I smile, recognising this scenario. So how do you keep them surprising, fresh, full of the joys of spring? I ask. 'For me, it's about capturing Vivaldi's fiery energy,' she says, 'and for that you go back to the score. I'm afraid it may sound like a cliché but it's always true, go back to the original, not to anyone else's recordings.'

It's about reading the instructions. The score holds the recipes for the seasons, but how you decide to mix Vivaldi's ingredients is your own personal blend. The skill is then communicating that to your fellow musicians, and the audience. 'During the rehearsal, I'll allude to the programmatic elements,' Rachel continues, 'I'll say "Hey, in the rustling bushes moment can we do this?", or "It's not cold enough", or "Cello, I'm drunk here but you're the person steadying me because you're the bass line – if you're as drunk as me, we'll all end up in the gutter," and if they don't know what I'm on about they've got to find out exactly what's going on. Fast.' It sounds again as though Rachel's drawing on her ideas of staging, choreographing, setting the scene for the monologue. 'What makes it fun is when the audience arrives; even though you have your plan and you know the story, it's always different.' This is the musician's intuition, their ability to read a room, both in rehearsal and performance. Acoustics, and the mood of the people within the space, always bring challenges, but add into that a piece that everyone thinks they know, and these issues are compounded. 'If it's a kind of gala event and people are checking their watches, then I'm out to shock,' Rachel grins, 'I'm playing in a way that says, "Oi, you! Look up and pay attention. I'm not having that."' That's exactly the situation Vivaldi was in, playing to people in theatres and milling around court, perhaps another reason why these concertos give so many opportunities for such wild contrast in performance.

My enduring impression from talking to Rachel is that when you play Vivaldi's *Four Seasons* you must *embody* it. It's not painting a scene in music, there are no caricatures; it's more like life: messy and risky. In this light, the middle movements of the *Four Seasons*, such as this one in *Spring*, are poetic, personal *and* practical. Far from being hackneyed stalwarts of the repertory, these concertos contain multilayered, multi-textual music that remains exciting and challenging to play. Rachel makes a final analogy with acting and the stage. 'Actors so often say "Every night is a first night", and this is no different. Every performance you give is to a different combination of people, you owe it to that audience to bring the passion, to show how radical Vivaldi's seasonal visions are.' Put like that, it's a whole year in a single night's performance. No wonder playing these concertos is exhausting – it's meant to be.

Tea drunk, beautiful bone china greatly admired and our spirits refreshed by gossip and the glories of this music (exactly Thomas Twining's intentions for the ladies' tea-room, I'm sure), we each head on to more engagements in London. It's dark by the time I drive home, back through Regent's Park. The street lamps are on and I'm drawn to their beautiful old lantern-like design. They're electric now, rather than the original gas, but you can still imagine the lamp man lighting them for the evening. There's something in their glow that captures Rachel's approach to performance using period instruments to a tee. There is no dulling with the years thanks to the modern electricity; they capture the original feeling – both the practicalities and the magic their designer intended. Similarly, Rachel evokes Vivaldi's age and aesthetic using materials of the day, but powers them with modern energy. If her goat-herd wears modern garb, and dreams of twenty-first-century concerns, she's still reclining in a meadow flushed with blooms with her canine companion by her side. If musical interpretation is going to appeal to modern listeners and still feel right, then it can't help but be influenced by modern elements; after all, we can't backdate our ears, and why would we want to? We are the product of all the intervening musical years, but like those first audiences, we still want to be captivated and shocked by *The Four Seasons*.

III: Allegro pastorale

Listen now
as the merry bagpipes sound.
Deft as air, the shepherds
and all the spirits of the wood
take to their feet
and dance
and dance
in the brilliant light of spring.[1]

Across Europe, the word 'spring' in different languages reveals different aspects of the season. In Old English, 'springan' is the time when plants literally spring up from the frozen earth. In modern Italian, 'primavera' is literally 'first spring', the first flush of the year. But the Latin root is even more evident in the Spanish 'primaveral', pointing to the vernal equinox that occurs every March. Ancient rites and customs to mark the spring equinox vary between different cultures, in both mystical and practical ways. This turning point in the year signals the time to plant seeds, to spring-clean homes or bodies, or to rise early to greet the sun at daybreak. It's a time of rejuvenation, of new intention; an old, magical time in which colour returns, and blossom brings hope. From the green shoots under their feet to the canopy of stars above their heads, everything conspires to make Vivaldi's spirits and shepherds want to dance in the brilliant light of a *Spring* concerto finale.

Bluebells cluster round the old oak trees at Kenwood House in Hampstead one Saturday in April as my friend Hattie McCall Davies and I set out to walk my whippet and talk Vivaldi. Like me, Hattie has Ehlers-Danlos Syndrome, and neither of us moves quickly on either feet or wheels, but the whippet makes up for it by running rings round us both as we head out towards Hampstead Heath. I've known Hattie for years as a professional cellist and TV producer, but I've rarely asked her about her not-so-silent secret passion: the bagpipes. Come on then, I say, Vivaldi's bagpipes that begin the last movement of *Spring* — we're not talking about a Highland fling are we? She laughs and confirms that the instrument Vivaldi heard 'couldn't be further from most people's understanding of what a bagpipe looks or sounds like'. The 'Great Highland Bagpipe' is the perennial image of a piper carrying an instrument associated with national importance, with mourning, with war — a long way from Vivaldi's light-heartedness in *Spring*. 'The Highland bagpipe is certainly an instrument of rigid society, essentially a Victorian invention,' Hattie tells me, 'but bagpipes originally symbolised peacetime, dancing and happiness — they were the instruments of the shepherds.'

My wheels spin between the dusty stones on the path: mercifully it hasn't rained during the past week, otherwise this would be a different and very muddy story. But there's good reason to brave this route. The 790 acres of Hampstead Heath were once farmland: sheep grazed on the Heath until the 1950s; there was an active dairy at Kenwood, built in 1794–6; and shepherds and livestock merchants would stop here for common grazing en route to the London markets. The shepherd is key to the bagpipe story, and if you wanted to hear a piper close to the city, this rural spot would have been as good a place as any.

'Whether in the Middle East, India, North Africa or Europe, the people who have easy access to an animal skin are shepherds,' Hattie says, 'and bagpipes likely developed from a tradition of wind instruments with double reeds – forerunners of oboes – that were used for dancing.' The sound of a bagpipe evokes pride and place, and as Hattie points out, you don't need too much kit to construct one: a bag of hide or animal skin, wood to make a blowpipe, and some cane to make reeds. It makes sense that itinerant shepherds brought both the latest tunes and news from fields and roads to villages and courts, and that their sounds were an aural invitation to dance or celebrate. This is all sounding more spring- and Vivaldi-like by the minute, though 'you have to play one to appreciate it', says Hattie. I give her a withering look.

She's right, of course, and later, in the privacy of my living room, she presents me with two sets of bagpipes. I am a flautist, so the idea of playing the chanter – a pipe that looks like the body of a recorder – feels relatively natural. As far as I'm concerned, the rest of the instrument is an intimidating alien creature. I gravitate towards the smaller one. To state the obvious: the bag is the main event; attached to it are large wooden pipes with internal reeds – they produce the continuous drone, the accompaniment; and the chanter, again with a double reed inside, is the means of playing a tune. Success hinges on filling the bag with air, then applying pressure to expel the air through the drone pipes and chanter to produce the sound. Believe me when I tell you it's easy enough to make a noise – an uncannily sheep- or goat-like bleating noise – but a noise is really *all* I can credit myself with making. The drones pipe up readily enough, but achieving a smooth sound takes all my concentration. It's as if I've just acquired an external, unpredictable extra lung. But the very act of holding, of hugging the bag brings me closer to the notion of this as a very earthbound instrument, animated by air.

'There is something really organic about playing the pipes compared to any other instrument,' Hattie says, 'because you have, or at least you *had*, back in the day (now they're mostly made of synthetic materials), a formerly breathing animal in your arms.' That air is vital, not just in the way it's controlled by the piper, but in the effect it carries to the ears of the people compelled to get up and dance. In Hattie's arms, the small pipes bring that to life perfectly, making a whimsical sound far more evocative of sheep in the pasture than the view of an army barracks. 'The tunes may be specific to a place or time,' Hattie adds, 'but it's the constant drones that bring a true sound of homing, of grounding; they connect you or bring you back to something you can't necessarily describe but that you recognise as the countryside – your homeland.'

This seems to me to be the effect Vivaldi wants to achieve at the beginning of this final movement of the *Spring* concerto: the bagpipe section isn't long, but it's enough to form a connection with a place and a feeling. Its association with spring is deepened by the corresponding element of air required to make the sound – air that flows through this entire concerto, from the breezes in the first movement to the heavy breathing of the sleeping goat-herd, and now the bagpiper inflating the instrument as he calls everyone to dance.

In Vivaldi's sonnet, the word for bagpipe is *zampogna*, and a quick internet search reveals an enormous instrument, the size of an entire inflated goat or sheep. Traditionally the skin was cured with salt (with the hair removed) and turned inside out to create the bag, but it's still strikingly animal-like – a big, pastoral presence. Like all bagpipes, the *zampogna* would vary by region, not only in the size of the bag, but also in the length of the drones and chanters, and, significantly, the number of chanters. In contrast to the bagpipes Hattie let me loose on, a *zampogna* had multiple chanters – which means that they could play in harmony. I click through different examples online, and the sounds that emerge from them are pretty wild: they have a nasal quality yet a simultaneous sweetness, lyricism and windy vibrancy that I wasn't expecting.

There's a logic, then, to the music Vivaldi writes at the beginning of this final movement of *Spring*, recreating the sounds of the *zampogna*: the lower strings – the bass – take on its multiple drones and the muted violins the instrument's characteristic double chanter over the top. But the drones are not continuous here – they re-start four times. Hattie has a theory. 'It replicates the start of the dance,' she says:

> You've got multiple double reeds to get going, which takes quite a lot of air. You need to get the pressure in your bag to a point at which enough air is forced over all those reeds at once, so there's always that feeling of winding up to the max, and Vivaldi's using that for swing, that propulsion and momentum.

In effect, the whole ensemble has momentarily become a *zampogna*: it may only be for twelve bars in this opening sequence, but it's enough to set up that link to the shepherds on the hills. Vivaldi reinforces this idea by including the description 'pastorale' in the brisk tempo description (Allegro), and creates a sense of dancing through the metre: a time signature of 12/8, which means each bar contains four sets of three swinging notes. 'It's the style of traditional Italian *zampogna* music,' Hattie confirms, and it's certainly a trope that other Baroque composers adopt, particularly in Christmas concertos to evoke the shepherds on Bethlehem's hills. 'Another reason for that', Hattie goes on, 'is because shepherds would play bag-pipes around a newborn child's crib, and not only at Christmas but at any new birth in a village.'

In replicating a *zampogna*, Vivaldi is drawing on known traditions of the time to signify new beginnings. For me, his incorporation of these traditions into music for courtly strings brings the rustic and the refined into conflict. Happily, Hattie has thoughts on that too. 'It's because both the shepherd and his bagpipes are becom-ing fashionable; suddenly, courtiers are fascinated with this *other life* that people are living, and so the instrument gets refined and becomes something of a pastoral symbol.' This feels significant if you're developing programmatic music, providing aural short cuts that listeners can latch on to, even if they are sanitised versions of the original. Hattie smiles, before adding, 'It situates them without their having to get involved with the smells of the stables and the reality of the wild side of the instrument – a little like the rise of the rustic-sounding musette in France. Aristocrats didn't want to hold a whole goat, but they wanted that symbolism of nature.'

Vivaldi brings to the fore a springtime stage ready for dancing to the sound of an instrument that wholly

encapsulates the essence of spring. His music then continues with all the essential ingredients to create the classic
sounds of a rustic, pastoral celebration. The repeated
rhythmic patterns convey the steps of the dance; their predictability is a comfort, with nothing to trip up the revellers.
While the soloist's part takes the music to new places in
cascading notes and – suddenly, shockingly – changes
key around three-quarters of the way through to create
some jeopardy, any perceived threat from the sequence of
rising chromatic notes vanishes almost as soon as it has
appeared. The main bagpipe theme returns, and the
nymphs, spirits and shepherds join hands to reprise
the dance. While you might have expected a flashier
finish for this concerto, the lack of one is a reminder that
there is more to come. This is spring's promise, the
season signifying youthfulness and inspiration.

—

The end of *Spring* takes us back to where we began the
season, in Venice – and it was late spring when I first
visited the city, a decade ago, in search of Vivaldi's real-
life nymphs and spirits: the girls and women of the
Ospedale della Pietà.

Before touching down at Marco Polo Airport, I had in
my mind a quixotic vision of floating around a city
already so familiar from countless films and paintings.
My reality was somewhat different. I knew that navigating the cobbled streets and countless bridges in a
wheelchair was going to be an interesting prospect. I'd

been using one for a couple of years at that point, and yet was still learning the hard way about the practicalities of life on wheels. I was at a crossroads in life, faced with the decision of whether or not to continue trying to make a living as a flautist – but before potentially closing the door on this aspect of my career, I wanted to get to the Ospedale della Pietà, an institution synonymous with Vivaldi. Let's call it my Pietà pilgrimage.

The Pietà was a hospice, rather than a hospital, one of eighteenth-century Venice's four illustrious charitable institutions. The other three comprised the Ospedale di San Lazzaro e dei Mendicanti (the Mendicant, where Giovanni Battista was employed), which served war veterans, the homeless and fallen nobility; the Ospedaletto, for orphan boys headed for military service and for the ailing; and finally, the Incurabile, which housed those with incurable diseases – alongside repentant prostitutes. The Pietà was markedly different from the others as the only one that exclusively took in orphans and abandoned children. Its name translates as 'compassion' or 'pity', and it accepted any child of illegitimate birth with no limit on the number, resulting in more than four thousand residents in Vivaldi's lifetime. Governed by around thirty wealthy Venetians, the Pietà received provisions in food and wine from its sister house in the country; it had its own bakery, bank and general shop, and, as with the other three institutions, held music at the heart of daily life. Once a year all four institutions joined musical forces, but for the rest of the time there was a healthy sense of competition between them. However, in contrast to the others, the Pietà would not allow affluent families to take advantage of its facilities – you could not pay for your child to attend. Some said that it suffered from not actively seeking out musically gifted 'legitimate' children – but it maintained an orchestra and choir regardless. Under Vivaldi's charge this was no ordinary group, but a top-flight, professional-standard ensemble, and one comprised entirely of women.

While this was unusual, there was good reason for the all-female talent. In the Pietà, boys were separated from the girls at the age they could learn a trade. They were given a different (better) diet and regime, became apprentices in stonemasonry, carpentry, cotton-beating or weaving, and left for jobs when they were sixteen. Girls, on the other hand, were separated into two categories. The first, the *figlie di comun* (community daughters), studied embroidery, weaving and cookery, learnt to take care of the institution and sold their work in the Pietà shop. The other comprised the *figlie di coro* (daughters of the choir): the musicians. Not only did music bring joy and creativity to this community, but the sixty or seventy girls and women of the *figlie di coro* found status within the Pietà. They had their own separate rooms and apartments and could earn a living. Some paid their way by raising and teaching the younger girls, or accepting occasional performances outside the Pietà, and a select number were permitted to tutor a *figlia in educazione* (daughter in education), i.e. a daughter of a local noble family who wished to learn music privately – although as previously mentioned, these students were not permitted to join the music-making in the Pietà itself. Music brought a new identity. All the girls and women were expected to sing and play, but as they specialised, they assumed surnames that came from the instruments or vocal types they excelled in: for example, instrumentalists Angelica dal Violin, Lucieta Organista and Stella dalla Tiorba; or singers Oliva dal Sopran[o], Cecilia dal Contralto, Vittoria dal Tenor and even Aneta dal Basso.[2]

The idea of a historic place of female music-making held an immediate allure for my pilgrimage, but even more so as the girls and women in Vivaldi's orchestra performed out of view, high up in the church of the Pietà. They were hidden behind iron grilles, so no one was distracted by their gender, nor did they clock whether they had disfigurements or disabilities. Neither hindered their music-making, and the fact that the women couldn't be seen meant that there was no distraction if they had, say, unconventional techniques. I'd spent so long surreptitiously shifting in pain while in full view on stage that the idea of being hidden from view was enticing. In this scenario, no one would see if I stood on one leg, I'd not have to hide winces or the pall of exhaustion, and the effect of pain on my posture would be invisible. The idea that you could move around without anyone knowing or caring was suddenly liberating, and judgement-free. It is the freedom I'd later find in making radio, but that was a long way off at the point of my Pietà pilgrimage. I just wanted to see this space, the mechanics of it, the proportions, and discover the magical acoustics.

The Pietà is just around the corner from St Mark's Square: a ten-minute walk, or wheel, brings you to the waterfront of the Grand Canal, the Riva degli Schiavoni. It's a road you immediately recognise from Canaletto's canvasses of the waterway. However, my plan to see Vivaldi's church, Santa Maria della Visitazione, unravelled almost immediately on meeting the Vivaldi scholar Micky White in the Hotel Metropole. That's because the hotel is now on the site where the church once stood – a great place to recover from the cobbles, but a bump in the road on a Pietà pilgrimage. And it's not even a near-miss. In 1760, less than two decades after Vivaldi's death, its replacement was completed: the Santa Maria della Pietà (also still known as Santa Maria della Visitazione). Once a sacred space used by the Pietà in exactly the same way as the original church Vivaldi knew, it now doubles up as a concert hall, one that boasts innumerable performances of *The Four Seasons.*

Vivaldi was well aware of the building project: a plaque outside records that he was consulted on the acoustics before his death, and the concealed performance areas of the new church replicate the environment of the original chapel more than enough to help me understand how it worked.

Fig. 2: Facade of Santa Maria della Pietà.

The outside of the church was designed by Giorgio Massari. It's relatively simple compared with other ornate Venetian churches, but, rather appropriately, there is a large bas-relief over the main entrance depicting Charity, made by the artist Marsili around 1800. After the blazing heat of midday Venice, crossing that threshold brings cool relief. Inside, the church sweeps around in an egg shape with a vaulted, frescoed ceiling. Did Vivaldi see the paintings hanging on the walls by the sixteenth-century artist Alessandro Bonvicino, also known as Il Moretto? We don't know if they were moved from the original church, but it's possible. The main fresco on the ceiling, *The Coronation of the Virgin*, is by Giovanni Battista Tiepolo, a near-contemporary of Vivaldi, and includes many musical figures playing string, wind and keyboard instruments, including a possible depiction of Vivaldi himself, violin in hand, with a couple of red curls giving away his identity.

The altarpiece is *The Visitation* by Giambattista Piazzetta, a rococo painter and another Venetian contemporary of Vivaldi, active in the city at the same time. (The painting was completed by his disciple Giuseppe Angeli.) Inspired by Caravaggio, Piazzetta's art has the same sense of drama and light and shade, pulling the viewer into the scene – effects that you might well also feel on hearing Vivaldi's music written for the Pietà and in *The Four Seasons*.

On each side of the church are the two choir lofts from which the women performed. In a shock development, the eighteenth-century architects didn't install lifts so I couldn't get up there, but even in the stillness of that moment, I felt a profound longing for that historical musical experience.

Micky White was living in the Ospedale at the time of our meeting, researching the lives of the women who called Pietà their home. Her eyes lit up as she told me of their individual characters, and she went out of her way to lift the curtain and escort me backstage to the *real* parts of the Pietà. She pointed out the buildings in which the girls and women lived, and a long upstairs room where they were taught, played chamber music together, rehearsed for services and gave private concerts for visiting nobles and dignitaries. Ironically, most touching of all was the staircase up to that room, a space in which light from a window falls beautifully, as it always has over smooth worn steps, testament to the number of women who dawdled there before heading up to perform.

My visit ended in the modest Pietà garden, a place of calm behind the formal buildings, which would have provided the same sense of sanctuary in Vivaldi's day. He would have sat here, as his terracotta bust does now, taking in the leafy shade. His association with the Pietà held fast throughout his life – even in periods when he wasn't technically on the books – until he left Venice for good to end his days in Vienna, but if his spirit lingers on in this verdant little oasis, it's because Antonio spent the springtime of his profession here.

Fig. 3: Bust of Vivaldi in the Ospedale garden.

There's still magic in the way the shafts of light play across the courtyard, and in the sounds that bounce off the walls of the surrounding buildings. You get a sense of being right in the bustle of the city – the boats coming in, footfalls on cobbled lanes and the babble of the crowds – just as it was then. Admittedly this is a vastly romanticised view of an institution that undoubtedly saw a huge amount of suffering. But it was also a place in which lost souls found hope, where women who would otherwise have lived in the worst alleyways of society were given purpose and fulfilment in a life of music.

By the end of the eighteenth century, however, the Pietà was largely bankrupt: Vivaldi's music was considered a thing of the past, the instruments were sold off, and its doors closed for good. Unbeknown to Vivaldi, though, he'd helped create a model that would be used in future centuries by musical conservatoires – nurturing the new talent that is the lifeblood of music-making. He had witnessed the institution's heyday, a time in which festive sounds resonated around the chapel, and the women, like his spirits and shepherds in this finale of *Spring*, played and danced (Why not? No one could see!) in the brilliant springtime light of their lives.

The Life Cycle of *The Four Seasons* – Roots and Shoots

The First Performances

Vivaldi's *Four Seasons* took root in the eighteenth century with performances he gave himself. From there it grew shoots from manuscripts he sent to musicians or copies of published editions that found their way into numerous institutions – shoots that continue to spring up today. We like to imagine Vivaldi at the Pietà, and in Venice. It fits a convenient image of the composer, but in reality he spent huge amounts of time away from his home: he was renowned in cities across Italy and north of the Alps as a composer of operas and concertos.

Vivaldi's first opera *Ottone in villa* received its premiere in May 1713 in Vicenza, a city forty miles to the west, and part of the Republic of Venice. A year later, the composer cemented his fascination with all the facets of production by joining his father at Venice's Teatro Sant'Angelo. This was the start of a career not just as an opera composer – his initial role – but also, eventually, as an impresario. Over the years, the Sant'Angelo became known as 'Vivaldi's Theatre', a small, rather unfashionable opera house on the Grand Canal, but one in which he had the opportunity to get involved in every aspect of productions. This was a time in which the composer of an opera was ranked lower than the singers and often the librettist, so Vivaldi relished the habit of playing violin concertos in intervals – another chance for this showman to draw in the crowds and dazzle in his own right.

Could Sant'Angelo have been the setting for the first performances of *The Four Seasons*? We don't know when exactly he began writing these concertos or how long they percolated through his musical mind. We also don't know whether he produced prototype versions, or if they emerged as the finished product. A set of manuscripts has come to light revealing that *La tempesta di mare* (The Storm at Sea), a violin concerto from the op. 8 collection that included *The Four Seasons*, was written in 1716. This was while Vivaldi was still at both the Pietà and Sant'Angelo, so perhaps that's where the seasonal seeds were sown.[1] However, it's more likely the project began in the comparatively rural setting of nearby Mantua where, in spring 1718, Vivaldi took up a position at the court of Prince Philip of Hesse-Darmstadt directing the music of official occasions.

For centuries, Mantua had been a dukedom ruled by the Gonzaga family. The last duke, Ferdinando Carlo IV, had always been more interested in theatres of art than theatres of war, and lost both his possessions and his city to the Austrian Empire. On his death in 1708, Mantua was declared a hereditary duchy of the House of Austria, and by 1714 it was in the governing hands of the aforementioned Prince Philip. Like a giant hermit crab, Philip's court moved into a new home, a palace stripped of its artwork and furniture; however, the prince had grand schemes to restore its former artistic glory, especially when it came to music and theatre. Such was his enthusiasm and investment that in 1735 he was recalled to Vienna on account of his extravagance. Vivaldi would be long gone by then, but on his arrival in spring 1718 he could enjoy the prince's considerable injection of cash into the arts. It would prove to be the only time that he took a court position and the only regular employment he held outside Venice. He stayed little more than two years, leaving on excellent terms in 1720 when the court went into mourning for the Dowager Empress Eleonore Magdalene and all the operas were cancelled. However, in these two years, Mantua offered connections to other courts, a lifelong link to Vienna, and the hands-on experience Vivaldi longed for.

As Mantua's *maestro di cappella da camera* (director of chamber music), Vivaldi was the man in charge of everything, from daily instrumental chamber music to large-scale celebrations and, within a year, opera. It was a secular post, so he didn't write any church music in Mantua, but his compositions flowed freely for the twenty-three members of the court orchestra. He staged four of his own operas in his time there, and some forty cantatas, but the high point of his tenure was intended to be the 1719 wedding of Prince Philip to Princess Eleonora di Guastalla.

The bride-to-be had been born in Mantua in 1686 to the then-ruling Gonzaga clan, and in her early twenties was married off to the forty-eight-year-old Francesco Maria de Medici in an effort to provide a male heir for the Florentine Medici line. Eleanora made every effort to avoid her ageing, unattractive husband, and within two years was widowed and enjoying her own literary circle in Florence.[2] Come 1719, political machinations were in motion again and she was poised to marry Mantua's Prince Philip. The date was announced and preparations made, but suddenly the wedding was called off. The definitive reason for this remains unclear. It could have been a Viennese intervention – the imperial court fearing potential claims Eleonora could have made to her birth city – or it may have been the result of odd, unsubstantiated rumours that Eleonora had illegitimate children in Florence. However, while what might have been a consolidatory and political match for the region didn't happen, the party had been planned, and the music written. The wedding had been intended to coincide with the 1719 Carnevale, and *Tito Manlio*, one of two operas Vivaldi wrote for that season, remained dedicated to Eleonora. Had things gone to plan, Vivaldi would have overseen the extensive secular side of the wedding festivities and provided concertos galore. He may well have been aware of Reinhard Keiser's 1702 matrimonial and seasonal opera *Pomona* (Roman goddess of fruitfulness), that we met earlier and as a result been prompted to write *The Four Seasons* for the wedding. It's conjecture, but even if he'd begun the concertos before he arrived, *The Four Seasons* would have fitted the occasion and reflected the marriage of artistic minds: theatrical instrumental music that played into Philip's desire for grand spectacle and Eleonora's love of art and poetry.

Wedding party possibilities aside, Mantua's rural location plays into the musical landscape of Vivaldi's seasonal violin concertos, combined perhaps with his memories of Venice. Add to this his commitment to set designs for Mantua's Archducal Theatre; Vivaldi brought the artist Antonio Meneghini with him from Venice, and the pair experimented with new visual effects in his Mantuan productions.[3] This artistic role brought Vivaldi new perspectives, and in *The Four Seasons* we can see him easily bridging the gap between the action on stage and the musicians in the pit. The solo violinist takes a position previously held by a storytelling singer, and the string band become set designers, painters, architects of special effects. The fact that Vivaldi borrowed music from his operas for these concertos *and* vice versa shows how his musical mind flitted with ease between instrumental and vocal genres, and how visually he conceived *The Four Seasons*. For example, he adapted the opening swinging melody of *Spring* for his 1724 opera *Il Giustino*, where it appears in the same key and with the same uplifting effect, forming the Sinfonia to Scene 5 of Act I, a vision of the Goddess Fortune as she makes her entrance and steps out into the light.

Assuming Vivaldi was living in Mantua when he wrote *The Four Seasons,* it stands to reason that the concertos were played there. Even though they could not have featured at Prince Philip's aborted wedding to Princess Eleonora in 1719 (which would have brought the great and the good of European aristocracy to the city), they may have been played between acts at the opera during Carnevale. We know for certain that an early performance of them made an impression on the Bohemian Count Wenzel von Morzin.[4] He and his sons made stops in both Venice and Mantua on their Grand Tour of Italy, and heard what must have been a prototype version of *The Four Seasons* with Vivaldi as soloist.[5] As a result of his seasonal encounter with Vivaldi, Morzin took a score of *The Four Seasons* – quite the Grand Tour souvenir – home to his palace in the Malá Strana district of Prague, where he maintained an orchestra of some ten to twelve players. In return for this and the promise of more concertos, Morzin made Vivaldi his *maestro di musica in Italia,* and records show that throughout the 1720s Vivaldi sent him numerous creations in return for handsome sums of money.[6]

———

Performances spread far and wide once the concertos were published in 1725 in Amsterdam. They quickly became test pieces for leading violinists of the age and instantly appealed to the duelling virtuosos of La Serenissima. Vivaldi's fellow Venetian Giuseppe Tartini set up a violin school there in 1726, attracting students from all over Europe including Domenico Ferrari and André-Noël Pagin, and anyone who came to study with him would have encountered the solo parts of *The Four Seasons* as they became central to the standard repertoire of the day.

While Tartini anchored himself in Venice, Vivaldi was on the move. After a couple of years in Mantua, he briefly returned home before travelling to Rome, where he spent three Carnevale seasons, played for the Pope, and met Corelli's former patron Cardinal Pietro Ottoboni. Ottoboni would play a significant part in the dissemination of *The Four Seasons*, as we shall see when we come to look at *Summer*, and before that, the concertos became known in Rome after Vivaldi took the opportunity to furnish the cardinal with bespoke manuscript parts.

By 1752, the Berlin-based composer and flautist Johann Joachim Quantz was writing that Vivaldi 'supplied almost half the world with his concertos', which might have been a slight exaggeration, but perhaps it felt that way.[7] Not only did they find their own routes across Europe in print, but Vivaldi's excellent connections ensured they became known to a whole network of musicians, headed up by the leader of the renowned Dresden court orchestra, Johann Georg Pisendel. Pisendel had originally studied with the violin virtuoso

Giuseppe Torelli before settling in Dresden in 1712, and during a tour to Venice and Rome in 1717–18 he caught up with Vivaldi. Pisendel was interested in both violin and composition and eventually returned to Dresden with numerous concertos by Vivaldi that he'd copied out while studying with him. Over the years, he acquired many more, and continued to champion the Italian composer's music after his return to Dresden, where he became leader of the court orchestra in 1729. It's very likely *The Four Seasons* was played in Dresden with Pisendel as soloist, and that Johann Sebastian Bach heard the work there. Almost as confirmation, in 1726, the year after the concertos were published, an echo of the first movement of *Spring* appeared in Bach's church cantata *Wer weiß, wie nahe mir mein Ende?* (Who knows how near to me my end?) BWV 27. Vivaldi's theme is clearly identifiable in the opening alto aria with accompanying organ and oboe da caccia, setting the words: 'Welcome! I will say when Death steps to my bed. I will joyfully follow, when he calls, into the tomb, I will take all my troubles with me.'[8] That Bach should choose to refer to *Spring* when setting words about death might appear a little contradictory, but his Lutheran faith made him see death not as the end but a new beginning.

If Vivaldi's fame and *The Four Seasons* were rapidly spreading through Saxony, he had really taken off in France. A veritable Vivaldi fever gripped the French capital, and captivated both court and king. Vivaldi was

heralded in the *Mercure de France* as: 'le plus habile com-
positeur qui soit à Venise' (the most accomplished
composer in Venice), and these concertos further propelled his success.[9] In 1725, their year of publication, the
Concert Spirituel was established. One of the first public
concert series, it was designed to provide entertainment
during the Easter fortnight and similar religious holidays, when other venues such as the Paris Opéra were
closed. The Concert Spirituel's programmes featured
sacred choral works and virtuosic instrumental pieces, so
Vivaldi's recently published seasonal concertos fitted the
bill perfectly. Records show that audiences had to wait
until February 1728 for a performance of the full set, but
as testament to their immediate popularity *Spring* and
Summer were heard again two months later, and *Spring*
alone some twelve times over the next few decades.

Spring was a particular French sensation. King Louis
XV himself requested to hear it in 1730, when it was
played at a concert by a band made up of members of
the nobility. There was something about this music that
captured the Parisian vogue for optimism – and held it
for an unusually long time, too. In 1739 Nicolas
Chédeville published – under his own name – *Le printems
ou les saisons amusantes – concertos d'Antonio Vivaldy*
[*sic*.] (Spring or the Seasons of Amusement – Antonio
Vivaldi's Concertos), arranged for musettes (bagpipes)
and hurdy-gurdies, with accompanying parts for violin,
flute and continuo. Really playing up the pastoral

associations with more traditional shepherds' instruments, Chédeville's version comprised half a dozen three-movement mash-ups of _The Four Seasons_ with Vivaldi's other op. 8 concertos, but crucially left out any disagreeable depictions of harshness or anxiety. Chédeville was keen to reframe the seasons to reflect the general French attitude, which exaggerated the sunnier aspects of the year, so sprightly spring, as opposed to stormy summer, was brought to the fore. Even by 1775 this feeling was still in the ether as the composer, writer and philosopher Jean-Jacques Rousseau published a version of _Spring_ for unaccompanied flute.

Perhaps the most eyebrow-raising of all the French spin-off performances and arrangements of the time was Michel Corrette's 1765 grand motet _Laudate Dominum de coelis_ (Praise the Lord from the heavens), in which he set words to _Spring_ to bring the concerto into a religious sphere. The first two movements (of six) are Corrette's original music, hinting at what's to come with pastoral motifs and intricate wind and string parts. But then, in the first full chorus, the strains of _Spring_ begin. Singing 'Laudate Dominum' (Praise the Lord), the voices and instruments present every note of Vivaldi's score, and Corrette adds more. He includes harmonies Vivaldi only implied, filling out the textures and occasionally meandering off into new pastures as the mood takes him – especially with more intimate break-out vocal solos and duets. However, the very identifiable music of the concerto keeps returning with full effect, and includes all the virtuoso solo violin lines in the string parts. In the middle movement, 'Montes et omnes colles' (The mountains and all the hills), Corrette sets his take on the sleeping shepherd for tenor and chorus; there's no sign of the dog in the text, but it's still there in the music. Then, after two more solo numbers, the full chorus strikes up the final movement, mirroring the celebration of Vivaldi's nymphs and shepherds with young and old men and women praising the name of the Lord.

It's fair to say Vivaldi took France by storm – in spirit and music, though not in person. In July 1723, still two years before *The Four Seasons* appeared in print, Antonio returned to Venice from his post-Mantuan travels, and secured a new contract with the Pietà. He agreed to resume his position as *maestro de' concerti* (director of concertos), and supply two concertos every month, by post if travelling. Vivaldi agreed to direct rehearsals and performances, and also instigated a commitment to purchasing two new instruments each month to increase the range and scope of the orchestra. Writing in 1739, the French jurist and polymath Charles de Brosses recalled hearing the women play violin, lute, organ, oboe, cello and bassoon, concluding, 'There is no instrument, however unwieldy, that can frighten them.'[10] Vivaldi's concertos were the mainstay of concerts given on weekends and solemn feast days, which not only brought in a good deal of money for the Pietà but were a focal point in the Venetian social calendar. The Pietà's accounts confirm payment for over 140 concertos throughout the 1720s, but were *The Four Seasons* among them? No information about the pieces survives in the archives, but it's unlikely Vivaldi would have withheld them, especially as they spearheaded his next publication. You can just imagine him playing his concertos with the women in his charge on his return to the city – a postcard from his years away in Mantua. Personally, I like to imagine him selecting four soloists from among the women in future performances too – a living allegory of each season.

PART TWO
Summer

I: Allegro non molto

The summer sun burns with a terrible fire.
We droop and fade under its force.
The animals grow weak.
The pine trees are lost to their thirst.

The cuckoo issues its call,
joined by goldfinch and turtle dove.
A soft breeze begins to blow
but is swept up into the hard north wind.

The shepherd is frightened.
He knows what a storm awaits;
its greed and ruin,
how it will spoil his crops,
waste his hope.[1]

Vivaldi's north Italian *Summer* does not conjure up long mountain holidays, afternoons lounging in the sun with a gelato, or evenings sipping Aperol spritz in cobbled courtyards. His concerto depicts the harshest of agricultural summers, as oppressive heat sweeps the region. The worst-case scenario was the arrival of the *temporale*, a violent storm whipped up in the Sahara that typically hit Italy in the summer months and obliterated crops and livelihoods. This was certainly the reality Vivaldi encountered in rural Mantua, where he would no doubt have heard stories of the impact of the weather on surrounding farmland. Fear pervades this opening movement of *Summer*, right down to the key Vivaldi chose to write in: G minor, long associated with storms and violent music. Unlike in the other concertos, he uses the same key for all three movements, which suggests that we're heading in a straight line for trouble, with no sheltered detours.

The music immediately signals tension, the surprisingly quiet notes of the opening bars revealing how uncomfortable this summer season can be – airless, windless, and sticky with heat. The violins play in harmony, but always at the interval of a third – it's as if they are stuck like that, unwavering in an oppressive atmosphere. Against this backdrop, the shepherd and his flock droop – signified by pairs of falling notes. They swelter in the heat and are exhausted even before the storm arrives. In these dog days of summer – so called because the dog star, Sirius, rises and falls with the sun – understandably paranoid farmers were quick to look for any signs of threatening weather. The soft, gentle south winds that eventually stir the air in this first movement of Vivaldi's *Summer* are merely passing comfort, essential brief breezes sweeping through the violins to dry the wheat and hay. However, they are whisked aside by the violent North wind – the wind of change that spells disaster – commanding that the whole ensemble join and rage.

If spring is the season of sound, then in the realm of the senses, summer is historically associated with sight. As the storm brews, Vivaldi's solo violinist, the shepherd, scans the horizon, but for now all he sees are the birds. In *Spring*, the birds took centre-stage, representing the best of the season; here their presence signals the opposite. This time Vivaldi very deliberately names them in the soloist's part: the cuckoo, turtle dove and goldfinch. Their calls are no refreshing dawn chorus; rather, they are fateful songs of premonition, signalling the start of the fury and fast pace of *Summer*. Keen to know how realistically they are nesting in the music, I consult my ornithologist friend Tom McKinney once more.

——

Wind whips the trees, and the rain lashes down my car windows as I pull up in the car park at RSPB Lakenheath Fen one early summer morning to meet Tom. As seasoned presenters of Radio 3's Breakfast shows, a sparrow-fart start doesn't both either of us, but I'm a town mouse these days and my mobility scooter has a habit of getting stuck in reverse if its electrics get too wet. I don't let on about that as Tom waves and jokes that he's arranged the weather of Vivaldi's *Summer* for our visit. Pragmatically, I don every item of clothing I can find in the car.

A muntjac deer darts ahead of us, a ducking and diving swirl of brown in the ditch turns out to be a weasel, and when the trail forks, an extended family of geese and their goslings waddle nonchalantly up the path we don't take en route to the reedbeds. In spite of the rain, it seems as though turning out early *without* the dog this time has its rewards. We arrive at our first hide to a crescendo in the wind that Vivaldi himself would have been proud of, and I immediately clock the place has no roof, as we turn to face the rain head on.

'The landscape Vivaldi experienced on the Venetian lagoon and this one on the Suffolk fens are actually not that different,' says Tom. 'Both are man-made – these reedbeds were once drained for farmland, before being rewilded to their original state.' The net result is that the reed-loving migrating birds, the warblers and so on, are common to both regions – in fact, the very birds around us could well have stopped in Venice on their way here. All of a sudden, the sounds that inspired *The Four Seasons* 300 years ago in Venice and Mantua appear to be here on our doorstop.

As the rain beats down on the pitifully minimal shelter of the hide, I make Tom listen again to the opening of Vivaldi's *Summer* from my phone, and it's well worth getting my pocket score out – and soggy.

When Vivaldi published *The Four Seasons* in 1725, the concertos did not appear in a neat score like mine; rather, they were printed as individual parts for each string player. On acquiring a set, the musicians would also notice a lettering system across their music. At first glance the letters look like modern rehearsal marks – the kind that allow all the players to pick up at a given point – but in fact they mark the precise moments in which the music depicts various poetic effects. Vivaldi ascribed each line of his accompanying sonnets a letter, which corresponds to the letters marked in the parts. It is confirmation of his musical devices: rather than leaving things to chance or our imaginations, he reveals the exact moments he intends effects to be heard.

In addition to this, there are further written annotations of features or images that are not otherwise mentioned in the poetry, similarly labelled at the precise moments they are depicted in the music. For example, in the opening bars of *Summer* the sonnet begins by describing the burning sun and the drooping and fading of the shepherd, but Vivaldi adds 'laziness from the heat' to the falling sequences of notes, suggesting the feeling for how it could be played. This is how we know that Vivaldi introduces each of his summer birds in turn, and can be sure of identifying their characters in the music.

Wiping the rain from my score, and as much scepticism from my voice as I can, I ask Tom what the chances are of hearing Antonio's cuckoo, turtle dove or goldfinch in all this rain. 'Actually, pretty high,' he says, and we press on.

Being radio presenters, Tom and I are used to listening to at least two things at once through headphones, whether the music, our own voices or that of a producer. It seems Tom extends this to the avian world, because while our conversation is in full flow he suddenly stops and points up. And there it is: clear as a bell, the soft clarinet-like tones of a cuckoo call through the rain. I look in the direction it's coming from. 'Nah, that one could be a long way off,' he says, 'that call carries for miles.' But it is unmistakably a cuckoo. Ironically though, from a musical perspective it seems to be a *highly* mistakable call, with quite some variation among the composers who choose to imitate it. Gustav Mahler opts for the interval of a falling fourth in his First Symphony, Beethoven goes for a falling major third in his 'Pastoral' (Sixth) Symphony, and Delius a falling minor third in *On Hearing the First Cuckoo in Spring*. The one we hear at Lakenheath Fen is *definitely* a minor third. But what does Vivaldi do? He takes another route entirely. In *Summer*, the falling call of the cuckoo is embedded in a twenty-one-bar torrent of notes on the solo violin. There is no soft cooing here; the falling minor third harsh, and frenzied. Why? Because that is the character of the bird.

The footpath has become more a track, an increasingly sodden one, but at the point where my wheels start to spin, Tom puts an arm out again to stop. 'Straight ahead – at the treetops,' he says, passing me the binoculars. I focus in on a bird battling the wind, darting about above the branches; I would never have guessed it was a cuckoo. If pressed, I would have hazarded a guess at some sort of bird of prey. 'It looks like a sparrow hawk,' says Tom. 'In flight it has the same demeanour, proportions and action.' There's good reason for this; our cuckoo is far from a

pleasant sort. 'The reed warbler neighbours assume it's a
bird of prey too, and abandon their nests,' Tom explains,
'then the cuckoo swoops in and lays its egg among the
others in the deserted nest. On their return, the reed
warblers continue to sit on the eggs as if they were all
their own.' This is certainly a redefinition of maternal
instincts on the part of the nest invader. 'Cuckoos are
pure evil,' says Tom, 'the first act of their hatched chick
is to murder.' Cuckoo embryos have been observed to
move far faster than any other species while still within
the egg; on hatching they are therefore immediately
strong enough to kill any other chicks they find in the
nest and demolish any remaining eggs. They are para-
sites in host nests and, perhaps most shockingly of all,
the adoptive mothers don't notice the situation, but continue to feed and sustain the cuckoo chick until it fledges.
Out here on the fen, my attitude to the softly cooing birds
of novelty clocks changes entirely.

Having caught sight of a cuckoo on the wing, we
return to the main path, and a lull in the rain brings the
sounds of reed warblers. 'Ah, there are the potential host
families,' says Tom, and we spot one hopping among
reeds to its nest: a surprisingly tiny bird considering the
volume of its call. I'm angry with nature and the cuckoo,
and Vivaldi's furious line makes even more sense now.
The falling minor third is there in the music, audible
through a torrent of notes, but I'm still a little perplexed
that this representation is so far from the fabled call of

the cuckoo, however deceptive that sound might be. Tom has an answer to this, too. In most cases it's the male songbird that sings to attract a mate, but very unusually, female cuckoos sing too. I grudgingly admit that if you've arranged permanent childcare and you don't have to provide food and shelter, there's time for that. He smiles and plays me a sample of a female cuckoo's call. It's faster and angrier, more menacing; it sounds like the wrath of a woman scorned. Things are falling into place in Vivaldi's furious summer.

The other birds Vivaldi cites and presumably sighted for his *Summer* concerto were not only commonplace in northern Italy in his era, but are also the birds frequently evoked by Romantic poets, especially the turtle dove. Tom points out that Vivaldi's imitation – a stressed low note before a short high note and back to the low one – doesn't sound much like the purr of a classical turtle dove. It's not quite the call of the wood pigeon either – a song common across the British countryside. I bet you can call that one to mind: *short-long-long, short-short*, to which my daughter sings: 'None o—f your bus-iness.' Tom reckons that Vivaldi's turtle dove is more like a collared dove, and plays a pretty convincing sample of its song from an app on his phone. It certainly combines the two ideas, a purr and stress followed by a high-pitch point, and it corresponds much more closely with the score. 'Dove or pigeon,' Tom goes on, 'whatever Vivaldi heard was the sound synonymous with the season; he didn't have the Collins Guide to cross-reference; that sort of interest in birdwatching only got going after the Second World War.' What Vivaldi knew was that *that* was the sound of birdsong in summer, when the doves returned to the same spot for the breeding season. Poetically, they symbolise peace, loyalty and love; true love's gift on the second day of Christmas has it in a nutshell. But Vivaldi's portrayal is relatively short-lived, half the length of the cuckoo it rather ominously follows – best not to stick around long when pursued by a bird that symbolised madness, deception and betrayal, hence 'cuckoldry'.

Back at the Lakenheath Fen Visitor Centre, industrial-sized bird feeders attract all manner of feathery characters to the table. Tom explains the contraptions are slightly controversial, because if not kept clean – which these ones are – they can harbour harmful diseases that affect beaks and feet. A great spotted woodpecker rocks up, there are blue tits galore, and then our collared dove appears. 'We'd do well to find a turtle dove these days,' Tom says, 'they're disappearing from the UK.' 'Range contraction' is the term, caused by a dangerous triumvirate of climate change, hunting and farming – or at least changes in land use. Tom had called around contacts and other RSPB nature reserves in the weeks before we met to see if any had been spotted, but the usual turtle dove haunts turned up nothing. 'Not seeing one today *is* the story,' he says, 'the birds that Vivaldi heard in bountiful number are now being driven to extinction by excessive hunting in the Mediterranean and Middle East. When those that survive reach places that should be a haven for them, places like this, they find conditions changed, and their habitats not what they were.' Climate change plays its part in this picture too, challenging the instincts of the birds themselves. 'If there's a mild winter, they can arrive too early, and a late frost will then kill the eggs,' Tom explains, 'but it's the *unpredictability* of climate change that's the most destructive.' It seems that turtle doves once thrived across the UK, but now they are retreating to the south-east, and it looks as though their days are numbered there, too.

The final crew to turn up at Lakenheath's busy bird tables are the goldfinches. That's a full house for Vivaldi's *Summer* this morning. Even though this final bird only enjoys a few bars of song in the concerto, its jangly call would later go on to inspire Vivaldi to the heights of a complete flute concerto, one in which you can overlay its song with startling accuracy. In *Summer*, it's a flash of six bars, enough for an audience familiar with its song to envisage the bright colours of its yellow wing-bars and red face. In Vivaldi's day, goldfinches were as common in cities as the countryside, and when caged they were capable of being taught tricks or led about on a string. However, the bird has darker associations too, and appears in some of the more foreboding examples of Italian art. These include portraits of children who did not survive to adulthood, including Agnolo Bronzino's *Portrait of Giovanni de' Medici as a Child*, and images of Jesus as a young boy, such as Raphael's *Madonna del Cardellino*, as the goldfinch was also commonly seen as symbolic of Christ's crucifixion. The goldfinch has long associations with virtue and innocence too. Leonardo da Vinci observed how it would 'cling to purity, like a light that shines in the darkest place', and described how it would keep its sight fixed on someone destined to survive, 'as if curing them of their sickness', but also how it would look away from a sick person whom it knew would die.[2] The goldfinch appearing so fleetingly in Vivaldi's *Summer* is not a good omen; the bird arrives, but then rapidly darts away.

All three of Vivaldi's summer birds contribute in their own ways to the terror of the season. The 'cuckoo is heard', reads Vivaldi's original sonnet, with no further comment, but now we know this bird's true colours. The ensuing 'sweet songs' of the turtle dove and goldfinch are sung in the light of a threat to love and innocence, a portent of doom. As for the setting, the winds at Lakenheath are more than enough to convince me of the effect of the 'hard north wind' mentioned in Vivaldi's poetry, incongruous though it might be with our idea of an Italian summer. Here it whistles creepily through the reeds just as it would in the marshes around Venice's lagoon or Mantua's marshes; I need no more convincing of the threat of the storm, and the safety and warmth of the car.

—

On hearing Vivaldi's *Summer* concerto, his audiences would have been left in no doubt of the season's destructive nature. Even if they felt it was a harsh viewpoint, they knew very well that summer signified hot and dry conditions, and had ancient associations with fire and ruin. This first movement is volatile from the start, with its depictions of languid limbs, angry birds and squally winds, and by the end of it we meet the shepherd – or more likely the farmer – who is terrified by the threat of the impending storm. His crops are in danger, and his family will face starvation as a consequence. The solo violin takes up his plight, and as suggested in the sonnet, it's not only his crops but also his hope that will be wasted. Vivaldi's mournful writing goes beyond a mere portrait to capture the psychological impact of the situation, and in the sudden bare musical textures beneath the cries of the violin lament, we know the shepherd is entirely alone. His anguish increases with every mounting chromatic twist before the solo evolves into a heartbreaking wail. But neither time nor weather show compassion for the shepherd's plight; the strings regroup and bring back the summer winds, portents of the approaching storm, which swirl the movement to its close.

II: Adagio e piano – Presto e forte

From fitful sleep the shepherd wakes,
his body shocked and gasping,
gripped by sky's threat.
A cloud of flies,
thick and black as night,
frets and hisses at his fear.[1]

The second movement of *Summer* brings a musical sequence of almost unbearable tension. We awake, with the soloist, to a sinister scene: black clouds gather and prepare to do their worst. The solo violin quietly takes up a plaintive melody – slow, sighing and built around falling phrases. It leave us in no doubt that the shepherd is disheartened and dispirited. You can feel the prickly heat and moisture down the back of your neck as accompanying violins take up the taunt of the flies – and wasps (Vivaldi adds to the printed edition), the worst of summer pests. The viola, and the cello and remaining continuo instruments, are initially silent, adding to the atmosphere of anxiety, until they interrupt with a sudden change of tempo for a fast, deep and loud rumble of thunder. It's a dramatic effect that's heightened by the subsequent threatening silences, before the violin soloist and accompanying strings resume their hum. The effect is repeated, but not with any predictability: there is no telling when the thunder will roll, but after each of its appearances the laboured lament and buzzing goes on. The whole movement is a mere twenty-two bars, but in that short time we see and feel the emotions of a shepherd gripped in fear, and utterly worn down by an oppressive summer.

This music carries a dark undertone that audiences may not have expected in Vivaldi's courtly, refined circles in Mantua or Venice. The birds that have characterised both concertos so far have vanished, and that is significant. In *Spring*, they sang their hearts out, and returned after the rain to bring renewed joy, and in the first movement of *Summer*, they were at least still singing, albeit as harbingers of doom. Now they've disappeared, leaving the shepherd entirely alone. A sighting of rooks staying close to their nests would have signalled rain was on the way, while swallows catching insects high on warm streams of air would have indicated that conditions were settling. With neither on the agenda, there's no certainty and no comfort. This is a moment that hangs in the balance, and the unpredictable music emphasises that. If the rainstorm arrives before the harvest is gathered, it will spell disaster, financial ruin and hunger; there is a lot at stake in this eerie isolation.

With fear woven into the fabric of the music, we might ask whether this middle movement is merely a morbid picture postcard of impending doom, or whether there was more seasonal psychology at play in Vivaldi's experience of the time of year. To me, this middle movement of *Summer* emerges as one of the most personal moments in the entire *Four Seasons*, and I believe it could point towards the composer's health. As noted, Vivaldi suffered from what he described in one of his letters as a *strettezza di petto*, a tightness of the chest, and although he doesn't articulate it here in the poetry, I sense it in the unbearably taut lines of the violin solo and the widespread discomfort portrayed by the rest of the ensemble.[2]

—

For a long time, the common thinking has been that Vivaldi had asthma, or at least a congenital constriction of the larynx and chest that resulted in asthmatic symptoms. This is my starting point in exploring how we might hear this particular movement as a respiratory-impaired experience of summer. Anyone, in any age, who, like me, suffers from respiratory problems knows how uncomfortable, unpredictable and at times frightening they can be. And so, as the action slows in this middle movement, we have another opportunity to glimpse Vivaldi through the seasons of his life. In the middle movement of *Spring* we saw his early career; in *Summer*, as he reaches maturity, his medical condition seems to come to the fore in his music. Prompted by the potential effects of the season on his health, I search out expert medical advice and meet up with Andrew Bush, Professor of Paediatrics and Paediatric Respirology at Imperial College London. Incidentally, Andrew is the son of the British composer, academic and author Geoffrey Bush, who in addition to his considerable musical credentials was a keen student of detective fiction. In our own pursuit of a historical medical conundrum, we attempt something of a retrospective consultation for Antonio.[3]

Andrew agrees that a chronic tight chest points to a respiratory issue, but has a qualified scepticism about about the oft-cited diagnosis of asthma, considering Vivaldi's own insistence on attributing his condition to the circumstances of his birth. This was something very likely perpetuated by his parents, and certainly maintained by the composer until the end of his life. Andrew suggests that Vivaldi might have had more than one condition: an early-onset, non-asthmatic disease that caused immediate respiratory distress at birth, and, later, something more akin to asthma. Venice was not short of doctors, and asthma (or 'asma' in Italian) was a known condition at the time, but no medical reports survive, and Vivaldi makes no specific mention of it in any surviving letters. Whatever he believed his illness to be, his own perception is paramount, because it would have affected how he sought to treat it.

One of the greatest clues we have in this matter comes from a letter Vivaldi wrote to Marchese Guido Bentivoglio in 1737, explaining that he could only leave home in a gondola or coach because of his 'chest ailment' or 'constriction of the chest', which did not permit him to walk.[4] This is a shocking piece of information; I had not considered Vivaldi in this way before, as someone who, like me, was not able-bodied. Yes, I'd envisaged him as a wheezy person, with a condition that might have restricted activities, but not as someone completely debilitated by it.

In the same letter from 1737, Vivaldi revealed that after his ordination in 1703 he celebrated Mass for a year or so but then stopped, 'because my ailment forced me to leave the altar three times without finishing'.[5] The act of leaving the service before the preparation of the altar, or – worse – immediately before the consecration of the sacrament was particularly shameful. Rumour had it that Vivaldi had been caught out looking distracted, then been seen nipping out the back to write down a fugue – not really the sense of priorities the Church was looking for.[6] But could the incense in church in fact have made his symptoms worsen, I wonder? 'There are many irritants,' Andrew acknowledges, 'dust, smoke, house mites – incense might have been problematic.' Vivaldi's respiratory problems and general ill-health as a child probably contributed to his parents securing his training in the Church, but equally could have made it difficult to execute the profession. He'd already had exemptions from preaching because he got out of breath during sermons, and not being able to complete services prompted him to renounce his active calling.

Vivaldi's health very likely affected his employment at the Pietà too. Contracts were arranged on an annual basis and, in order to be reinstated, an employee had to receive a majority vote from the governing body. Vivaldi didn't always achieve this, and his health may account for his absences from the institution in his early thirties.[7] It was certainly a good reason for the composer to train up deputies among the musical women in his charge, a crucial element in maintaining standards when he was away.

It is difficult to equate a debilitating health condition with Vivaldi's reputation for dramatic and flamboyant performances, but I know first-hand that an exciting performance is something that you can go to great lengths to achieve, at private cost. It can also have a huge impact on temperament, and communication. Vivaldi might have been a brilliant musician, but he was far from an easy character, and had a reputation for being aloof and difficult. He was prone to exaggeration, a notorious boaster who made wild claims about his abilities and famously blurted out that he could compose a concerto in all its parts faster than it could be copied out. His habit of inflating his achievements certainly did not endear him to his contemporaries – but could it have been because he was compensating for his physical limitations?

Whatever the case, his ailments never impeded him as a performing musician. In the summer of his own life-span, a thirty-five-year-old Vivaldi appeared undeterred and even unconcerned by what others thought of him, and embarked on an operatic career, putting on productions between, and indeed during, Pietà contracts.

One thing is certain: however badly Vivaldi suffered from his tight chest, he was able to teach, execute wildly virtuosic concertos, and direct operas. So, what treatment might he have sought?

———

An older contemporary of Vivaldi, the English physician John Floyer, throws the most interesting light on respiratory problems and their treatments at the turn of the eighteenth century.[8] His 1698 *A treatise of the asthma* sets out theories based on his personal experience, outlining respiratory problems as systemic conditions brought on by an imbalance of bodily fluids.[9] Floyer believed the membranes of the lungs and the network of blood vessels were irritated by 'windy spirits' – anything that would obstruct either blood or air vessels. He cites as aggravations everything from smoke, winds and heat to the phases of the moon, and believed that sedentary artisans, such as Vivaldi, were particularly susceptible. His conclusions chime with a vision of Vivaldi's suffering as presented in this slow movement of his *Summer* concerto.

Floyer also confirmed that respiratory problems were more severe and more frequent in summer than winter, and in his case also worsened on his arrival home to the Staffordshire countryside after his studies in the more urban environment of Oxford.

Over in Italy, and at the time he wrote *The Four Seasons*, Vivaldi was living either in Venice or, more likely, Mantua.

If Venice was notoriously humid, Mantua was famously swampy. It might not have been technically afloat like Venice, but in Vivaldi's day it was surrounded by water on every side. Intended as a defence mechanism, four lakes had been constructed in the twelfth century, drawing on water from the River Mincio, a tributary of the Po that ends up in Venice. Three still exist today (the fourth dried up at the end of the eighteenth century), and as a result there has been little opportunity for urban sprawl. Mantua has barely changed over the centuries hence its nickname: 'La Bella Addormentata' (the Sleeping Beauty).

There's little doubt that Vivaldi would have suffered in either city, just as his fellow composer Claudio Monteverdi had done a century earlier. Mirroring the protective care of Vivaldi's father, Monteverdi's father Baldassare, an apothecary and surgeon, wrote to the Gonzagas in Mantua requesting his son be discharged from his court duties 'so that he might find other air for his health'. Claudio was already out of favour in Mantua, but this letter sealed the deal on his move, and his health at least improved on moving to Venice.[10] In the early eighteenth century, the Englishman John Breval described how Mantua stood on 'a marsh rather than a lake', and confirms that the water 'stagnates in most places, to the great annoyance of the inhabitants in the hot months'.[11] Beyond the swampy parts, the Mantuan landscape Vivaldi found in 1718 was much more agricultural than Venice, one in which dust and pollen could have been further triggers to exacerbate his tight chest. Already, the middle movement of *Summer* is starting to emerge as a possible response to these surroundings.

In terms of weather, Andrew Bush points to increased respiratory problems as a storm approaches. 'Even people with very mild respiratory conditions can have big flare-ups in the run-up to a storm,' he says, on account of the combination of 'a high pollen count *and* thunder'. The hypothesis is that lightning shatters the pollen grain, and Andrew describes how 'tiny grainlets get trapped in the respiratory system, aggravating and causing inflammation in the airway lining, which makes inhalation difficult and results in tight chests and problems breathing.' Back in the eighteenth century, Floyer went into greater detail to explain why the threat of bad weather spells trouble, noting that he had frequently observed attacks before great storms.

The pressure of the air being weakened by the vapours, the windy asthmatic spirits expand themselves, and inflate the pneumatic nerves and membranes, and so on occasion the asthmatic fits before great rains.[12]

The moment the mercury fell in a barometer, Floyer was on high alert, recounting that his respiratory problems were more 'frequent and grievous' in summer, when temperatures soared and expanded the 'animal spirits' in the 'rarified air'. It may not be the language of modern medicine, but anyone who has had anything like an asthma attack can attest to the feeling of animal spirits at work in your body, taking control of your breathing and tightening your chest. Floyer states that the 'Great Changes of the Year' could give rise to what he called 'Anniversary Asthma', the annual dread of irritants carried on summer winds converging in a perfect storm.[13] 'The relationship between respiratory conditions and anxiety is complex,' Andrew explains. 'Clinical psychologists spend a lot of time considering anxiety's impact on the most severe respiratory patients, but it's impossible to tell the extent to which they feed off each other. It is of course easier to panic and hyperventilate if you've had a really bad attack before; you know what it feels like, and you think, "No, no, no: I'm getting another one."'

—

Andrew and I agree that asthma couldn't be the sole explanation for Vivaldi's medical condition, and before I leave, we return to the composer's belief that his ailment began at birth. 'One common assumption would be that he suffered from Infantile Respiratory Distress Syndrome (IRDS) if he was born prematurely,' Andrew says. IRDS is a dramatic moment at birth in which premature lungs resist being inflated, and there would have been signs for a seventeenth-century midwife, such as rapid breathing, flared nostrils, a pulling in of the ribs and blue skin. However, Andrew explains that in the days before any intensive care and oxygen therapy, the outcome for a baby in this situation was either death or, at the other end of the spectrum, virtually complete recovery.[14] 'Long-term consequences of IRDS could not account for Vivaldi's lifelong illness,' he concludes.

Vivaldi scholar Giuseppe Gullo has put forward a hypothesis that Vivaldi developed Eisenmenger syndrome, a condition that affects the direction of blood flow around the body and usually presents in adulthood.[15] Gullo points out that the lower extremities – from the waist down – are worst affected, and that a sufferer would experience fatigue, chest pains, palpitations and cramping. Left untreated, Eisenmenger syndrome wouldn't pose an immediate risk to life and would explain why Vivaldi's illness seemingly worsened in adulthood, with increasing pain and breathlessness. Where summer is concerned, Gullo confirms that those who suffer with this condition often have a reduced tolerance to high temperatures.[16]

It's fascinating to speculate, but speculation is certainly the watchword. Conditions such as Eisenmenger syndrome, and other possibilities such as Ebstein's anomaly or primary ciliary dyskinesia, may explain why Vivaldi was able to use his upper body to play, direct, compose and so on while not being able to walk any real distance. It may also account for his choice of the priesthood rather than a more physically active occupation, and the fact that he was rarely on his own. In Venice he lived with his family, including two unmarried sisters who probably acted as housekeepers, and the lack of such a support network in Mantua may have contributed to his return after only a couple of years. Indeed, the need for practical help explains his reliance on a pair of sisters in later life too: Anna Girò and her half-sister Paolina Trevisan. Girò was an opera singer whom Vivaldi had met in Mantua, and her platonic presence throughout the rest of his life is very likely accounted for in a carer's role. However, it was the suspicion of scandalous reasons for her spending so much time in his house that contributed to the Ferrarese authorities denying Vivaldi access to their city, and prompted the very letter to Guido Bentivoglio in which Antonio outlined the limitations of his health and requirement of hired help.[17]

We are into the territory of gleaning potential health conditions from Vivaldi's biographical details, and any verdict is at best inconclusive. I know very well from personal experience just how long it can take to receive a diagnosis for abnormalities in pulmonary and respiratory systems, and I'm presenting a living body to modern medical experts. Andrew smiles before concluding: 'the thought that we could be certain about a patient who has been dead for nearly three centuries is wild.' That said, this summertime investigation into Vivaldi's health has already changed my perspective of the composer, and I feel a deep affinity with the figure in this middle movement of *Summer*, who faces impending terror.

—

Is it really possible to express any of this in music? I was surprised to find a definite direct musical representation of asthma from the eighteenth century: an instrumental piece by Marin Marais, who was a virtuoso viol player at the court of Louis XIV.[18] In 1717, the year before Vivaldi arrived in Mantua, Marais published his fourth book of viol pieces. It comprises dances typical of the day: sarabands, gigues and so on, many with descriptive titles, and among them 'Allemande l'Asmatique'. In contrast to the gravity of the disease and the often-stately nature of the Allemande, it seems at first glance to be a relatively light-hearted movement, with the playing instruction 'très gai'. Marin Marais often wrote complex chords into his melodies to show off the viol's chordal capabilities, but here the focus is all on the interplay between the melody and bass part – a breathless conversation alternating individual notes, as air is snatched, with wheezy sighs. However well it's executed, it is an uncomfortable listen, with sudden changes in both note lengths and directions.

It is far easier to catch on to the notion of an asthmatic character in Marais' piece than in the slow movement of Vivaldi's *Summer* concerto; however, the diagnosis is in the detail of my reading of this music. With its alternations between an ominous melody and the sounds of irritant flies and rolling thunder, nothing ever happens the same way twice. The phrases are different lengths throughout, which means you can't predict when the thunder will rumble. In contrast to Marais' conversational evocation of wheezing, Vivaldi's melody line in the violin is slow, high and drawn out, corresponding, I think, far more closely to Floyer's description of asthmatic symptoms being something of a 'high, slow, rare, and laborious respiration'.[19] The fact that Vivaldi specifically notes tired limbs 'robbed' of rest could be another reference to how most respiratory conditions caused attacks at night, at which point patients were taught to sit up – and stay up – as their breathing became difficult. Floyer's argument that asthma was a full-body experience (affecting the lungs and also the stomach and head), manifested not only in breathlessness but extreme drowsiness, taps into Vivaldi's fatigue. Furthermore, Floyer cites thunder as a trigger for sudden shortness of breath and audible irritation of the airways; the exasperating sounds of buzzing flies might be another trigger, or might simply amplify the struggle to breathe. There seems little doubt then, that Vivaldi's tight chest could be directly affected by storms, and the anticipation of one arriving could certainly have increased his symptoms both physically and psychologically.

It makes me consider whether music could have been either a remedy or therapy for Vivaldi. Picking up his violin to play would have focused his mind on counting in time, breathing in time with the music, even as a string player. The benefits of playing wind instruments for asthmatics are now well advocated, and I certainly never recall having an attack while playing my flute. The

ADAGIO E PIANO – PRESTO E FORTE

outcome of regulating breath through phrases of music could well have been enough for Vivaldi to distract himself from hyperventilating, and to have had a calming effect on both his nervous system and his airways, especially in a slow movement such as this. Music-making demands your whole attention; everything around you becomes secondary to the physical and mental act, and – setting aside nervous or performance adrenalin – playing in solitude can certainly slow the body's pulse.

Here in this middle movement of *Summer*, as the violin soloist re-starts his long, high melody after every rumble of thunder, it's as though Vivaldi is openly demonstrating the treatment that worked best for him. By the end of the movement, the violin maintains a single note, a poignant finality, as the shepherd's tired limbs are robbed of rest. I don't think for a moment that the fear Vivaldi writes about in this middle movement was *only* the considerable dread of losing crops – it was also the threat of not being able to breathe. If this movement is a snapshot of his experience of the height of summer, there is no doubt that he was sometimes frightened and felt alone with his condition – perhaps especially so in Mantua, away from his family network. After all, the untreated effects of respiratory illnesses, let alone pulmonary ones, can still be dangerous today.

III: Presto

And how the storm comes to meet this fear.
Lightning splits the sky
and hail smashes at the ground.
The crops are struck and crushed
and all is lost.[1]

With the final movement of Vivaldi's *Summer*, worst fears are realised. The violent storm, the *temporale*, arrives, recreated in a veritable tempest of string writing. It's a tale of inevitable suffering and destruction, played out across Vivaldi's ensemble as winds converge and spiral, thunder roars and hail ruins the crops.

This would be a catastrophic event in any era, but Vivaldi was born into a period we now refer to as the Little Ice Age. Some say this cold phenomenon began in the Middle Ages and extended as far as the early nineteenth century, but the term is most commonly used to refer to the period spanning the late sixteenth century to the beginning of the nineteenth. Although the Earth itself records many of the effects of the Little Ice Age in layers of its strata, scientists don't agree on what caused it. Some suggest it was the result of volcanic activity, in which ash blocked out the sun, causing temperatures to plummet; others that it was the effect of sunspots: darker, cooler regions of strong magnetic fields on the sun.[2] Whatever the cause, global temperatures were reduced by around two degrees Celsius, and the results were wide-reaching. Not only did polar ice caps and glaciers grow, altering the salinity of seas, but ocean currents were affected, and climates radically disturbed. This led to severe meteorological events – increased storms, frosts, floods, droughts – which in turn caused famines and related catastrophes such as disease and displacement. The enduring impact of the Little Ice Age, prompted by its name, was of much colder, brutal winters, but the summers were adversely affected too, with storms and extreme temperatures that would have been the norm for Vivaldi and his contemporaries.

By the time *The Four Seasons* was published, Europe had experienced more than a century of agricultural upheaval. The drop in average temperatures had not only resulted in rainy summers with violent storms, but also almost three weeks of lost annual growing time compared to the mid-sixteenth century. Crops were slow to ripen, and sometimes didn't fully ripen at all. Failed harvests, grain rotting in the ground and hail damage were long-term crises across the continent. It would be the mid-eighteenth century before farmers would experience yields to match the bounty of harvests before 1570. This would have been a stark reality check for Vivaldi, moving inland from the coastal trade town of Venice. In the countryside, most people were reliant on grain to some extent, so the harvest was not only nutrition but also a source of currency and power.[3]

It was a long-standing tradition that a harvest would be divided three ways. The family livestock would consume one third, another would be kept back to be sown the following spring, and the final third would be paid in tax to the landowners. Most people wouldn't come into contact with money, instead living by this exchange of goods. Tax was paid by the success of the harvest, with landowners always looking to raise funds in order to keep rule, defend lands and retain their social standing. This included patronage of the arts, something that would have been at the forefront of Vivaldi's mind. It was an inflexible system, and if crops failed, then not only did people go hungry, but epidemics were also far more likely to take hold, and people more liable to riot. A storm like the *temporale* could portend economic and social upheaval.

When Vivaldi's storm hits, it does so with considerable force. Any memories of the soft breezes and argumentative gusts portrayed in the first movement of *Summer* are blown away by this tempestuous music. Vivaldi had form when it came to creating this meteorological effect; he'd written several concertos depicting *tempeste di mare* (storms at sea), and this finale to *Summer* epitomises his musical treatment of stormy weather. There is a specific texture that he uses: an exhilarating effect in which all the musicians abandon their harmonic roles and join forces to play as one in unison octaves.

You can trace the moments when Vivaldi deploys this effect across each concerto in *The Four Seasons*. In those in which he idealises the year, it happens sparingly. There is just one instance of the ensemble coming together to play in unison in *Spring*: the first movement's low-register tremolo thunder. There is also just one example of this in *Autumn*: to represent the hounds on the hunt. However, in his more malignant seasons, *Summer* and *Winter*, it's a major feature. In *Winter*, the unison ensemble illustrates effects such as people falling to the ground, ice cracking and whistling winds; and here in *Summer* we see the most protracted use of all, portraying thunder and violent wind.

Vivaldi employed this specific orchestral texture at the end of the first movement of *Summer*, as the shepherd feared the building storm. After his languishing and lamenting in the heat, the sudden contrast as the winds picked up and the strings all joined forces in unison scales made the reality of a potential full storm's destructive powers even more shocking. Their descent to unanimously rest on a low G at the end of the first movement – the lowest, most gravelly note the violins can muster – ensured Vivaldi had our full attention. In the middle movement of *Summer*, the thunder prompted him to use the unison effect again and the impact was very physical, as the entire ensemble rumbled to

interrupt the soloist's pained song. Come this final movement, Vivaldi presents us with the most extensive
depiction of wild wind and weather. The violence of the
storm is once again exaggerated by the effect of full
strings in unison as the wind blows in all directions, as if
carrying each player with it. Vivaldi creates a giddy swirl
of intensity, with downward leaps and repeated notes
depicting the hailstones, before gusts of wind lift the
musical lines again. When multiple musicians play the
same part, whether at the same pitch or at octave intervals above and below it, new resonances are created, as
the open octaves create overtones: higher pitches that we
hear in the frequencies that ring above the ensemble. It
feels like the sonic impact of nature herself. Vivaldi was
not the first to use the effect of an entire ensemble suddenly playing in unison; in opera it had long been
associated with barbarism, with negative emotions, or
had simply been used as an abrupt device for getting
audience attention.[4] In *The Four Seasons*, Vivaldi seems to
combine all these associations as the concertos harness
the power of emotional suggestion.

—

Vivaldi's original handwritten score of *The Four Seasons*
may have met a fate as dramatic as those of the crops
destroyed in his summer storm. Whether they are missing,
destroyed or sold off into obscurity, the musical notes and
information that he sent to the publisher Michel-Charles
Le Cène in Amsterdam are nowhere to be found. For a

long time, the only source for this most famous of pieces was a single copy of the first edition from 1725, which is held in the Bibliothèque nationale de France.

There are however, a few other copied-out excerpts that have turned up around Europe, and oddly enough they are all of this *Summer* concerto. An early version is in an archive in Genoa: it doesn't include the sonnet or any clues to the seasonal scenes in the music, but it is note-for-note the same music. There's another copy of *Summer* in a library in Lund, Sweden, which has cue letters referring to the sonnets, but no copy of the sonnets themselves. This Swedish connection is almost certainly through the composer Johan Helmich Roman, who personally copied a number of Vivaldi's concertos when he stayed with him in Venice in the 1730s. The fact that these manuscripts have turned up across Europe is testament to their appeal, and the spread of Vivaldi's fame.

The greatest finding, however, is an eighteenth-century copy of *The Four Seasons* in full that was discovered in the 1970s in Manchester in the UK, and proved that the winds of Vivaldi's summer storm could blow his music far from home. To trace its journey from the Grand Canal to the Bridgewater Canal, though, we must return to Venice.

On the feast day of St Louis, 25 August 1726, the year after *The Four Seasons* had been published, a performance of Vivaldi's grand serenade *La Senna festeggiante* was given at the French embassy. It was to mark a great diplomatic event: the visit of Cardinal Pietro Ottoboni, Protector of the Affairs of France at the Vatican. Ottoboni had damaged relations with Venice – and France – by accepting the appointment from his great-uncle, the Pope, in 1712 and thus appearing to pledge loyalty to the French, but, nearly fifteen years on, the breach had healed sufficiently for him to return to his native city in triumph. Not much actually happens in *La Senna festeggiante*: three characters – L'Età dell'oro (The Golden Age), La Virtù (Virtue) and La Senna (The Seine) – lament the sorry state of the world, before ending up at the royal palace, singing praises to King Louis XV and predicting a glorious future.

A glorious future is what Vivaldi also had in mind, if only he could impress Ottoboni with his music. Already a patron of George Frideric Handel, Arcangelo Corelli and many others, the cardinal could change Vivaldi's life and fortunes with his sponsorship, and so along with the serenade, Vivaldi presented him with choice sonatas and concertos, including a bespoke copy of *The Four Seasons*. Ottoboni returned to Rome with the treasures – but, his patronage was not forthcoming.

It is a like-minded friend and literary collaborator of Handel, in fact, who carries this story onwards: Charles Jennens, the man who most famously provided the libretto for *Messiah*. Jennens was a great connoisseur of music and an avid collector; he subscribed to Handel's publications and owned a good number of copies of his original manuscripts. However, his interests were not confined to British shores: he was fascinated by Italian compositions of the day, and his means of obtaining them was via a third man, the Neo-Latin poet and classical scholar Edward Holdsworth.

While travelling Europe, Holdsworth was able to secure scores for Jennens by the likes of Domenico Scarlatti and Johann Adolph Hasse, and in Venice in 1733 he met Vivaldi. The encounter was not fruitful: although Vivaldi was prepared to sell him manuscript copies of various concertos, Holdsworth didn't feel confident to spend a large sum of Jennens's money without knowing exactly which ones he wanted. The next trip in 1742 was, however, considerably more successful. Two years after the death of Cardinal Ottoboni (and a year after Vivaldi's death), there was an auction of the cardinal's private music collection. Holdsworth took a punt – not on a specific piece, but on more than '150L weight of musick', and immediately wrote to tell Jennens that he had done so. This mighty stash of music came from a distinguished source and had works in it by 'celebrated hands', including Handel, Scarlatti and Benedetto Marcello.[5] Opening the case back in England, Jennens found himself the recipient of ninety-six assorted concertos and instrumental pieces. He had them bound for his private library, and that was that – there was no mention of Vivaldi or the fact that *The Four Seasons* nestled between the pages. Either Jennens hadn't noticed, or he wasn't particularly interested.

On Jennens's death, the collection was inherited by Heneage Finch, the 3rd Earl of Aylesford, and remained in his family for around a hundred years. Some of the wider collection was then auctioned off in 1873, and Sotheby's received the rest in 1918 when it was sold to Handel's biographer Newman Flower. The Handel angle remained the main interest when, in 1965, Manchester Public Libraries acquired Flower's collection. They published a preliminary list of the Handelian manuscripts, but the rest were consigned to the archives. That was, until 1973, when Vivaldi scholar Michael Talbot came across the volume containing works by Vivaldi.

'I have to admit, I enjoy making finds,' Michael tells me. 'So many discoveries are made in libraries, and yet the librarians themselves are the unsung heroes and heroines.' He'd gone to Manchester to look at a work incorrectly attributed to Albinoni, and distinctly remembers his excitement at being presented with a whole pile of unexamined music acquired from Newman Flower. The handsome manuscript of twelve mostly unknown Vivaldi sonatas (now referred to as the 'Manchester Sonatas') was the find of the day, but the existence of *The Four Seasons* among the manuscripts secured Michael's existing hunches about Vivaldi's practice of preparing bespoke parts for different benefactors.[6] 'In the end, the fact of the discovery is less important than what one makes of it afterwards,' he concludes.

—

The fact that the only complete eighteenth-century manuscript parts of *The Four Seasons* are held in Manchester turns out to be propitious: it's an ideal almost-halfway point between my home in London and celebrated British violinist Daniel Pioro's in Edinburgh. Daniel has something of a lifelong obsession with these concertos and jumps at the chance to see the manuscripts up close.[7] The Manchester Public Library is particularly quiet at the end of August, and we have the archive search room pretty much to ourselves. A stack of leather-bound, marble-effect-covered books of music lie in waiting: a Solo, Violin 1, Violin II, Viola, and Basso, for a keyboard player – all an ensemble needs save for the missing cello part. There's no evidence of any missing duplicate parts, which suggests Vivaldi played in a small dynamic band.

Each volume contains a mismatch of paper pages, with numerous concertos written out on different papers of varying sizes, and yet because I know they are in there, *The Four Seasons* concertos are not hard to locate; the familiar notes of the score leap off the page. It's just pen and ink on old paper, yet there's a magic in these pages. The handwriting is not Vivaldi's, rather that of copyists working for him, but these are pages he must surely have seen himself, perhaps played from himself. It's a strong touchstone back to his time, the air he breathed, the sounds that filled his study, and the pages of music that papered his desk. It's clear enough even to our eyes that there were two different scribes working on these concertos – two different pens, each with a different sweep to their quill across the beams and note heads, and different flourishes on their lettering. It was thought for some time that one of these two was Vivaldi's father Giovanni Battista, who was an accomplished copyist, but Michael Talbot tipped me off before the visit that it was more likely this scribe was Vivaldi's brother-in-law, the professional copyist Giovanni Antonio Mauro.[8] What is clear is that the owner of the quill was working against the clock, as their handwriting becomes more hurried as the score goes on. Nevertheless, there is considerable care taken in fitting complete movements – like this last movement of *Summer* – onto a single side, or double-page spread, so that performers didn't have to turn a page mid-drama.

These handwritten parts were copied from Vivaldi's master score, a document that certainly pre-dated the printed parts made in Amsterdam – in 1725, even though these parts could have been prepared a year after the published edition came out. They actually make the Amsterdam publisher, Le Cène, seem hurried and scatty by comparison, as these private scores include passages that are more detailed in articulation, with additional chromatic notes and figures for the bass line. More than that, they give a much more 'musical' account of the music they contain compared to the 1725 publication, in sharp contrast to the regimented printed page of modern

Fig. 4: Manchester Manuscript of the soloist's part of
Vivaldi's *Summer*, Movement III.

123

editions. 'There's something about seeing the human hand that makes you realise that it's open to feeling,' Daniel says, 'it's showing you the truth, not dogma.'

There's also something brilliantly intangible about the way these manuscript parts show that these concertos weren't played the same way twice. It's in the freedom of a handwritten part: you can imagine Vivaldi playing from them for Cardinal Ottoboni and in no way slavishly sticking to what was on the page. We pore over the flick of slurs (the markings that signal to the performers to play smoothly), the whimsy of pen-lines that suggest direction and flow, and pauses that seem to invite an improvisation in the moment. Visually the score says so much about the energy of the piece, whether in the rush of notes or the gaps for rests (the silences that punctuate it). 'It's as if the score itself is in flux,' Daniel says. 'It makes me want to take a manuscript copy to all first rehearsals for anyone who thinks they know how it goes – just to see this variation, inconsistency or insistence on an effect.'

Daniel highlights aspects that have influenced his interpretation – details that down the years have become distorted by influential recordings, such as a long high G in this stormy *Summer* movement that players most often resolve down to an F, of which Vivaldi shows no indication. In these parts are brief passages that contradict the printed edition of 1725: they correct errors, mostly minor ones, that were made by the printers. 'It's liberating,' says Daniel, 'almost as if a modern score can gaslight you – even if you know the answer musically, how it should sound, you can't usually prove it.' When you see notes on a printed page, they are generally identical in size and similar in shape, but here, light and shade is in the movement of the handwriting. 'It's as if you hear the lines and the direction of the music,' Daniel agrees. 'Even just the thickness of the pen suggests an energy and reminds you it's a gesture rather than a fact.' These are working documents that actively encourage creative freedom.

Imagination and freedom are words that are not usually suggested by a score, but looking at handwritten manuscript parts we get a sense of the spaces between the notes, the musical aspects that only arrive after years of playing these concertos and hours of experimenting with them. I wanted to look at the manuscript parts in Manchester specifically with Daniel because, whether he knows it or not, he embodies the practical outcomes of going back to sources and taking their essence into the modern world. But there's another reason I wanted to bring him here and it concerns another detail integral to the score: the sonnets.

—

It may still surprise people who have known *The Four Seasons* for years to discover that there is specific poetry wound around them, but Vivaldi's sonnets explicitly reveal his vision of the turning year. However, they are, and always have been, the unheard element in performance. The preface to the 1725 publication explains how the sonnets and descriptions were *added* to the music, leaving us to presume that the original manuscript copies made little if any reference to them. That's not to say that Vivaldi hadn't had all the elements of each season in mind, or even had the poetry itself to hand when writing the concertos, but there is a general consensus that there were just titles to begin with, and the texts followed.[9]

The Manchester manuscripts show the text of the sonnet written out in full in the Basso continuo – the keyboard player's part. Mirroring the scheme we've already seen in the printed parts, each line of the poetry is preceded by a letter, and those letters then appear in

Fig. 5: Manchester Manuscript of the sonnet for Vivaldi's *Summer*.

the score of each part to show the exact moments in which particular effects are portrayed in the music.

In contrast to the published parts, here in the manuscript the lines of music are freed from the messy clutter of the words that are squeezed around the notes. It makes them startlingly clear; they really look like parts for people who know what they are doing. You could say that the published parts keep reminding the players which detail of the scene they are depicting, but these manuscript copies clear the way for a wider, freer interpretation.

Despite Vivaldi's best efforts to align the words to the music in his published score, it remains the task of the performer to decide the extent to which they inform their interpretation and how evident the poems'

Fig. 6: Excerpt from the first movement of *Summer*, first edition. (*Il cimento dell'armonia e dell'inventione*, op.8 (No.2) (Amsterdam: Michel-Charles Le Cène [1725]). Plate 520.)

meanings are to an audience. Programme notes or album sleeves are the texts' natural habitat, and many performers now summarise them before playing – which can be a real eye- (or ear) opener for listeners. As we remember from *Spring*, Rachel Podger enjoys having an Italian musician playing in her band who can read the poems in the original, and there's the rub: musicians tend to agree that in English translations they don't have the impact you'd hope – they're not polished jewels, certainly not Shakespeare. This was my motivation to commission poet Kate Wakeling to make the new translations that head up each of my chapters. Her creative rendering of the original Italian might appeal for reading in performances, yet it still honours the original author, who is widely thought to be Vivaldi himself.

In the decade during which Vivaldi trained to be a priest, he amassed knowledge of religious texts that went on to serve his sacred works, but, considering his humble upbringing, it seems improbable he had the time or means to devote himself to literature and classical studies. However, this was something he sought to rectify later in life, especially as his operatic career blossomed. He became a champion of young Venetian librettists such as Antonio Maria Lucchini, who wrote texts for three of his operas (*Tieteberga*, *Farnace* and *Dorilla in Tempe*) and whose other librettos included *Giove in Argo* (Jupiter in Argos), set by Antonio Lotti and Handel. Vivaldi also played an active role in the crafting of librettos: original drafts of his operas reveal that he made inconsistent and often inconsequential alterations to aria texts, and often rewrote portions of recitative.[10] The fact that the sonnets for *The Four Seasons* include Venetian variants of specific words also used by Vivaldi in his own letters – words such as 'mossoni' rather than 'mosconi' (blowflies), and 'canni' in place of 'cani' (dogs) – suggest that he may indeed have been the sonnets' author.[11] He certainly doesn't seem to have lacked the confidence to write in verse.

The choice of sonnets above short pieces of prose perhaps reveals something about the workings of Vivaldi's mind at the time. Translated as 'little sound' or 'short melody', the sonnet was an important Italian poetic form (also popular in England), with inherent musical connotations. Through his use of it, Vivaldi taps into a tradition of making the sonnet a tool to explain another art form, such as visual art, another kind of literature – or even card games. There is also a performative angle, as sonnets were commonly chosen for recitation (and publication) by literary reformers within the Venetian societies or accademias, based on the model of the Accademia degli Arcadi (the Academy of the Arcadians) in Rome. There's no evidence that Vivaldi was a paid-up member of any such society, but they were highly influential, especially for the librettists Vivaldi worked with for his operas. The sonnets of *The Four Seasons* certainly conform to the Arcadian hallmarks of good taste, which included an accessible narrative and the portrayal of real-life situations.[12]

For all this, the poetic value of the sonnets lies in what they imply rather than what they explicitly portray, and Vivaldi's artistic imagination is only fully revealed in the music. What is certain is that the more time you spend with both manuscripts and sonnets, the more you realise they are inextricably interlinked. The music may be timeless, but whether the poetry in its original format is evergreen is up for debate, and that's where Daniel Pioro's interpretation re-enters the fray.

As a British performer, he faced the familiar feeling of anticlimax on reading the standard, very literal translation of the poetry. 'It's a bit like explaining the magic of a snowflake rather than experiencing it directly,' Daniel says, 'yet it's vital to be able to square the sonnets with the musical elements and storytelling.' His solution was to reach for the phone and talk to his old friend and collaborator Sir Michael Morpurgo. 'It just made sense that it would be him, a man for whom classical music is a great joy, and who writes not just for children, and not just for adults, but for people.' What Daniel wanted was a retelling of the sonnets for our time, something that would resonate with the impact of, say, Prokofiev's *Peter and the Wolf.*

Following the 2023 premiere of Michael's version, when he joined Daniel and the London Sinfonietta to read his sonnets on stage, I met up with this national storytelling treasure at the Hay Festival. Between literary events, and rainstorms that Vivaldi would have raised a knowing eyebrow at, Michael and I shared an appropriately seasonal summer-berry-slathered panna cotta. He'd just come off stage where he'd held an audience in raptures, talking, appropriately enough, about the importance of *retelling* stories, capturing new imaginations with old tales from antiquity and Shakespeare. We carried on that theme over our pudding, chatting about the importance of not sugar-coating stories, but making them relevant and relatable. If we were to re-imagine the poetic content of Vivaldi's sonnets from *The Four Seasons* today, what would their focus be – flash floods and forest fires? For Michael, Vivaldi is there to remind us of what we are destroying, all the things we love but rarely articulate. 'Seasonality goes beyond weather forecasts,' he says, and his new sonnets prove once again how the seasons offer us time-less – and timely prompts to stop, watch and listen. It's a chance to mirror Vivaldi's love letter to the year, with a personal one of his own:

Summer
Welcome happy days of sun and summer.
Welcome back, you skimming swallows,
You screeching swifts,
You buntings and godwits,
How we have longed to see you again,
You found your way back.
You bring our summer with you,
Make your summer homes with us,

Be again our family and friends, lift our spirits,
Warm our hearts.

Here we are to greet you again.
Woken now from winter sleep.
Honeysuckle and campion,
Dog-rose and foxglove,
Buttercup, and daisy,
Bright-eyed daisy by day, closed tight at night,
And every morning, every dawning,
Each one gladly opened up again,
By summer sun, by you.

As we are too.

Cuckoo calls, unseen, from far-off wood,
Summer's echoing herald.
Lark rises high in the blue, and is lost.
But her song still sings.
Hay dances in the warmth of the breeze,
Sways and waves with the whispering trees.
The world has come alive again.
And it is wondrous to us.
On days like this, sweet summer,

You make it so.

We may swelter often in the heat of the day.
As we shear our sheep and make our hay.
Summer storms may flash and rumble,

And blow in wild on gusty winds
With squally hail and lashing rain.
They can roar and rage all they like.
We do not care. It cleans the air.
We are watered, filled with newness,
Like the fields, like the flowers, like the trees,

Like the whole wide world.[13]

This is the sort of summer we want to experience; it's the season we seek to reclaim if we've stopped listening to the rhythm of the year in the frenzy of modern life. The summer sun on our faces is what we long for every cold winter, but this poem also undeniably reveals Michael's very personal evocation of the woods and fields of Devon, which is a long way from the landscapes of Mantua or Venice. There is a universality of feeling, though, that unites the two, and the culture of living in the countryside is not that different. 'When I'm in Devon', Michael says:

I feel the connection to the past, to the eighteenth
century and beyond. The hedges were dug by the
Saxons over 1,000 years ago, the buildings are
hundreds of years old, everything comes from the land.
In summer, the people, in either Devon or Mantua,
hunkered down in their little cottages while the wind
roared outside; that's what we still do. It still *sounds*
exactly the way that it did at this time.

That's a connection to the seasons that transcends time and place. In his poetic response to the music, Michael proves that longing for a season is as important as the season itself, and he laughs as he admits that it's wonderful to be aware of summer's qualities *without* cursing the weather.

Vivaldi's texts were precisely annotated at very particular points in the score, but that's not necessarily the case with Michael's. The birds, for example, do not correlate exactly with Vivaldi's or appear at the same moments – but to make them do so perhaps misses the point. Michael's poems are a retelling, not a translation: his *Summer* depicts the birds and flowers of our own time. But one of the biggest differences between the original poetry and this retelling is that Vivaldi ended *Summer* with utter devastation, whereas Michael finds resolution in cleared air. I ask him about that notion of riding out the storm, and his answer is bound up in his role as the modern-day teller of Vivaldi's seasonal story.

> I always feel that life is full of storms, and we all wait
> for the big hurricane at the end of our lives, but the one
> wonderful thing about the human spirit is that in the
> midst of fear, of human and natural disasters, there's a
> sense that we'll get through and come out the other side.

This might not be what Vivaldi's sonnet suggested, but we know that autumn and all the celebrations it brings are only moments away. In a retelling, this is the resilience we can learn from nature and the cyclical rhythm of the seasons. 'All my life I have been focused on the importance of our connection to the world about us,' says Michael, 'and one of the reasons I think *The Four Seasons* is so loved is because it fosters something we want to feel – a sense of belonging to what's around us.'

If you know the concertos or are familiar with the original sonnets, Michael's poetry plays with your expectations, inviting you to add modern layers of nuance and colour to Vivaldi's musical canvas. These are not themes that take us to the edge of understanding, they are the everyday things that transcend time and place. 'The more you read Michael's poems, the more you realise they will affect you as much or as little as you are willing to allow,' Daniel says, 'I would love it if they became the gateway into this extraordinary music for generations of people to come.'

—

Both Michael's and Daniel's words echo in my head as I take the train home from Manchester to London. The late-summer sun casts long shadows across the acres and acres of golden stubble that streak past my carriage window, the relic of crops that have been safely gathered in. Right in the centre of one field, miles from anywhere, a tyre swing hangs from a huge old oak tree. Someone comes here to feel free, to watch the trains perhaps, or the turning colours of the year. Judging by the size of the tree, combine harvesters have circumnavigated it for decades, and the swing looks as though it could have been hoisted up there at pretty much any point over the last hundred years. There it waits, impervious to summer storms, ready for the next person to drink in the view and feel the wind in their hair. Vivaldi's manuscripts of *The Four Seasons* in Manchester seem to me to be like that too: sitting in glorious isolation in North-West England, waiting for the next person to open them and head back to eighteenth-century Italy.

The Life Cycle of *The Four Seasons* –
Branching Out

The 1725 Publication

The turn of the season into summer is often used as a metaphor for maturity, as is a tree branching out and appearing in full leaf. This season invites the natural world to develop: spring's shoots have grown and established themselves, able to spread further and also to weather any storms. And so, Vivaldi's *The Four Seasons* comes of age under a hot north Italian sun, the concertos proving their maturity and longevity in their publication.

The 1720s saw the heyday of Vivaldi's instrumental composing career, and he received commissions aplenty from European nobility and royalty.[1] Hailed as 'the famous Vivaldi' and known to be the 'best composer in Venice', his reputation preceded him, whether in Venice or Mantua, Milan or Rome. [2] He'd made his name not only from his operatic ventures and virtuoso performances, but also in print; however, he chose not to publish at home. Venice had once been the pioneering centre of printing music, but by the turn of the eighteenth century this had changed. Two firms now dominated the Venetian printing scene: the houses of Giuseppe Sala and Antonio Bortoli. Both were considered technically and commercially backward, their products reputed to lack clarity and their sales reach very modest. So Vivaldi initially published in Rome, but then looked north of the Alps for further business opportunities.

The firm in question was that of Estienne Roger, a francophone printer, bookseller and publisher of sheet music based in Amsterdam. Roger was renowned for his repertory of Italian composers, and the publisher's trademark was the supreme quality of assiduous, exquisite printing from copperplate engravings. Between 1696 and 1722, Roger printed more than five hundred works (not including reprints) and was the premier continental publisher for composers working in Italy, Northern Germany, England and the Netherlands.

In stark contrast to the publishers Vivaldi encountered in Venice, Roger was at the cutting edge of printing innovation. He and his London rival, John Walsh, had sparred over their various attempts to publish the definitive edition of Arcangelo Corelli's op. 5 collection of violin sonatas, and as a result caught the attention of many more Italian composers. It isn't known if Vivaldi met Roger; it's more likely the publisher met with the composer's father. Around 1709, Giovanni Battista was absent from his post as a violinist at St Mark's and it isn't known why. He was the one who managed the family finances, and so it's possible that during this time he brokered a deal for his son in Amsterdam.

Vivaldi had originally published his first two collections – the twelve trio sonatas op. 1 (1705) and the twelve
violin sonatas op. 2 (1709) – in Rome, but Roger was
happy to run with second editions of both. Having established this relationship, in 1711 the Dutch publisher
presented the first edition of Vivaldi's hugely influential
op. 3, a set of twelve concertos entitled *L'estro armonico*
(Harmonic Inspiration). 'Their greatest distinction will
now be their engraving by the famous hand of Monsieur
Estienne Roger,' Vivaldi wrote in the dedication to Grand
Prince Ferdinand of Tuscany, and the benefits were
mutual.[3] Roger, who'd not yet published many concertos – then a new musical form taking northern Europe
by storm – now had the monopoly on one of the most
influential collections. Within op. 3, Vivaldi had combined tradition with innovation, creating a collection
that drew on more than a decade's worth of concertos – a
winning combination from Roger's perspective, as he
could sell them to those who loved the likes of Corelli
and Torelli while also introducing the latest Italian ideas.
As a result, a commercial boom beckoned for Vivaldi, one
that positively catapulted him to celebrity. No other publication had had such an instant and captivating effect,
and over the next thirty-two years it would see no fewer
than twenty reprints.

Roger's near-monopoly on eighteenth-century music
publishing was due both to an international catalogue and
a highly effective distribution network of agents in centres

from Rotterdam to Berlin, Leipzig to Paris, and Hamburg to London. He attracted the trust and business of major composers and established the practice of publisher's numbers, i.e. numbering all his publications – now a vital system for twenty-first-century musicologists fathoming the chronology of long-dead composers' works.

Vivaldi and Roger's business partnership flourished. The twelve violin concertos of Vivaldi's op. 4, *La stravaganza* (The Eccentricity) appeared in 1716, then followed in quick succession the six sonatas of op. 5, the six violin concertos of op. 6 and the twelve concertos of op. 7. There is some speculation that Vivaldi wasn't enamoured of the haste in which this all took place: opp. 5, 6 and 7 lack dedications, all three opuses include mistakes, and some of the concertos in op. 7 are possibly not written by Vivaldi, which suggests they appeared without his express permission. If Vivaldi was growing disenchanted with this arrangement, it didn't stop him offering Roger his op. 8 collection, which begins with *The Four Seasons*.

However, in 1722, before op. 8 could be published, Roger died. He had two daughters – both of whom had designs on the business. The elder, Françoise, had married the aforementioned publisher Michel-Charles Le Cène, who had worked with his father-in-law on non-musical books for a couple of years after the wedding. However, Roger had named his younger daughter Jeanne the successor to his business, and from 1716, six years before his death, cemented this by using her name on publications. She had been the one to issue Vivaldi's recent publications – the ones published with apparent undue haste. But then tragedy struck again, Jeanne fell ill and promptly died in December 1722, just five months after her father.

It would seem her sister, Françoise, had ignored Jeanne's needs on her sickbed. In the nick of time, Jeanne cut her out of her will, leaving the business to her trusted employee Gerrit Drinkman.[*] They say bad things happen in threes, and within months he was dead, too. Waiting in the wings, Françoise and her husband Le Cène stepped in to buy, rather than inherit, the family printing firm from Drinkman's widow. Any triumph they may have felt was sweet but short: two months after the acquisition, Françoise died too. The only one who seemed to enjoy good health, her husband Michel-Charles Le Cène, then carried on the business alone for the next twenty years. He capitalised on old successes by advertising the firm as 'Estienne Roger & Le Cène', and, with a considerable eye for talent, added new composers to the catalogues, including Handel, Tartini, Telemann and Locatelli.

Vivaldi was in good company among those names, but needed to regain control of the rate and accuracy of the publications appearing in his name. As he had offered op. 8 to Roger shortly before the latter's death, there was a delay in publishing the concertos and, to avoid his latest music and ideas stagnating or seeming old hat, Vivaldi apparently considered changing his publisher in order to release concertos by subscription, i.e. as demand and funds allowed: something of a proto-type crowdfunding model that would see them released individually rather than in complete collections. Such a rumour may just have been enough to spur Le Cène into action, and in 1725 op. 8, complete with *The Four Seasons*, was ready for release. It appeared as individual parts rather than a full score, which was typical prac-tice, and, as per the new approach Roger had established with Vivaldi's op. 3 violin concertos, it was released in two volumes of six concertos each. The cover of each sported an engraved portrait of Antonio by François Morellon de La Cave.

From Vivaldi's perspective, op. 8 was a milestone pub-lication, an anthology of concertos spearheaded and inspired by *The Four Seasons*. Tradition dictated that he couldn't have published just those four concertos alone – they needed to be part of a set of six or twelve – so he added more concertos with extra-musical themes. In contrast to previous collections, which had mainly show-cased his latest ideas, here he included concertos that dated back a decade or so in order to comply with his plan, such as *La tempesta di mare* (The Storm at Sea) and *Il piacere* (Pleasure) to complete volume one, and then *La caccia* (The Hunt) in volume two. It shows a new way of thinking, though it's a shame he couldn't find five more concertos with titles to complete the second volume.

Fig. 7: Antonio Vivaldi (engraving by François Morellon de La Cave, from Michel-Charles Le Cène's edition of Vivaldi's op. 8, Amsterdam, 1725)

Throughout the 1720s he wrote plenty more concertos on extra-musical topics, which suggests that Roger and Le Cène had been in possession of *The Four Seasons* for some time. With the exception of *La tempesta di mare* the contents of op. 8 mostly reflect agricultural concerns and pleasures of nature that relate as much to his time working in Mantua as to the port of Venice, so it's likely that Le Cène had had them at least since 1723, but possibly much earlier.

Opus 8 would have added prestige to the freelance position Vivaldi took up at the Pietà in 1723: an anthology demonstrating that the composer was still innovating with the concerto form, and showing how vibrant and descriptive it could be. Vivaldi had also cottoned on to the idea that, in a saturated market of concertos, attaching a name to a collection garnered greater attention; it had worked well with *L'estro armonico* (op. 3) and *La stravaganza* (op. 4). This latest set of concertos warranted an even more enigmatic title: *Il cimento dell'armonia e dell'inventione* (The Trial of Harmony and Invention). It's sometimes translated as a contest rather than a trial, but there's no real suggestion that harmony and invention are at odds; rather that they may work in tandem, or even fuse, to bring new meaning to music.

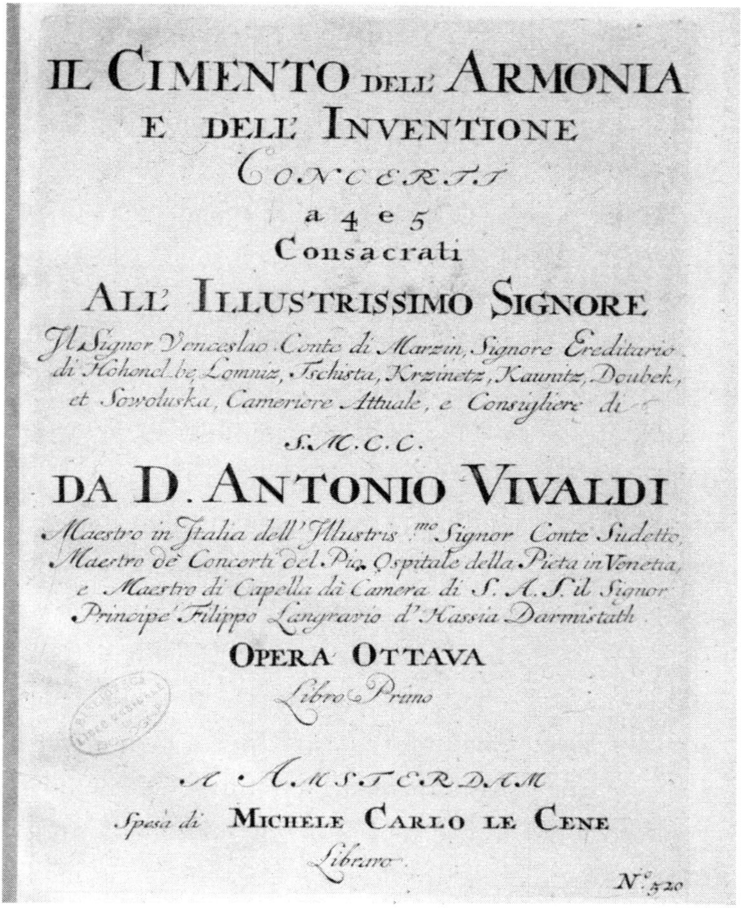

IL CIMENTO DELL' ARMONIA
E DELL' INVENTIONE
Concerti
a 4 e 5
Consacrati
ALL' ILLUSTRISSIMO SIGNORE
Il Signor Venceslao Conte di Marzin, Signore Ereditario
di Hohenelbe, Lomniz, Tschista, Krzinetz, Kaunitz, Doubek,
et Sowoluska, Cameriere Attuale, e Consigliere di
S. M. C. C.
DA D. ANTONIO VIVALDI
Maestro in Italia dell' Illustris.mo Signor Conte Sudetto,
Maestro de' Concerti del Pio Ospitale della Pieta in Venetia,
e Maestro di Capella dà Camera di S. A. S. il Signor
Principe Filippo Langravio d' Hassia Darmistath
OPERA OTTAVA
Libro Primo

A AMSTERDAM
Spesa di MICHELE CARLO LE CENE
Libraro
N.º 520

Fig. 8: Frontispiece for *Il cimento dell'armonia
e dell'inventione*

One of the first things to leap off the title page of the printed edition is the dedication: to the 'most illustrious' Count Wenzel von Morzin, a man with a list of titles as long as your arm. This is the same Morzin we encountered in *Spring* on the Grand Tour with his sons. He'd met Vivaldi, possibly in Venice, more likely in Mantua, heard *The Four Seasons*, taken a copy of the concertos back to his musicians in Prague, and made Vivaldi his *maestro di musica in Italia*. Vivaldi lists that specific title in the dedication, alongside his being concert master of the Pietà in Venice *and* being *maestro di cappella da camera* to Prince Philip of Hesse-Darmstadt in Mantua.

Inside, there is a much longer dedication, in which Vivaldi is quick to flatter Morzin's musical prowess, his 'supreme understanding of music', and his 'most accomplished orchestra'. Could Vivaldi have heard this ensemble in Prague? His certainty that his concertos 'will enjoy that eminence which they do not deserve' could suggest he had; it's certainly a knowing tone.[5] The otherwise grovelling manner of the dedication is typical of the age, but reading between these lines written in 1725, there is a sense of his impatience in getting this publication out into the world. He states that he 'blushed' when reflecting on the fact that until this point he had not demonstrated in print the 'profound veneration' in which he held the count. As Morzin's *maestro di musica in Italia*, Vivaldi had sent him multiple concertos over the years since their first meeting, proof of which can be found in surviving receipts from the court in Prague. There is also evidence that Morzin had paid Vivaldi a 'reglo', a subsidy for the publication of op. 8, and therefore the delay would have been even more embarrassing.[6]

Morzin was evidently a generous benefactor, and one that Vivaldi was at pains to keep sweet; therefore it's significant that he singles out *The Four Seasons* in the dedication as concertos that have 'long enjoyed the indulgence of "Your Most Illustrious Lordship's kind generosity".' Crucially, he notes that he's 'added to them [. . .] a very clear statement of all the things that unfold in them', concluding: 'I am sure that they will appear new to you.'[7]

There is an implication here that manuscript copies of *The Four Seasons* circulating prior to this publication might have just had seasonal titles and lacked the poetry that may have inspired them. It certainly suggests that this edition offers a new degree of clarity, and that Vivaldi realised he had hit on a novel idea for the concerto-buying public: the as yet undefined genre of programme music – instrumental music that renders an extra-musical narrative.

At long last, on 14 December 1725, the *Gazette d'Amsterdam* announced the publication of Vivaldi's *Il cimento dell'armonia e dell'inventione* op. 8. After weathering summer's storms, *The Four Seasons* had finally flown the nest.

PART THREE
Autumn

I: Allegro

The workers are merry;
the harvest is now gathered safe
and so they sing and dance.
Each drinks their fill
from Bacchus' brimming cup,
before each glad and weary body slips
towards the soundest sleep.[1]

Venice is surrounded by water, but also by vineyards. Today, the Veneto region generates the greatest volume of Italian wine each year – no small matter in one of the world's major wine-producing nations. Grapes have been grown in the region since Roman times, but in the 1420s Venice expanded its borders on the mainland, and with that came a modern approach to farming and viticulture. Beautiful villas were built amid vineyards, orchards and fields of crops. In response, the 1450s saw innovative glassmakers in Murano produce tableware to match. Their creative goblets and bottles offered a way to appreciate the colour of the wine and to watch the way it moved, enhancing the drinking experience at banquets. Vines were also grown to create shady areas for walking and sitting, their leaves adorned Venetian porches, and the imagery of

Bacchus with which they were associated suited the town's revels well. For a time, moving glass and grapes between Lebanon and London made Venice – a city of ships and merchants – a true capital of wine. A prized product revered for its exotic origins, it was a lavish status symbol, and Venetians knew how to capitalise on it. They taxed it at every opportunity, with guilds not only controlling imports at the point of entry but also as the wine was transported on, re-sold and even served. Throughout the fifteenth and sixteenth centuries, Venice traded wines from the Greek islands in the Aegean Sea, the Eastern Mediterranean islands of Cyprus and Crete, the Ionian Islands and the Dalmatian coast, bringing the city financial success and immense power.

Even though political machinations saw that trading monopoly decline before Vivaldi's time, his Venice was still one of the most wine-centric cities in Europe. The wine business Vivaldi knew was given a last hurrah with the surge of tourists on the Grand Tour, and especially those who flooded the city for Carnevale. To meet their demands, Venetians imported from Germany, Hungary and France, but still relied heavily on home-grown wines from the southern Italian states as well as the Veneto. Viticulture around the lagoon itself has always been precarious, owing to the salt-rich soil and brackish waters, which risk sterilising vines at high tides. Whether or not Vivaldi actually observed the grapes hanging on the vines, being harvested or turned to wine, he certainly would have heard talk of the grape harvest in Venice, and with a declining wine trade, a successful harvest gave even more reason to celebrate.

That's exactly what we find in the first movement of Vivaldi's *Autumn*: the villagers dancing and singing in cheerful F major. It is one of the most repetitive moments in the whole set of concertos, a dance-like theme that is introduced and repeated, again and again and again. This creates a sense of stability, a toe-tapping reassurance that includes syncopated moments for extra revelling, but nothing to trip up dancers of any age. The tune is quickly familiar, one that everyone could soon sing, and in which predictable phases and catchy rhythms have the power to set simple dance steps flying.

Music and revels established, specific characters emerge as depicted by the musicians, all audibly affected by the wine. Fired up by Bacchus's liquor, the soloist is the principal drunken member of the party, and is soon joined by the cellist, the pair of them losing their footing in falling phrases. The full band arrives as if to hold them up, before revealing that they are drunk too, a fact confirmed by Vivaldi marking 'Ubriachi' (drunkards) by the relevant phrases in each part. Short rising motifs appear like hiccups, and long descending scales suggest the dancers falling to the ground. Twice the ritornello – the dancing chorus – returns as the harvest revellers rally and regain their footing to join in again, but the movement overall is one of the most drawn-out drunken scenes in Baroque music. Vivaldi keeps up the memos to remind the soloist and other band members that their characters are inebriated, insinuating that they might enact this in the delivery of their phrases, keeping up their flailing and loud declamations. The soloist in particular is spurred on to ever-greater feats of virtuosity, depicting wilder and wilder dancing in their outrageously arpeggiated line. However, between the organised leaps, their music slides under slurs, the notes tumbling to illustrate their staggering and tottering about. Eventually, in what is often delivered as a comedy slow-motion effect, the soloist's drunken character falls to the ground, and Vivaldi confirms that they have become 'l'ubriache che dorme' (the drunkard asleep). Initially only a pair of violins stay with them, quietly accompanying the long, held notes of the sleeping protagonist. A viola eventually joins too, but the bass instruments are nowhere to be seen or heard. Presumably they've only headed off back to the bar, because at the point when everything has gone really quiet, the entire band strikes up a final ritornello. The swinging chorus is heard one last time, and all the revellers, and perhaps the soloist too, resume their singing and dancing to the end of the movement.

—

In 1718, Venice signed the Treaty of Passarowitz, a deal in which the city's ally Austria insisted it ceded former Venetian colonies in Greece and the eastern Adriatic to the Ottoman Empire. The result was a free-trade treaty in which Austrian and Ottoman superpowers bypassed Venice, their former broker in the Mediterranean, and diminished her hold over the wine trade. Mere months before the signatures dried on the parchment, Vivaldi had set out through Venice's vineyards, en route for Mantua and his new post under a member of the Habsburg dynasty.

It's early October when I head for Mantua, a North Italian town unjustly neglected by tourists making a beeline for Juliet's Balcony in Verona, or the glamour of Lake Garda. Verona is the closest airport, and on landing I sympathise with Vivaldi's complaints that travel was expensive for a person of limited mobility. How could my taxi driver not know the way to Mantua's Ducal Palace? As we circumnavigate roundabouts multiple times, the meter skyrockets. Oldest trick in the book.

The road from Verona to Mantua cuts through wetlands and flat arable land. Vivaldi probably travelled from Venice to Mantua by carriage, although it's possible that sections of his journey were undertaken on the River Po and the waterways built for trade. It's the sort of landscape across which you could well imagine a storm gaining momentum and causing mayhem before hitting the Dolomites on the horizon, but as summer turns to autumn, wheat, apples and pumpkins grow plentifully on the well-watered plains. However, there are not many vines out here, I note – marshland doesn't lend itself to viticulture. After learning more about

Vivaldi's debilitating tight chest in summer, I really can't imagine him in the fields witnessing the revels of this first movement of *Autumn* – but they were certainly waiting for him in Mantua as the spoils of the harvest were gathered in town.

Historically, the European harvest was bookended by two important holy days in the church calendar: the Feast of St Michael the Archangel (Michaelmas) on 29 September and the Feast of St Martin, patron saint of winemaking, on 11 November.

The Feast of St Michael at the beginning of the harvest coincides with the initial gathering in of crops, the bounty of the earth brought home and celebrated. The purpose of it was principally to honour the Archangel Michael, the greatest of all the angels, revered in the Book of Revelation for defeating Lucifer in the war of heaven. Michaelmas was recognised throughout Western Christianity: a legal 'quarter day', and a Holy Day of Obligation on which the faithful were expected to attend church. After Christmas and Easter, it was the third biggest feast of the year, a particularly auspicious date for masses of festive proportions. However, it was a feast day enjoyed principally by the wealthy and clergy – which would have included Vivaldi. The poor peasants would attend services, but otherwise would put in long hours in the fields, continuing the harvest.

The Feast of St Martin, on the other hand, occurs at the end of the harvest process. Martin was known for his generosity and was canonised after he found a beggar shivering in the cold and cut his cloak in half in order to share it with him. At the moment that his sword cut the cloth, the clouds parted, the sun came out and the temperature rose. That night Martin dreamt he had met Jesus, and the next morning he awoke to find his cloak restored to its former glory. Thanks to this parable, St Martin's Day is also associated with the phenomenon of an 'Indian summer': the last flush of sun before winter. Where wine is concerned, old sayings such as 'A San Martino ogni mosto diventa vino' (On Saint Martin's Day each must [new grape juice] becomes wine) and 'Per San Martino si spilla il botticino' (On St Martin's Day you tap [open] the little barrel) refer to the magical moment in which the most recently harvested grapes ferment into wine, and the farmers open the barrels for the first time to taste it.

Thursday is market day in Mantua. I'm woken early by traders busy setting up their stalls in the Piazza Sordello. Under the watchful gaze of Mantua's Cathedral and Ducal Palace, rolls of material are hauled out for inspection, cashmere sits alongside discount T-shirts, the pasta van smells delectable, and cauliflowers, beans, grapes and the season's first pumpkins fill the fruit and veg stalls. *Tortelli di zucca* is Mantua's signature dish: pumpkin-filled pasta parcels, the sweet vegetable made sweeter still by the addition of crushed amaretti biscuits or *mostada* (preserved fruits in mustard syrup), served with sage butter and plenty of cheese. It's an autumnal colour palette worthy of the burnt oranges, umbers and browns of the Mantuan architecture. Come lunchtime, my tortelli arrive with a nice glass of something, and I try not to taunt Ron Merlino, the New York-based music and wine historian, as I call him from my table. (It's early morning in the Big Apple, so I'm the only one drinking.) Taking a sip, I ask him how the first wines of the harvest taste.

'At this time of year, the young wine has just about finished its fermentation in the vessels and vats,' he says. 'This means there's still a bit of carbon dioxide in the juice – so it's fresh, a touch fizzy and light. It's only just crossed the line between grape juice and wine, which means it's a moment when all classes of people, from peasants to nobles, can celebrate and drink.' Looking round the market right now, that certainly rings true, and Ron reminds me that back in Venice the new wine is referred to as *vino novello, acqua pazza, acquarello* or *vinello* – and still drunk with special St Martin's Day biscuits called *cotognata*.

St Martin's Day denotes a dividing time for different styles of wine. It renders the previous year's wines 'old' or 'aged', which has legal implications on storage and price, but for the year in question, it also has great technical significance. 'St Martin's Day signifies the demarcation line between normal wines and late-harvest wines,' Ron explains.

From this day forward, grapes are intentionally left
on the vines or twisted to hang without water and
nutrients as the weather shifts and concentrates their
sugars. This is the beginning of the process of making
the famous Venetian sweet late-harvest 'Vin Santo' too,
as this is the time from which grapes are harvested
and laid out on straw mats or hung on rafters inside
wineries to dry out and sweeten.

As a priest, Vivaldi would have been intimately
acquainted with the sacred, musical and culinary traditions of the feasts of both St Michael and St Martin, and
Ron has me persuaded that he surely understood something of the significance of each harvest feast date in the
cycle of winemaking. So, is one of them depicted in
the first movement of his *Autumn* concerto? Neither
seems a perfect fit, but the atmosphere of communal festivities and ritual is certainly present.

Tortelli finished and glass drained, it's time for me to
head inside Mantua's Ducal Palace and tread the paths
and boards Vivaldi would have known when he was
appointed the city's *maestro di cappella da camera* (Director
of Chamber Music).

———

When the Habsburgs seized control of Mantua in 1708,
much of the city had already fallen into disrepair: the
Gonzagas were a legendarily cash-strapped dynasty and
the last of them hightailed it to Vienna, with as many

possessions as they could muster. A thousand paintings were stripped off the walls of the Ducal Palace and taken away, along with furniture, statues and books. When Prince Philip of Hesse-Darmstadt was installed as Governor in 1714, he had to prioritise the parts he wanted to restore in his quest to return the artistic fortunes of the city to their former Gonzaga glory.

Vivaldi played a part in this restoration, arriving around four years later to take charge of composing and directing secular music; he was a band leader in priest's clothing. We don't know whether he lived within the palace complex (although it seems likely, as musicians and artists such as Andrea Galluzzi did before him), nor do we know whether he was, in fact, paid partly in wine, as his forbears had been under Gonzaga rule. Let's assume both were distinct possibilities. Inside the Ducal Palace is a labyrinth that covers some 35,000–40,000 square metres and the director, Stefano L'Occaso, meets me to plot a route through the possible performance spaces for seasonal concertos.

We start with the theatres, two sizeable venues that could be accessed from covered walkways without having to set foot outside. Stefano explains that over the centuries they've both been referred to as the Archducal Theatre, which has led to much confusion. Neither is a theatre now, but we begin in what was known as the *New* Archducal Theatre, a venue being renovated while Vivaldi was in Mantua – and not completed until many

years after he left, although a number of his operatic productions were mounted there. In the nineteenth century
it was turned into a market, and it's now the Archaeological
Museum. The other, the Comic Theatre, was well known
to Vivaldi during his tenure, and he certainly put on four
of his own operas there between 1718 and 1720; it was
demolished in the late nineteenth century and is now,
somewhat incongruously, a museum of firefighting.
Vivaldi had form performing concertos in the intervals
of his operas, but these spaces have long been converted
so it's not possible to garner any specific acoustic or
potential artistic influence on *The Four Seasons*. A smaller
theatre found high up in the original fourteenth-century
Castello di San Giorgio is a different matter.

The majestic four-tower battlement was always
intended to be a symbol of absolute power, commanding
wide views of the lakes and countryside, and Stefano
shows me the site of the former theatre, a space we esti-
mate could have seated around 100 courtiers. This venue
between the north-east and north-west towers seems
ideal for some of the forty serenatas Vivaldi is known to
have written for Mantua, but the theatre space, which
would formerly have been covered with frescoes, is now
divided into two museum rooms, so it's another workout
for the imagination. Adjoining them is the former Bridal
Chamber, or Chamber of the Spouses, frescoed to the hilt
with scenes of the Gonzagas and their court in the
countryside, with imagined images of Rome, perhaps

Tivoli, and the classical world painted by Andrea Mantegna in the fifteenth century. Although all the palace's paintings were removed by the Gonzagas, the frescoes were a fixture, and Vivaldi certainly could have seen these. If the Bridal Chamber had been used by the Habsburgs it would have been as an entertaining space, and music such as *The Four Seasons* would have made a huge impact in this generous acoustic. However, there's a theory that they used it for storage rather than living, so I'm keen to keep looking for further possible sites of influence for Vivaldi's *Autumn*.

I ask Stefano about more domestic places in which chamber music might have been played. He takes me to the Hall of Rivers, decorated today as it was in 1773, and which was most likely the refectory in the early eighteenth century. The arched windows of the huge banqueting hall would originally have opened onto the hanging garden outside, a feature even more remarkable when you realise that the floor here is not at ground level; the rooflines beyond remind us that we are a sizeable level higher. The thought of a celebration of the harvest, with wine flowing and the vines curling around the arches, certainly brings to mind Bacchus, god of wine, and the celebrations this room must have witnessed. Even if this wasn't the performance space for Vivaldi's *Autumn*, it could easily have been an inspiration.

Stefano is called away, but before he leaves, he points out a feature of the room's acoustics. Where the walls meet the ceiling there is a soft curve, a vault constructed with woven swamp reeds. It was a technique used by the celebrated architect Vincenzo Scamozzi for the Ducal Palace's music rooms, and it's the same feature that we see in the nearby Hall of Mirrors – a space beloved by Claudio Monteverdi for his Friday-afternoon concerts. The thought that Vivaldi wandered the corridors of this frescoed old palace seeking out the best places to perform chamber music makes the centuries between us feel irrelevant. The challenge for us is working out which of the rooms appealed. There seems little doubt Vivaldi would have also appreciated the acoustic in the rooms we've seen so far – spaces that could have seen the premiere of Monteverdi's 1607 opera, *L'Orfeo*.[2] These were splendid places for banqueting and entertaining, in which the images of nature seem to invite revelling.[3] They are plausible performance spaces for *The Four Seasons*, but I continue to wonder whether they may also have played a part in inspiring the content of the concertos too. Paintings of vines also bedeck the walkways and corridors I get to see away from public view, to say nothing of the four considerable gardens within the palace walls, all of which are ideal for training vines and creating the classic tableau of autumn's harvest celebrations.

Each of the movements of *The Four Seasons* we've encountered so far has been situated outside, but seeing Vivaldi's workplace first-hand makes me wonder whether the action of the first two movements of *Autumn* could conceivably be set *within* the walls of the Ducal Palace. This idea of bringing the outside inside is heightened by the lack of birdsong in this movement. Birds still nest, as they always have done, in the Ducal Palace, but not in the numbers that Vivaldi would have experienced had he been out in the fields. Their absence here suggests a harvest watched from a window, the glories of the season and the effects of the new wine enjoyed without the need to ever leave the palace gates.

Fig. 9: Giardino dei Semplici at the Ducal Palace in Mantua.

—

I leave the Ducal Palace with some questions answered and many more swirling around my head. If I have potentially found places around the palace in which *The Four Seasons* could have been played or even quasi-staged, who, then, was getting drunk? If the music reflects parties held out in the fields or at the market, then the farm workers and traders easily fit these roles. If the scene is brought inside the Ducal Palace, then courtiers fill the peasant roles, under the vines of hanging gardens or frescoes. But the soloist serves up the main-character energy, and their line depicts the key drunkard.

This makes me wonder about Vivaldi's experience of wine. His role as master of secular music and opera impresario might well have required him to have a working knowledge of wine; he would have arrived in Mantua knowing that part of the job was to feed and water the musicians in his charge. Later that night, over polenta and local stew – with a large glass of red – I call Ron again.

'As a member of the clergy, Vivaldi would have had access to a whole world of wine in Venice,' he says, 'from church vineyards to traders and visiting dignitaries – he would have tasted wines from all over the continent.' There's a surviving account from the diaries of Johann Friedrich Armand von Uffenbach, a wealthy lawyer and aristocrat from Strasbourg, who visited Venice in 1715 for Carnevale. He attended several operas during his stay and, as an avid collector of Vivaldi's music, arranged a meeting with the composer to buy manuscripts from him directly. His diary offers an intriguing glimpse into the presence of wine in Vivaldi's life: he begins 'After supper I received a visit from Vivaldi [. . . I had] a few bottles of wine fetched for him, knowing that he was a cleric. He let me listen to his very difficult and quite inimitable fantasias on the violin, so that, being close at hand, I could not but marvel even more at his skill.'[4] Did Uffenbach inform Vivaldi that he had wine waiting, as an added incentive for him to agree to meet? Or was he offering wine as a sign of respect for Vivaldi's priestly position?

'My personal guess is that Uffenbach is likely giving Vivaldi wine from his own personal collection,' says Ron, 'wines he may have brought with him from France as gifts, wines that would have been wildly popular in Venice yet not easy for Vivaldi to purchase. What's more,' Ron goes on, 'it's possible Vivaldi already had a reputation as a wine connoisseur when Uffenbach met him, because he had other powerful wine-producing friends in the form of the two brothers von Schönborn.'

Back in 1709, these two Hessian counts, who owned some of the most important vineyards in the Rheingau region of Germany, visited Vivaldi to purchase trio sonatas and commission cello concertos. They took the music home to Germany and also to Moravian wine-growing regions that, Ron tells me, the Schönborns had purchased from none other than the Morzin family, whose descendant, Count Wenzel von Morzin would become the dedicatee of *The Four Seasons*.

The more I learn of this, the more the worlds of wine and music collide. In Venice, Vivaldi very likely drank both white and red wine, alongside the highly coveted sweet wines Vin Santo, grown in church vineyards that were only available to members of the clergy. Could we hazard a guess at the bottles in his wine cellar, I ask Ron? I might as well have asked him if the Pope's a Catholic. By the end of the evening, we'd agreed a list, and some historical tasting notes:

Whites

Garganega (Soave): The ancient white grape behind the iconic wines of Soave, Garganega offered peach-blossom aromas and green-apple and green-herb flavours to complement the eastern spices added to classic eighteenth-century Venetian banquet dishes like *risi e bisi* (rice and peas).

Glera (Prosecco): Glera, the grape that makes Prosecco, was planted in the Venetian doges' state vineyards as early as the fifteenth century – but its history stretches back to the very beginnings of Venice. The official wine of the Republic, Vivaldi's Prosecco was was, as the name suggests, dry and often bitter – nothing like the off-dry, gently fizzy aperitif wine we drink today.

Malvasia (Malvasie): The ubiquitous grape of Venice, Malvasia was an extensive family of ancient white grapes. Sold in shops also called Malvasie and served in Venice's opera houses, bottles of these wines – which ranged from the fragrant and sweet to the grassy and dry – were available only to the most privileged members of society.

Reds

Raboso and Friularo: Two related rugged red Venetian grapes that initially delivered deeply coloured, intensely sour, aggressive wines but when made sparkling with added sweetness could blossom into a flavour festival of red cherry, plum and pomegranate framed by violets and lavender. They were wines loved by the great Giacomo Casanova and praised in verse by Vivaldi's collaborator, the librettist and playwright Carlo Goldoni.

Marzemino: One of Italy's oldest grapes, Marzemino was prized by Venetian nobles for its floral, perfumed and peppery melange of crushed dark berries and fresh mint. One of the last grapes to ripen in the vineyards, Marzemino was the traditional Venetian toasting grape for the St Martin's Day harvest feasts that signalled the end of the wine-gathering season.

Refosco: A robust, tannic, earthy red grape with bold acidity and long life in the cellar, Refosco remains one of the most historically important still-surviving grapes from the early eighteenth century. It was a go-to Venetian red wine for the ceremonial hog roasts staged on St Mark's Square during Carnevale.

Vivaldi potentially had a wide-ranging palate when it came to wines like this from the Veneto, and may have collected bottles from abroad, too. Ron points out that given the city's rising fashion for non-Venetian wines in the early eighteenth century, Antonio may well have enjoyed prized bottles from Germany such as the Rhine wines made from the white Riesling grape, or France – their Bourgogne or Burgundy wines made from red Pinot Noir grapes. Even if he was not a big drinker, this was a time in which consuming at least watered-down wine was safer than straight water. 'Don't forget', Ron says, 'that in the 1670s the average per capita consumption of wine in Venice was more than 1.5 litres per day.' That's two full bottles.

When Vivaldi was living in Mantua, his wine cellar might have looked quite different. It depends, of course, on whether he lived in or out of the Ducal Palace. In the nineteenth century an inventory was taken of the palace that listed forty-five cellars, and who knows how many of those stocked wine. 'Mantua drew on two wine regions,' says Ron. 'To the north are the vineyards below Lake Garda, as important then as they are today for producing Bardolino and Valpolicella.' He confirms these are light, easy-going wines, made principally from the red Corvina grape. They are wines that the Mantuans (and the Venetians too) had prized for centuries – Isabella d'Este took pride in showing off her collection to visiting dignitaries long before Vivaldi arrived on the scene. Then to the south there are the Lambrusco vineyards – the only major Lambrusco region outside Emilia Romagna.

'The Lambrusco Mantovano is a deep, dark-red sparkling wine – typically dry,' Ron explains, and 'one of the most ancient grapes on the planet'. It has a heritage that can be traced back to the Etruscans and Romans, and is a variety that's been grown in Italy longer than almost any other. 'But here's the thing,' he says, 'as a result of its longevity, there are many different variants, including the Lambrusco Gonzaga, which implies there must have been a significant focus on those vineyards that we have to imagine was still going strong when Vivaldi was there.' It's certainly not a category of wine that has ever gone out of fashion; the 1970s and '80s may have led it to acquire a tarnished reputation as an inexpensive, low-quality product, but recent decades have seen a resurgence in refinement.

This is only a snapshot, but it makes me wonder about Vivaldi's opinion of the drunk person in this first movement of his *Autumn* concerto. He must have been the original soloist, so is he poking fun at himself? Did his health condition make him something of a lightweight? It's done in high art, but could it be high stakes too?

Vivaldi would have risked embarrassment by depicting himself as drunk in front of his employers, or scandal if he was imitating a courtier — perhaps one who was famous for getting drunk on the new wine of the season. Alternatively, he may have been wise to courting trouble and the movement may portray fiction, an allegorical tale from a fresco.

We've no evidence that Vivaldi visited the nearby pleasure palace, Palazzo Te, or even what state it was in when he arrived in Mantua, but had he done so he'd have seen the extraordinary frescoes that survive to this day, including a depiction of *Dioniso ebbro* (Drunken Dionysius) by Giulio Romano, where the god of winemaking is being held up by his friends. It's tempting to see this movement as a morality tale from a cleric composer, but the music seems to suggest a staggering — literally staggering — wild virtuosity about the drunk reveller himself drinking from 'Bacchus' brimming cup', something that only Vivaldi as both composer and violinist could have effectively pulled off.

II: Adagio molto

The last celebrations pass to stillness
and the air grows fresh and cool.
It bids all those who rest
to dream without care,
to dream loose and deep and free.[1]

Revels ended, the autumn air clears, and sleep ensues for Vivaldi's ensemble of merrymakers. Even the solo violinist joins in the long lines of the deep-breathing string slumber party. This is the sort of sleep that wasn't possible in *Summer*: a deep, heavy sleep in which you might, as the sonnet says, 'dream without care'. Vivaldi instructs the players to play their long, sustained lines – Adagio molto – with as much ease as they can muster; but it seems that entirely restful contentment, or the literal 'sweet sleep' of the original Italian sonnet, is impossible. The harmonic (chordal) continuo players – the harpsichordist, organist or lutenist – take on the job of propelling the movement forward. Vivaldi instructs them to play arpeggios (spread chords), but those chords are anything but ordinary. He takes the bass line to weird harmonic corners, and the ensuing slinky chromaticism creates a deeply disturbing atmosphere. These continuo instruments bring the return of that ominous dark streak that weaves its way through *The Four Seasons*, and refuses to be ignored. The whole movement lasts fewer than three minutes, but the psychedelic visions it holds have the power to haunt your dreams for a long time.

I put it to violinist Adrian Chandler that it doesn't feel like a slumber song, and he responds with the universal truth: 'Sleep after a skinful is never a good sleep, is it?' Unsurprisingly, drunken dreams can be unnerving, however 'loose and deep and free' the sonnet might suggest them to be. Adrian also shows me a little more about why he thinks that's the case here. 'Vivaldi uses three levels of quietness,' he points out: '*piano*, then *più piano*, and *pianissimo*, but he doesn't place them until the end of the movement.' I'd not noticed that before – nor have lots of musicians, it would seem. This is no softly sung lullaby, but a wild fantasy. Adrian points to the eighteenth-century flautist and writer Johann Joachim Quantz, who says that just because you have a mute on your violin doesn't mean you have to play softly; it's just a different tone. 'Add in the chords Vivaldi writes for the continuo,' Adrian says, 'and whether on harpsichord or lute, they are nothing short of disturbing – it's utter genius.'

The deeper significance of this movement starts to emerge, not as a refreshing sleep, but as a dream of ancient Greek mythology. Hypnos, god of sleep, was a son of Night, a friend of the Muses, goddesses of literature, science and the arts, and the twin brother of Thanatos – death. The River Lethe – forgetfulness – ran through the cave in which he lived on the island of Lemnos, which he claimed as his own dream island. Seen through this lens, the fitful, dream-streaked sleep of the drunk revellers is the work of Hypnos, with the tricks and half-light of his realm. 'I reckon there's a moral message underpinning this middle movement,' Adrian says, 'a memento mori; a reminder that you are mortal.' It plays into the seasonal associations of autumnal decay and foreshadows the hunt of the final movement.

——

As the autumnal party sleeps, we glimpse Vivaldi as a mature character, in his third age – the autumn of his life.

Antonio had left Venice as a violinist, priest, teacher and composer of operas, and two years later arrived back from rural Mantua with both the necessary work experience and the money to set his sights on being impresario of the Teatro Sant'Angelo. He didn't receive an immediate promotion – he was initially still 'just' the composer – but when he mounted his first production *La verità in cimento* in October 1720 he got to cast all his own singers, which was a step in the right direction. He certainly made enough impact to be lambasted as the subject of his aristocratic colleague Benedetto Marcello's satirical pamphlet *Il teatro alla moda* (The Fashionable Theatre). Marcello published anonymously in order to castigate what he saw as the artificial plots and stereotyped music and poetry of the latest operas, along with their extravagant set designs, and the vanity and ineptitude of singers. The pamphlet unfolds as a series of chapters offering ironic and seemingly straight-up 'advice' to each member of the creative and production team on how they might put on a theatrical event. For example, librettists should *never* read the ancient authors because *they'd* not read the modern ones, and modern composers should possess no knowledge of the rules of good composition. Marcello comes across as a dry wit with an axe to grind. Despite his elevated status, he was perhaps jealous of Vivaldi's triumphant return to the operatic scene in Venice, and his family were embroiled in legal disputes over the Teatro Sant'Angelo itself. Lest we are in any doubt of his directing his ire at Vivaldi, the pamphlet is attributed to Aldiviva Licante, anagrams of both Vivaldi's surname and that of the famous singer Caterina Cantelli.

The cover art shows three figures in a typical Venetian boat. Vivaldi is represented by the little angel at the helm on the far left. He sports a priestly hat while playing the violin with one foot on the rudder and the other raised as if dancing. The large figure rowing the vessel is the current impresario of the San Angelo, Signor Modotto, a man who'd previously been in the boat trade. Finally, atop a barrel of wine sits a bear, thought to represent Giovanni Orsato. The impresario of the Teatro San Moisè at the time, Orsato was a notorious operator in the operatic world, famously slow to pay young singers, and in the habit of bringing in travelling troupes to save money. He made his (small) fortune by taking productions onto the mainland to places like Padua or Vicenza, where the nobles had their villas. Since his role as impresario required him to provide food, wine and housing for most of his cast members, Orsato was also well known for trading in wine from these estates. While attending out-of-season productions in the provinces with Orsato, Vivaldi would have been thrust headlong into the wine trade, which would have been excellent training for his own forthcoming period as an impresario, and given him plenty of time for sampling and feeling the effects as portrayed in this middle movement of *Autumn*.

Did the publication and fame of *The Four Seasons* bring Vivaldi any contented sleep, as at least the sonnet suggests for these drunken revellers? We don't know. Aside from endorsement of the performances and contemporary imitations of the concertos, as outlined in Chapter IV in 'Spring', a 1761 account by Vivaldi's literary collaborator, the playwright and librettist Carlo Goldoni, recalled that he was 'famous for his instrumental works, especially those entitled *The Four Seasons*'.[2] However, Vivaldi's other published collections, especially his op. 3 *L'estro armonico*, were arguably just as successful, both at home and abroad.

At this point in *Autumn*, we leave an industrious Vivaldi in Venice, because, with regard to *The Four Seasons*, the 'dreaming without care' of his sonnet might have been a fantasy about the fruits of the concertos' harvest far beyond the eighteenth century. The impact these four seasonal concertos would have in future performances – and especially recordings – was beyond Vivaldi's imagination: for a piece to be remembered even throughout a lifetime was exceptional in his day. Yet this dream sequence of a middle movement invites us to explore the notion that he would be rediscovered, revered even, in subsequent centuries. And so, as *The Four Seasons* sleep, and like a fine wine mature in silence, we fuel Vivaldi's wildest dreams and glimpse his music's future.

—

The nineteenth century merely whispered Vivaldi's name, and only really in relation to early scholarship on J. S. Bach. Bach had learnt his compositional craft copying out Vivaldi concertos, though none of these copies were published in his lifetime. When they finally appeared in print in 1851, Siegfried Wilhelm Dehn, one of the editors at the publishing house of C. F. Peters, admitted that, more than a century after their first publication, 'original works by Vivaldi have long been musical rarities'.[3] He had no way of expanding a Vivaldian catalogue either, until 1860, when a cabinet of musical manuscripts was discovered at the Catholic Hofkirche (Court Church) in Dresden. It had been untouched for a century. Julius Rühlmann wrote up his findings, identifying some eighty-three violin concertos by Vivaldi that had presumably been played at the

Dresden court by the violinist Johann Georg Pisendel, and in the process of his analysis, presented the first historical portrait of Antonio as a man and musician.

Not everyone was as complimentary as Rühlmann. His contemporary Wilhelm Joseph von Wasielewski held the opinion that Bach had taken Vivaldi's 'thin and lifeless skeleton' and through his arrangements put flesh back on the bones. He was the first to cast shade on Vivaldi's productivity, accusing him of being a 'scribbler in the worst sense of the word' who lacked substance and found meaning in 'every kind of superficiality'.[4] This was not an atypical view, especially as German attitudes at the time were pretty damning towards Italian music in general, and Italian Baroque music in particular. Despite this, inventories of known manuscripts and surviving printed copies began to appear, and occasional concertos found their way to publishing houses. However, Vivaldi's posthumous reputation leapt forward with two events in 1905. The first was the publication of Arnold Schering's book on the history of the concerto. In it, he enthusiastically compared Vivaldi's concertos to Corelli's celebrated sonatas in terms of their invention, innovation, expression and technique, and asked: 'does not *one* of our concert directors wish to see whether one of these magnificent concertos is still viable or not?'[5] One did. Violinist Fritz Kreisler subsequently caused a musical scandal by adopting an age-old trick of attributing one of his own pastiche concertos to

Vivaldi. It was enough to get people talking and, in 1922, to secure a published thematic catalogue of virtually all the music Vivaldi had published in his lifetime, including op. 8 and within it *The Four Seasons*.[6]

In the reawakening of Vivaldi's music from its long slumber, one single event catapulted the situation beyond anything anyone could have imagined thus far. In 1926, the Salesian monks of the Collegio salesiano di San Carlo in Borgo San Martino (Monferrato) put a collection of music up for sale. The musicologist Alberto Gentili was dispatched to investigate and advise whether or not the Turin National Library (now the Turin National University Library) should buy it. What he found was an incredible ninety-seven-volume collection, fourteen of which were manuscripts by Vivaldi, many of them in his own handwriting. There were 140 instrumental works, twelve operas, twenty-nine cantatas, an oratorio and multiple fragments – a huge range of works from throughout his entire life. It was far beyond the means of the Turin National Library to buy this treasure trove, and they found a backer in one of the city's stockbrokers, Roberto Foà, who donated it back to them in memory of his infant son. That was not the end. It quickly became apparent that these manuscripts had been part of a larger collection, and what the library now had in its possession represented just 50 per cent of the original stash. Scholars began an epic historical treasure hunt, which led them to Genoa and the Durazzo family.[7]

In 1754, Count Giacomo Durazzo had become super-intendent of the imperial court theatres in Vienna. During his time there he bought a huge number of old concertos from Jacopo Soranzo, a Venetian collector who had held them since around 1745. This tranche of Vivaldi's works, comprising scores, parts and original manuscripts – including sketches and fragments – has since been proved to be the 'working stock' of the composer's own library.[8]

On the count's death in 1794, his sons had inherited the collection, and Gentili speculated that a living descendant of Marchese Marcello Durazzo would know the full story. Giuseppe Maria Durazzo was Marcello's (ageing) nephew – and had been previously responsible for bequeathing part of the collection to the Salesian monks. After much persuasion, he revealed that he still had the rest of the collection, and eventually agreed to sell it to the Turin National Library so that both parts could be reunited. This time the library's financial backer was a Turin textile manufacturer, Filippo Giordano, who, like Roberto Foà, had lost a son in infancy and similarly wished to donate the manuscripts in his name. The collection became 'The Foà-Giordano Collection' but is now commonly known as the 'Turin manuscripts'; it has revealed more about Vivaldi than anyone could have dreamt, but the original manuscript of *The Four Seasons* was not among its folios.

The pieces of the Vivaldi jigsaw started coming together with a huge undertaking of editing, publishing and disseminating. Efforts were hampered by the economic and political climate of the 1930s, but just before the outbreak of the Second World War came the first major musical event in the rediscovery of Vivaldi. In autumn 1939, the Accademia Chigiana hosted a Vivaldi Week in Siena, mounting performances of concertos, vocal works and even an opera. However, momentum in the Vivaldi revival was then inevitably lost over the course of the Second World War.

A new wave of enthusiasm picked up in the later 1940s and with it the re-emergence of *The Four Seasons*. The Vivaldi Institute (the Istituto Italiano Antonio Vivaldi) was founded in Venice in 1947 by Antonio Fanna and Angelo Ephrikian, and through its auspices the music publishers Ricordi committed to releasing the composer's complete known instrumental and vocal music. In addition to this, seminal books by Mario Rinaldi and Marc Pincherle changed perceptions of the man behind the music, and the Danish scholar and doyen of Vivaldians Peter Ryom set out to create a definitive catalogue – which is why works by Vivaldi are followed by an RV (Ryom-Verzeichnis (index)) number.

More than any of this, the sounds of Vivaldi's world and *The Four Seasons* were set to come alive with recordings, the enduring fruits of the rolling year. These are discussed in the last chapter of this season; for now, we let them slumber in Vivaldi's intoxicated dreams of autumn.

—

I confess that I struggle to love Vivaldi's *Autumn*, whatever recording or performance I listen to. The season of the year might be my favourite, but among these four concertos this one doesn't speak to me as I wish it would, and I flit between recordings in my own quest to animate the dots on the page. I ask both violinist Adrian Chandler and recorder player Erik Bosgraaf (who has made his own arrangement of this concerto) to help me understand why I have this reaction, why I get irritated by some elements of the piece, and how I might see it through different eyes to appreciate it more.

'Put it back in context,' said Adrian:

The Four Seasons is a tough mudder of a piece, a forty-five-minute slog, and generally what happens is that you get to the end of *Spring*, and you think 'this is okay'. Then by the end of the first movement of *Summer* 'still relatively fresh', the second movement 'yeah that's fine', but by end of the last movement's storm, if you really do what it says on the tin, you're on the floor. *Autumn* is probably the hardest one, it's tricky, it's in a nasty key for violins (F major), and it requires concentration, technique, precision, all while pretending to be drunk.

That certainly explains the practised art in live performance – a highly performative concerto that's not pulled off convincingly can easily become pantomime, or

just sound chaotic. Erik agrees but adds: 'most recordings are not nearly theatrical enough. You have to
embrace the overestimation of yourself, feeling that you
are on top of the world, being like Icarus flying higher
and higher before falling again.'

Here in the middle movement, the soloist's part joins
the first violin part in the band; it's a moment of repose,
but Vivaldi can't resist the urge to inject the sleep with
the effects of alcohol. The success of the Adagio rests on
the harpsichordist's ability to spin out the very many
weird chords, and the violinist's ability to resist the urge
to react to them: a serious challenge in steadying the
pulse and holding your nerve.

III: Allegro

By the light of dawn, the hunters meet.
They bring their horns and guns and dogs,
and spill across the land.
Their frightened prey runs its best
but the hunters do not stop.
Hurt and spent, its spirit at an end,
the creature stumbles to the ground
and breathes its last.[1]

As the dramatic harvest moon wanes, the traditional farming cycle ends and the rich autumn colours give way to a more severe backdrop, framed by bare branches. At first light, with breath beginning to condense in the chilled air, the hunt assembles. Horses and hounds streak across fields, and the golden leaves under hooves and paws turn to rotting mulch, a reminder of the fleeting nature of life and its pleasures.

The sounds of the hunt are controversial today, but in eighteenth-century Mantua, they would have been an obvious signal of the season for Vivaldi's audiences. Considering his health and disposition, it seems very unlikely that Vivaldi ever joined a hunt, but he'd have almost certainly seen and heard one in action, especially around Mantua. A representative sight and sound of autumn, the hunt is another reflection of the victory of man over the struggles with nature he'd encountered in *Summer*'s storms. With crops gathered and grapes crushed, the hunt now symbolises dominance and control over the season, and sees the soloist engage in the most extreme displays of virtuosity.

Mantua's ruling family at the time, the Habsburgs, loved their horses. Since the sixteenth century, they had been developing a very specific breed, 'Lipizzan' or 'Lipizzaner'; grey-white riding horses that could be trained to demonstrate the high art of classical dressage. The Lipizzan is a typically 'Baroque horse' in physique, sporting a long head with large expressive eyes, a sturdy arched neck, deep chest, high tail, and strong muscular shoulders and legs. The Mantuan horses did not necessarily do all the highly controlled, stylised jumps made famous by the Spanish Riding School of Vienna, but there was a showground within the palace walls, where the prize animals would be exercised. Prior to the Habsburg rule, the Gonzagas had also treasured their horses, and the specimens that grace the frescoes of the Ducal Palace, and the Hall of Horses at Palazzo Te on the other side of town, attest to the care and attention to detail they expected from artists capturing the equine physique for posterity. Besides any encounters with the animals who pulled his carriages, Vivaldi would have seen and heard the horses at court and might have watched them setting out across Mantua's bridge to the hunting grounds beyond.

Modern notions of sport and class aside, the hunt, as opposed to simply hunting for food, has always been a human solution to a problem of our own making. In a man-made agricultural environment, certain animals become largely unchallenged and can wreak havoc; think no further than deer who decimate woodland, or foxes who kill poultry and lambs. The Italian autumnal hunting season continues to this day and legally involves hunting quails, hares, woodcocks, foxes, red deer, wild boars, black grouse, pheasants and partridges. It is maintained not only for sport, but for the conservation and preservation of other species as the countryside becomes increasingly micromanaged by man.

The music of Vivaldi's final autumnal scene may be buoyant and a romanticised vision of the season, but there's a menacing edge to it, an aggression that prompts thoughts of mortality. The recurring theme is character-ised by the momentum of the hunt in motion. Finding the right tempo for this is not easy, especially if you con-sider the real-life gait of a horse, which suggests that riding was not in Vivaldi's personal experience. Hunting fanfares ring out across the skies with the entrance of the soloist, and the rest of the band responds, depicting riders cantering this way and that. The hunting party is well and truly established before the soloist takes on the role of the wild beast in flight. Triplet figures that we heard in the first movement — the out-of-control drunkard — now suggest the panic of the animal as the situation gets out of its control, and the other instruments take on the roles of the hunters with their guns popping, and hounds who cry and then begin to run. The main hunting theme alternates between the triplets indicating the running prey and the firing guns as the hunters take aim. We're musically drawn into the plight of the wounded beast, its attempt to escape, and then its final descending breaths before its death, and the most pitiful chromatic ascent of notes as its spirit rises.

This is the only real moment of confirmed mortal distress in the whole set of concertos, a single phrase in a short cadenza, before the hunt moves off in triumph. In many ways, this movement is a caricature of the event rather than an attempt at a realistic depiction, but it is consistent both with the way in which Vivaldi depicted the hunt elsewhere and the way that his audiences would have understood it. Alongside *The Four Seasons* in his op. 8 collection is the Concerto in B flat major, *La caccia* (The Hunt) — but while it's entirely dedicated to the topic, it's a concerto lacking any literary references to a sonnet, or score annotations of guns, dogs and prey.

Violinist Adrian Chandler points out that if you place *La caccia* side by side with this third movement of *Autumn*, however, you can work out what's going on in the former, even to the point that the quarry is caught. In this final movement of *Autumn*, there is a sudden shift from F major into F minor, as the beast gives up its spirit, and you see the same thing happen with a shift from B flat major into B flat minor in *La caccia*, presumably representing a similarly sad end to the creature's life.

—

Modern farming has overtaken the necessity of hunting for food, but in Venice there is another reason that particular haunches of meat appear in butchers' shops in late autumn. They would have been a very familiar sight for Vivaldi every November in the lead-up to the feast day of Santa Maria della Salute; mutton hanging in preparation for each household to cook the traditional dish of *castradina* (mutton soup). To understand why, we must look back nearly fifty years before Vivaldi was born, to when Venice had been watching her neighbouring cities, particularly Mantua, succumb to the ravages of bubonic plague.

The death of an heirless Duke Vincenzo II of Mantua in 1627 prompted the War of the Mantuan Succession. It was a three-year conflict between would-be claimants to the Gonzaga duchies of Mantua and Monferrato, and became, in effect, a proxy war between France and Spain. The French would eventually claim a short-lived victory, but in 1630 the action swung in favour of Spain, who with assistance from the Holy Roman Emperor Ferdinand II brought about the siege and sack of Mantua. Ferdinand's Imperial troops brought in plague, which they spread among the inhabitants of the city. A delegation then set out from Mantua to Venice to ask for help, headed up, perhaps a little unexpectedly, by Alessandro Striggio the Younger – composer, librettist and friend of Claudio Monteverdi. Everyone arriving in Venice had to quarantine for forty days – merchants remained on their ships, others isolated on island *lazzaretti* (medical centres), but an exception was made for Striggio, who was allowed to spend his quarantine on the island of San Clemente. In order to make it safer, the Venetian Senate employed a carpenter to build a fence and – yes, you guessed it – Striggio's infection of the carpenter has been claimed to have been the way the plague got out. Quite unintentionally, the Mantuans infected Venice with a particularly virulent strain, and in the terror of the three months that followed around 46,000 people perished.

On 22 October 1630, at the height of the epidemic, and just before he died himself, Doge Nicolò Contarini turned to the Virgin Mary for aid. For three days and three nights the Venetians kept a vigil, processing along the alleys and out into the fields. As the weeks passed, the disease slowed. Was it their prayers, the colder autumnal weather or newly established herd immunity? The senate, mindful not to underestimate the Virgin's intervention, decided to commission a new church and made a vow to visit it annually. The grand basilica was to be called 'Santa Maria della Salute' (Saint Mary of Healing), in the hope that the Virgin would continue to intercede and save Venice from the plague. Prayers were eventually answered, but by the time Venice was free of disease a quarter of her population had perished.

A site of great prestige and visibility on the Grand Canal in the Sestiere di Dorsoduro was chosen for the new church of Santa Maria della Salute – a monument that would change the city's skyline and ensure no one would forget the Virgin's mediation. The foundation stone was laid on 25 March 1631, a date rich in symbolism as it was believed to be the founding date of Venice in AD 421, and also coincided with the feast of the Annunciation. On 1 April, music by Claudio Monteverdi was sung in a ceremony to mark the start of the building works, and for a service on 21 November, when the epidemic was formally declared over, Monteverdi wrote a celebratory Mass.[2] The church then took fifty years to complete and was consecrated on 21 November 1687, by which time the young Antonio Vivaldi was nine, and well aware of its significance and of the autumnal pilgrimage to mark the feast day.

In his early days as a composer of operas for the Sant'Angelo, Vivaldi had worked with a young Venetian set designer by the name of Giovanni Antonio Canal – more recognisable by his nickname: Canaletto (the 'Little Canal', to distinguish him from his father Bernardo, who also worked as a set painter and was presumably the 'Grand Canal'). In 1718 they had gone their own ways: Vivaldi to Mantua, Canaletto to Rome to create opera scenery for the composer Alessandro Scarlatti. On their respective returns to Venice, Vivaldi became *maestro de' concerti* at the Pietà, and Canaletto became the most famous painter of *vedute* (views). Vivaldi's *The Four Seasons* and Canaletto's large-scale scenes of the Grand Canal share resonances in capturing the atmosphere and local colours of the artists' north Italian homeland. Each have roots in real-life scenarios, but also in operatic scenery and the telescoping of ideas to ignite the imagination. Around 1730, Canaletto painted *The Entrance to the Grand Canal, Venice,* in which he intended that our eyes would immediately rest on the iconic image of the Church of Santa Maria della Salute.[3] Vivaldi had been in Prague and Vienna that year, but, like Canaletto, was probably back in that very church on 21 November to commemorate the feast day. No ordinary year, 1730 marked 100 years since Venetians had called on the Virgin Mary to save them and had embarked on building this extraordinary church in remembrance.

—

I arrive in Venice on the eve of the feast of the Madonna della Salute. It's foggy, and Venice slowly emerges from mist as my waterbus zigzags a route across the lagoon. I disembark at San Zaccaria, and in the distance, across the Grand Canal, the Santa Maria della Salute is silhouetted against the late November light.

Fig. 10: The Church of Santa Maria della Salute
across the Grand Canal.

Fig. 11: Hotel Metropole on the original site of the Ospedale della Pietà, alongside the Church of Santa Maria della Pietà.

That's my destination tomorrow; tonight I'm a guest of Gloria Beggiato, general manager and owner of the Hotel Metropole, which, as I learnt on my first visit to Venice outlined in *Spring*, stands on the very site of the original Ospedale della Pietà. These walls once reverberated to the sounds of Vivaldi's music, and within them lived the women who brought it to life, especially so following his return to Venice in autumn 1720. 'Nothing happens by chance,' says Gloria, greeting me in the opulent hotel bar. 'This is still a meeting place for music and art, artists and musicians.' Gloria grew up here, just like Vivaldi's musical girls, but their circumstances could hardly be more different. She inherited the business from her parents, along with a dual passion for adding star ratings and ways in which a hotel might tell the stories of the past. She tells me the building was converted from the old Ospedale in the nineteenth century, and was initially a German-owned hostelry, visited by the likes of Thomas Mann and Sigmund Freud. These figures add to the identity of the place as much as the eastern influences Gloria has brought to it; as much a curator as a hotelier, she understands the dynamic between creating personality and preserving tradition. Historic treasures such as fans, crucifixes, corkscrews and books are the very objects and symbols that made Venice rich in Vivaldi's day, but now they sit easily alongside modern art in this luxurious cabinet of curiosities.

This meeting of ancient and modern is perhaps encapsulated most of all in the hotel bar, once the small chapel of the Pietà – Santa Maria della Visitazione. Two columns still stand in their original positions – columns Vivaldi very likely leant against, but that people lean on for different reasons now – and the words of Sigmund Freud run round the top of the wall, a tribute in neon lights by contemporary conceptual artist Joseph Kosuth. If echoes of *The Four Seasons* resound here still, it's because the concertos are performed regularly in the 'new' Chiesa della Pietà next door. Today in late November, however, the hotel bar is ablaze with the rich tones of autumn, from the red velvet upholstery to the flames in the fire, the pomegranates and the Campari.

Fig. 12: Column from Santa Maria della Visitazione, the original Pietà Church, now the site of the bar of the Hotel Metropole.

In 1730, Vivaldi's Venice had already changed from a centre for trade to a cultural hot spot on the Grand Tour. Today, Venice continues to rely on tourism to keep its economy afloat, but the many visitors also pose one of the biggest threats to its fragile structure. It's a precarious dynamic that makes one question the city's identity beyond the hotels, grand palaces, museums and emblematic waterways.

Traditions rely on citizens, though, not tourists, and this is a concern to Gloria. 'Venice is in a delicate moment with tourism,' she says. 'I suffer when I see that things lose their importance, and days like the feast of Santa Maria della Salute are vital for the city; families and friends return with their children to preserve its stories, its history. You need to eat traditional *castradina* soup tomorrow,' she adds, 'and go to light a candle for health at the Church of Maria Della Salute, but go really early as it'll be packed later in the day.'

I wake at 5 a.m. and open my window to reassure myself that the first vaporetti are really heading up the Grand Canal. It's just two stops to Salute, crossing the famous waterway and passing the familiar sights of the Doge's Palace and St Mark's Basilica, which are proudly floodlit against the dark sky. There's a soft glow from the windows of the church, and in the darkness she's a formidable presence, a feat of old Venetian engineering unchanged over nearly 350 years, save for a ramp that's been specially constructed for the feast day, and for which I'm eternally grateful. For anyone who can climb it, a majestic staircase leads up from the lapping water to the front door of this octagonal church, complete with mighty bell towers, and a dome that from the outside forms a crown and from inside looks like an upturned chalice.

Candle sellers are just setting up stall at 6 a.m. and I buy a votive before heading inside to Mass. The altar is the focal point, a triptych of statues by the seventeenth-century sculptor Giusto Le Court. It features the Madonna della Salute with her Child in her arms in the centre; on the left, a young girl symbolises Venice pleading with the Virgin to be freed from plague; and on the right, an old woman represents the plague fleeing at divine command. There are some things that have remained unchanged in the ensuing ritual since Vivaldi kept this same feast day. The candles are lit in the same sacred space, much of the same Latin liturgy is spoken and repeated by the congregation, the private prayers of thanks or pleading are made for health. These are the things that Venetians intended for this day in 1630, and that they have kept ever since. Surrounded by local worshippers and nuns, I suddenly feel part of something that still connects everyone who comes back to this place. This is the space where the whole Vivaldi family came on this date each year, no doubt praying for their eldest daughter Gabriela, then for Antonio's health.

While some things remain the same, music changes with the times, and the hymns I sing are definitely the product of the twentieth century. Back in 1730, however, there was an extraordinary musical experience. To mark 100 years since the founding of the church, three ceremonies were put on in Santa Maria della Salute and St Mark's, modelled on those of 1630–1.[4] This was a rare occasion on which Vivaldi (and Canaletto) would have heard the music of Claudio Monteverdi, and many of the liturgical texts as they had been sung a century earlier. Specifically, the musicians of both churches performed Monteverdi's *Selva morale et spirituale*, a collection of sacred vocal music published in Venice in 1640–41, but dedicated to Mantua's Eleanora Gonzaga: a meeting in music of the two cities most affected by plague. The collection was once viewed as a bit of miscellany, but is now understood to be a precise reflection of the Mass of Thanksgiving and Solemn Vespers services at Santa Maria della Salute and St Mark's.[5]

When I emerge from the early-morning Mass (via a service lift at the back of the church which just happens to take me past an enormous Tintoretto painting), dawn is breaking over the Grand Canal. Venice knows how to take your breath away. The light glistens on the white marble of Santa Maria della Salute, and high above the eye-popping Baroque facade, above the images of the saints, up beyond the columns and arches at the pinnacle of the dome, stands the statue of the Virgin Mary. She holds a stick and gazes out across the lagoon and the city. She is here to protect, a symbol to remind Venetians that the fate of the city is always in her hands.

Fig. 13: The Church of Santa Maria della Salute.

In Vivaldi's day, there would be two ways of heading home. Like me, mobility-challenged Antonio probably went by water, but the other option was walking over a temporary bridge back to the San Marco side of the Grand Canal. It's been constructed each year since the church was completed in 1687 – to help fulfil the vow that Venetians would return each year to keep the feast. When Vivaldi was a boy, it was a perilous bridge of boats placed side by side with gangways between them, but it's now a floating votive bridge that appears annually to mark the festival in the third week of November. Processions pass this way throughout the day and families enjoying the public holiday reunite to cross the bridge together on their way to and from Mass.[6]

You may be wondering what this has to do with Vivaldi's late-autumnal hunt. The answer lies in the tastes of the season and this very particular day of year. There were certainly no horses for hunting in Venice – Vivaldi must have been inspired here by his memories of Mantua or the Venetian mainland. But, as Gloria tells me, aside from the haunches of mutton hanging in the butcher's for the *castradina*, Vivaldi would have been well aware of the hunting season for waterfowl, and particularly ducks. 'It's a very specific time,' she says. 'The season is short, it begins in October and it's certainly finished by December, and involves standing up to your chest in freezing cold water at dawn. You need permission,' she goes on, 'and critically you need to know

Fig. 14: The floating votive bridge across the Grand
Canal by the Church of Santa Maria della Salute.

your birdcalls as you can only shoot specific birds, and in
the dark before sunrise you can't see them, you need to
recognise their call to make sure you shoot the right one.'
This reminds me of the fact that there are no birds in
Vivaldi's *Autumn*, and strengthens my theory that he
wasn't the one out doing the hunting, but rather had
heard stories about it since childhood.

As I'm here to mark the feast of Santa Maria della
Salute, my mind is less on the birds, more on the broth,
the *castradina*. Come evening, the palaces along the
Grand Canal light up one by one, and through their
pointed windows you can see ballrooms with gilded
mirrors, huge chandeliers and open-beamed ceilings.
The Church of Santa Maria della Salute is crowded
with people buying candles before the hourly services,
and *frittole* (fried doughnuts) afterwards. I restrain
myself, as Trattoria da Remigio in the district of
Castello is my destination for dinner; they advertise
their *castradina* in the window, and serve it in a dish
lined with a large raw cabbage leaf. Putting thoughts
of the brassica's famous remedy for mastitis to the back
of my mind (Santa Maria della Salute serving up relief
as only a mother could), I tuck into the stew of shred-
ded mutton in a cabbage broth. This dish clearly runs
the risk of being fatty, but this one is not: the broth is
clear, the cabbage soft and sweet, the meat melt-in-the-
mouth, and the whole thing finished off with generous
twists of black pepper. This is true soul food for the

cold, rainy November evening, and it was always intended to comfort and nourish.

Mutton had long been a mainstay on ships that criss-crossed the Adriatic. Dried, seasoned and smoked, it could be preserved for a long time and was not only traded at the destination, but also sustained the traders themselves en route. During the plague of 1630, the Venetians had no access to fresh meat and the Dalmatians and Croatians, on hearing of their plight, sent shiploads of smoked mutton their way. *Castradina* is therefore the true taste of the feast of Santa Maria della Salute, another reminder of a time in which Venetians needed aid, and it has been eaten on this day every year since the festival was established. This one at Trattoria da Remigio is a roaring success in my book, and also, it would seem, in the books of the students and senior Venetians who sit at surrounding tables. If this trattoria is anything to go by, the tradition is being passed on and embraced.

Back at the hotel, Gloria tells me that *castradina* is found in all sorts of old Venetian recipe books, and either these or advice from a local butcher is usually the starting point for preparing the dish. After that, though, it varies from kitchen to kitchen, some recipes adding bay leaves, juniper berries or wine. 'Really, it's all about the number of times you change the water the lamb's boiled in,' says Gloria, 'and the point at which you make the broth.' This process of softening the dried lamb and releasing the flavours is said to be the reminder of the

Fig. 15: The *castradina* at Trattoria da Remigio.

repeated prayers for deliverance from the plague, and the theatre is in the preparation as much as the eating. There is no doubt the sight of hanging meat, the lingering smell of boiled cabbage and the taste of *castradina* were a quintessential part of autumn for Vivaldi in Venice.

In order for the year to turn, for nutrients to be cycled back into the soil, and even for feasting to take place, there must death, or at least a little destruction. Whether the demise of a stag, the cutting of corn, or the yellowing of leaves that then turn to mulch, the earth sees decay before renewal, and a degree of sadness before new glories. It's the understanding that comes with time, with age, with autumn's maturity. For Venetians, this time of year is inextricably linked to the thousands of lives lost to plague in 1630; 21 November celebrates Venice's new dawn in its wake, but is also an annual commemoration. A season of highs and lows then, and a season associated with touch and texture, all of which is encapsulated in Vivaldi's musical representation of autumn. The music in the finale of this concerto reflects this with its unity of purpose, thanks to the chorus of musicians coming together and heading in the same direction. Their synchronised, rhythmic layers of sound and the glories of predictable harmonic resolution are bound in a tightly organised musical structure, which contrasts distinctly with the freedom of the wild beast's soul taking flight, breaking free of the score and earthbound terror.

The pieces of Vivaldi's hunt are coming together in my mind, and starting to challenge my earlier reactions and preconceptions about this movement. Even so, I call recorder player Erik Bosgraaf to chat about my lingering lacklustre feelings on the recurring themes. 'I think the third movement in *Autumn* is very often performed too slowly,' he says. 'I don't like it that way either, because it just seems to be so heavy all the time and stuck on the F chord; but Vivaldi writes it in 3/8 time, and music written in that time signature is never slow.' That is certainly true, and at a faster speed there is more contrast for the poignant moment when the beast gives up its spirit. 'I think *Autumn* is the most theatrical of all the *Four Seasons*,' concludes Erik. 'It has all of life in it, but our appreciation of it comes through our collective memory of recordings that we have heard.' That's the rub: while this movement may be exciting to play and theatrical in the moment when heard live, on recordings – whether they be vinyl, CDs or accessed via a streaming service – performers will only succeed if they are able to combine poetry with a knowledge of eighteenth-century performance practices. Get that right and I'm hooked.

The Life Cycle of *The Four Seasons* – Fruits and Flowers

The Age of Recording

In the life cycle of *The Four Seasons, Autumn* bears witness to the work's fruitful produce – a vast bounty of recordings. The question of who made the very first is a little hazy. There are surviving acetates of a French radio broadcast that aired in 1939 with Italian-born British violinist Alfredo Campoli as the soloist alongside the British Boyd Neel Orchestra, but the first formal electrical recording was made during the war, in Rome in 1942. Conductor Bernardino Molinari and the Orchestra dell'Accademia Nazionale di Santa Cecilia, presumably with their leader in the solo role, recorded for the label Cetra. Molinari retained Vivaldi's orchestration of strings and harpsichord continuo, but the generous full-orchestral sound of his recording, complete with reinforced grand statements and broad melodic sweeps, is the result of his liberal transcription of the score.

Hot on the heels of Campoli and Molinari came Louis Kaufman and the first American recording in 1947: a pivotal moment that turned the tide towards Vivaldi in Europe and America. The night before the first recording session, a once-in-a-generation snowstorm took New York by surprise, but Kaufman recalled that fate was on their side: the instruments stayed in tune in spite of the cold and the string orchestra (who arrived in a flurry from an unexpected last-minute session on a different recording with the conductor Leopold Stokowski) remained alert and excited. When they reached the middle movement of *Autumn*, principal cellist Bernard Greenhouse was wide-eyed at the harmonic structure and programmatic vividness, exclaiming: 'they just discovered everything in the eighteenth century.'[1] 'These records will go around the world,' prophesied violinist Emil Hauser, who had listened in to the sessions, and he was right.[2] The recording's incredible success was a major step in re-popularising Vivaldi on both sides of the Atlantic. It won the French Grand Prix du Disque in 1950 and in the first years of the twenty-first century was both elected to the Grammy Hall of Fame and selected for the National Recording Registry in the Library of Congress.[3]

The World's Encyclopaedia of Recorded Music of 1952 cites only two recordings of *The Four Seasons*. More than seventy years on, there are *hundreds*. Since the 1950s, the concertos have been a professional hallmark of violinists, conductors and orchestras alike. With the advent of historically informed performances, the number of recordings accelerated, and by the late 1980s, they appeared at a rate averaging nineteen per year.[4]

With so many versions of *The Four Seasons* available to listen to, there's something to be said for a shortlist to get you started. I've used descriptive categories to divide up the more than seventy-year history of recordings of the concertos, all of which are direct, rather than re-scored or re-imagined interpretations — we'll come to those in *Winter*.

———

Symphonic Vivaldi

Not every Baroque composer sounds good when played by a symphony orchestra. Vivaldi *can*. His musical lines are robust enough to withstand a rich treatment of strings, and initially this was the way *The Four Seasons* was heard. This category of recordings revels in the full drama of a symphonic treatment — not necessarily the full complement of orchestral strings, but a substantial number.

There are around thirty recordings made by symphony orchestras of various sizes. A good number are characterised by slow, heavily accented approaches such as the 1954 studio recording of the Philharmonic Symphony Orchestra of New York (with soloist John Corigliano Sr) or the Orchestra da Camera Italiana's particularly stately version from 1968. That's not to say, however, that they lack whimsy. Corigliano recorded the work again in the 1960s with the New York Philharmonic and Leonard Bernstein at the harpsichord, and the difference is astonishing, the concertos emerging as livelier, more textured interpretations. On the other hand, Herbert von Karajan's 1972 recording with the Berlin Philharmonic and violinist Michel Schwalbé is a smooth, purring Rolls-Royce of a historic recording, not without upbeat moments, but with some achingly slow tempos typical of its time and place.

The late 1970s and '80s saw further recordings by the likes of violinist Gidon Kremer with the London Symphony Orchestra conducted by Claudio Abbado, or the Israel Philharmonic Orchestra and conductor Zubin Mehta with either Isaac Stern or Itzhak Perlman. Again, these recordings do not feature a full complement of symphonic strings, but there are plenty to make a full orchestral noise, and as the decades go by, they increasingly sound more effortless. Stern's ornamented slow movements are certainly a step towards freedom from the score, even if they have a very twentieth- rather than eighteenth-century approach to decorating a melody. With advances in audio technology, these recordings benefitted from the ability to place the soloist within the orchestral sound, and then have them emerge from the textures with a pure tone. Perlman's first award-winning recording was with the London Philharmonic Orchestra in 1976; he directed the players from the soloist's spot, and it remains his best-selling record in the Warner catalogue.

From Vienna to Melbourne via Prague and Venezuela, symphony orchestras have embraced the richest palette of *The Four Seasons*, creating big-boned recordings that can bring equally big contrasts thanks to their ranks of players. They're not by any means restricted to historical recordings either. The various experiences of Canadian violinist James Ehnes are a case in point. Speaking to me between rehearsals in Baltimore, James wisely muses that there are now 'groupthink' stages to recordings of *The Four Seasons*: the decades in which interpretative fashions were very stolid and slow, and then more recent times in which they were as fast as possible or highly improvised. He believes that musicians can fall into the trap of thinking: 'my greatest sin would be to *not* be different'.

For James, authenticity and distinctiveness in this repertoire come from simply being yourself in whatever circumstance you are performing. He's played the piece with dozens of orchestras and ensembles over the years from the Boston Symphony to the Scottish Chamber Orchestra, and while visiting Australia, jumped at the opportunity to record them with players from the Sydney Symphony Orchestra. James favours a line-up of six first violins, six second violins, four violas, four cellos and two double basses: 'small enough to be nimble,' he admits, 'but also big enough to create a generous, orchestral sound and a real impact in stormy sections.' With a larger ensemble, you have a larger-than-life cast of characters to bring the music alive. 'A good rapport with the principal players is crucial to make this work,' James says, 'because it's a fine line between character and caricature.' As is the space in which you play. 'You can't expect to make the same impact with twenty players in the Sydney Opera House as you can in a smaller venue,' he adds. 'That's something to consider when recording, in order to capture the impact you feel when playing together live.'

When it comes to improvisation and ornamentation, James is the first to admit that his approach is minimal: he often feels ornamentation imposes on the music, and wants to hear Vivaldi's voice speak the loudest. He has a refreshing attitude towards the different approaches to *The Four Seasons*, also born out of his own experiences away from symphony orchestras. He programmed them at his chamber music festival in Seattle, rotating different players as soloist. 'We were all completely different in the way we approached it,' he says, 'I sometimes thought: "Well, I wouldn't do it this way, but I'm sure happy to hear *you* play it this way."' This is the essence of both sticking to your guns and staying open-minded, the very best way of honouring Vivaldi.

Rock Star Vivaldi

I'm under no allusion that this category revolves around one figure: Nigel Kennedy. Chances are his was the first recording of *The Four Seasons* you heard – no musician has done more to popularise these concertos. But before we get to him, it's worth considering that while we have recordings from some historic violinist 'rock stars' such as Isaac Stern and Itzhak Perlman, we have none from other legends such as Jascha Heifetz or David Oistrakh. Nigel Kennedy is the quintessential rock star – but who else fits the bill? There are Vivaldi rock stars in each of my categories – but here I would include the likes of Yehudi Menuhin, Anne-Sophie Mutter, Janinie Jansen, Tasmin Little and Viktoria Mullova, among the leading violinists of their generation. The bottom line is that Kennedy stands alone because of the impact he made, the way that both he and the record-breaking album were marketed, and the lasting impression his album has had on listeners.

In his no-holds-barred memoir *Uncensored!*, Nigel Kennedy wastes no time on diplomacy in reflecting on how Vivaldi altered the course of his life and career.[5] He has long been open about his very practical motivation to record *The Four Seasons* – that they mirrored the best rock, soul or pop albums that presented in the region of twelve tracks of around three minutes each. In the age of 78 rpm recordings, his favourite classical artists, such as Pablo Casals and Fritz Kreisler, had also released short pieces that had proved hugely popular, and it struck Kennedy that quite apart from their melodic and rhythmic appeal, *The Four Seasons* fitted this marketing strategy. 'No one has to think about the meaning of life to get through three minutes of Vivaldi,' he quips, 'it's just energetic music with good contrast.'[6] The record label EMI agreed with him, and they also agreed with his manager John Stanley that if they wanted this collaboration to work, they'd have to sell Nigel for exactly who he was, rather than make him fit any existing

mould of how classical musicians might present themselves and their music.

Kennedy says that for him, Vivaldi is set apart from
Bach, Handel or Scarlatti by his 'memorable melodies
allied with comparatively huge dynamic contrasts', the
very things he felt were missing in the interpretations of
his contemporaries. He positions his recording as an
'antidote' to two schools of performance, which he
describes as the 'prissy self-satisfied interpretations' of
period players and the 'cloying complacent heaviness' of
modern virtuoso performers. His winning formula was
to play 'fast tempos fast, slow tempos slow, loud passages
as loudly as the orchestra could manage and quiet passages intimately and almost inaudibly'.[7] With minimal
crescendos or diminuendos, there it was: the contrast.

Released in 1989, Kennedy's album of *The Four Seasons*
sold over two million copies and spent nearly two years
at the top of the UK classical album charts. 'Yeah, that
ugly Fucker Viv changed my life,' he concludes, reflecting back on the sell-out gigs, billboards, chat shows, and
his beloved Aston Villa comrades singing it back at him
en route to the match.[8]

For all the pyrotechnics and punk attitude, precision
and passion are the priorities in this recording. Kennedy
is, after all, from serious classical music stock. His father
was a cellist and his mother a pianist, just as his grand-
mother was a pianist and his cellist grandfather played
with Kreisler and Heifetz. After more than a decade of

training at the Yehudi Menuhin School in London and the Juilliard School in New York, Kennedy made his name equally in the classical world with a debut album of Elgar's Violin Concerto, and on the jazz scene playing with Stéphane Grappelli. Both his classical and his jazz training are essential ingredients in his technique and attitude to playing Baroque music. He may be dismissive of period players, but many of his ideas, such as performing without a conductor, having the ensemble stand, and delving into the detail of the score, are straight out of the eighteenth-century playbook.

Kennedy's *Four Seasons* were recorded in just nine hours, with a couple of re-takes to incorporate new ideas in improvised sections, but they are pitch perfect, balance perfect, and proved a game-changer in terms of pacing and freedom.[9] You can watch Nigel talking through the programmatic elements of the concertos on YouTube: it's a window into his mind, what he pictures as he plays, and how personal this is for him. 'Although I wouldn't say that Vivaldi is the best composer in the world there's an electricity when I play his stuff,' he says, 'his slow movements have a confessional aspect to them when in my hands. It just happens.'[10]

Period Drama Vivaldi

Both James Ehnes and Nigel Kennedy have alluded in different ways to period performers, and this category is a sample of the groups who play on original or replica instruments. Using the sonic effects of gut strings, they bring a sense of refined poise pitted against wild abandon. From a one-musician-per-part band to a more generous ensemble, these are the interpretations that offer fresh ideas on articulation and ornamentation, sourced directly from eighteenth-century information.

There are more than forty-five recordings, covering the wide palette of colours across the period-instrument spectrum. Name a group and it's likely that they've released a *Four Seasons* album at a strategic point in their histories. Nikolaus Harnoncourt's pioneering 1977 recording with Concentus Musicus Wien still has a thrilling, exploratory atmosphere. It is an interpretation that laid the foundation for so many that followed, such as violinist Simon Standage's 1981 recording with the English Concert – the classic benchmark for decades. The 1980s and '90s brought further excitement and refinement from period players honing their craft – as have the first three decades of our current century. Whether you favour the theatrical renditions of Brecon Baroque or Le Consort; the daring, creative, and dance-infused interpretations of Musica Alchemica, Venice Baroque, or Gli Incogniti; or the intense drive and passion of L'Arte dell'Arco, Accademia Bizantina and Europa Galante, there are different blends of period drama to suit every taste, and more appear with every passing season.

This category also offers the chance to hear multi-soloist versions – mirroring the historical allegories and personifications of the seasons in art. It's a trend that began with the Academy of Ancient Music and Christopher Hogwood in 1982, was taken up by the Taverner Players a decade later, then by the European Union Baroque Orchestra in 2010, and – perhaps most compellingly of all – in recent years by Concerto Italiano. Directing the four soloists Stefania Azzaro, Mauro Lopes Ferreira, Antonio de Secondi and Francesca Vicari on a multi-award-winning 2003 album, Rinaldo Alessandrini transfers his moment-by-moment account of the sonnets and music in the sleeve notes onto his direction of the ensemble, playing with the group's catlike agility to take risks and always land on their feet.

La Serenissima's 2015 recording has repeatedly been chosen as the top of the pops when it comes to the best period instrument account. It's the go-to version for performers, scholars and critics alike who admire its passion, precision and dramatic flair. But a decade on, the ensemble has another in the pipeline, part of a record-ing of the complete op. 8. When I quiz their founder and director Adrian Chandler on what he thought made the first one tick and why he'd want to go again, his answer is surprising. 'In the nineteenth century, Johannes Brahms said that a good musician would spend as much time with his head in his books, as he would practising,' he says, 'and I really feel that holds true.'

In the first recording it was Adrian's ambition to create a performance that 'did what Vivaldi's texts say', in both poetry and music – and that's how he accounts for its success. For him, it was never about finding a wild angle, rather about finding out the perspectives it already presents, 'particularly', he says, 'when Vivaldi gives it to you in a box with pretty ribbons around it.' That's what lots of musicians would say they do too, but this recording still stands out from the crowd for its conviction and detail. Playing from their own edition, informed by the manuscripts in Manchester, Adrian and the group also steeped themselves in the surviving accounts of string playing of the time. Tartini was useful, Adrian says: 'he advised learning ornaments so you know exactly what you're going to play, but also the trick of making them sound as though they're being played for the first time.'

With the enormous success of their earlier album, why would they record it again? 'If you listen to both recordings you'll hear familiar things,' Adrian admits, 'but by re-examining the texts even more closely, I've re-imagined the interpretation.' And we're not just talking about ornaments and decorations here, some of the easiest things to change on a refresh; they've also taken Brahms's advice and stuck their heads back in the books and scores. 'There's a bizarre bowing in one of the drunk bits in the first movement of *Autumn*,' Adrian continues.

I've always wondered why Vivaldi bothered to write it out, and before, I took it for an error, but in re-imagining the drunk and revisiting the moment, I suddenly realised exactly what he's getting at. So I've changed the way I play that phrase – where we push on or hold back, and it's the complete opposite to what we did in the first recording.

The most compelling thing in hearing Adrian talk about details like this is the realisation that the group has arrived at an interpretation that reflects the sonnets even more closely that before. It's in the pacing, the timing of jokes and the programmatic effects that they hope to land even better this time. 'Whatever any critic might be tempted to say, I think we've done a good job with the second one,' says Adrian. 'I think it flows a lot more.'

Free Spirit Vivaldi

Vivaldi originally specified a violin soloist for *The Four Seasons*. However, music of the time was not a fixed entity – if it was playable on a different instrument, there was no reason not to try it. Plenty of chamber music was published with instructions for a range of possible soloists, so why not open up *The Four Seasons* to anyone who wants to join the fray? You might be enticed by recordings released by the likes of the Venice Harp Quartet, the Flanders Recorder Quartet, Vienna Flautists or even the Chinese Baroque Players on traditional Chinese instruments – just some of the plethora of versions transcribed for a new medium. *The Four Seasons* sport new garb with relative ease, as attested recently by the sensational recording from mandolin player Jacob Reuven and accordionist Omer Meir Wellber with Sinfonia Leipzig, and in the past by flautists James Galway or Jean-Pierre Rampal. Why not play them on keyboard instruments too? Versions abound for one, two or even three pianos – the latter memorably with Matej Meštrović, Matija Dedić and Hakan Ali Toker, and there's a remarkable recording of Hansjörg Albrecht playing them on the Silbermann organ of the Hofkirche in Dresden.

Church bells peal outside the window of Erik Bosgraaf's hotel room in Mexico, as he confesses to me on a video call that playing *The Four Seasons* on the recorder was not his idea, nor did it initially appeal. He'd just finished recording Vivaldi's recorder concertos and had come to the conclusion that Vivaldi always wrote for the violin, even if it was not the solo instrument advertised. However, *The Four Seasons* unexpectedly confounded this view. 'They bring out certain aspects that the recorder can do better than a violin, especially the more bird-like things,' he says, 'and in some ways they work even better than the concertos Vivaldi wrote specifically for the recorder.' The recording with his group Cordevento is testament to the success of this arrangement, and how quickly he grew to love the repertoire. But following the liberation of this creative approach to the sounds of the score, a new commission led him much further.

Erik has worked for some time with Dutch avant-garde film-makers and photographers Paul and Menno de Nooijer, and when he was approached to make a multi-media experience of *The Four Seasons*, a collaboration with them was a natural extension of what he'd been doing with Cordevento. 'They were very interested in the performative element of film-making,' Erik says, 'because consuming film in a cinema is a very static undertaking, you're basically silent and it's one-way traffic.' This is anything but. The performers all wear white, contrasting with a black stage, and under changing lights, images of nature and the ages of man are projected onto the back wall. Erik too becomes a canvas. 'It's like breaking the glass window,' he says, describing the awkwardness of unbuttoning his shirt so that wilting flowers, flickering flames and hands building a recorder are projected onto his body. 'The concept itself becomes very much a ritual,' he says. 'The audience enters into a dreamworld, and it's all a bit psychedelic.'

The multimedia performance involves real-time looped recordings of the ensemble, and Erik improvises between concertos. These extra elements could be seen as distractions, and I admit that I began watching a film of the event with some scepticism. But I was won over. Above all, I was consistently provoked to question what would happen next, which is a startling feeling when you listen to music you believe you know well. I believe the success of the performance lies in the fact that any additional musical elements are heard between the concertos, and Vivaldi's original music otherwise remains completely intact. 'It's already enough that I'm playing it on the recorder,' Erik quips, 'but I really don't have to change much of Vivaldi's score.' The lines of the concertos are all there, preserved and respected. 'It's a bit like a cocktail,' he says with a twinkle, 'you want the whiskey to be of good quality, *alongside* whatever else you put in – I don't want to dilute the original.'

That's why this is an interpretation rather than a reworking. It's free-spirited Vivaldi, but still very much what he originally wrote. 'It's the essence of the German phrase *Aha-Erlebnis!*' says Erik: 'the "Aha" moment for the listener; something that works exactly because *The Four Seasons* is so famous. It means that you can depart from the expected, but when you come back, there's a palpable sense of "Okay, now I know where I am."'

Modern-Instrument Vivaldi

This category is for listeners who enjoy *The Four Seasons* with the drama of a chamber group, but prefer the sounds of modern instruments to period ones – with or without multimedia. This is a place for chamber soloists and small-scale ensembles – players with all the individual responsibilities of an intimate collective. For these groups, *The Four Seasons* remains a work in which teeth are cut, mettle tested and imaginations fired – as more than eighty recordings demonstrate.

The first recording of *The Four Seasons* from the Academy of St Martin in the Fields and conductor Neville Marriner was released in 1969 with violinist Alan Loveday. It was their first gold record and sold over half a million copies, but it was the second release in 1979 with Iona Brown as soloist that for many years was considered the definitive version. Crisp, clear and driven, it has a lightness and ease that still makes it a compelling listen. Fast-forward to 2008 and Joshua Bell makes a point of giving the academy's modern instruments just as much romantic gloss. Beauty of sound is the aim of the game; you won't hear any of the period-instrument tones or the dirty realities of nature.

Defining another approach: the historically informed modern-instrument ensemble I Musici has recorded *The Four Seasons* no fewer than seven times. The first, in 1955, established the piece's popularity in Europe with violinist Felix Ayo, who went on to record it again in 1959 – creating the very first stereo recording of the concertos. The group went back into the recording studio with Roberto Michelucci in 1969, Pina Carmirelli in 1982, Federico Agostini in 1988, Mariana Sîrbu in 1995, Antonio Anselmi in 2012, and most recently with Marco Fiorini in 2021. They are living proof that there is no definitive recording, and that the ideas and fashions of a group can change with every new generation of soloists.

One of the greatest challenges to modern-instrument performances of Baroque music is the integration of chordal continuo instruments: the harpsichords and lutes whose distinctive tuning systems only naturally and easily blend with historical strings. Get it wrong and it sounds as though a harpsichord has been added to the recording as an afterthought – but get it right and the magic begins again. There are three recordings that stand out in this regard and the first is Richard Tognetti's with the Australian Chamber Orchestra, from 2015. Their lively, lithe interpretation is nuanced, percussive when needed, and makes the most of the sweet tones of the modern strings. The second is from the Orchestre de Chambre de Lausanne and violinist Renaud Capuçon, who who has admitted that he'd been in no rush to record the concertos; in fact, he'd refused to play *The Four Seasons* after hearing one too many renditions in the tunnels of the Métro in Paris. But once he'd immersed himself in the score he changed his mind entirely, and his live recording is a savvy move to reflect that his ideas about them are always changing.

Finally, violinist Daniel Pioro and Manchester Camerata's 2025 album has me utterly under its spell. 'This is a piece that suffers from either cheap tricks or being extremely well-mannered,' Daniel tells me – and his recording is neither. It's a label-defying interpretation in which he isn't afraid to sacrifice tone for effect, the continuo team is entirely integrated into the ensemble sound, and the freedom injected into the result makes you feel as though it's the first time you've heard the work.

Special-Effects Vivaldi

It's rare to have that 'first time' feeling with *The Four Seasons*, and as the recordings keep coming, musicians seek ways to redefine their interpretations. The recordings in this final category go beyond musical tones to express the sonic ideas in the sonnets and score. Take the recording made by period ensemble Il Giardino Armonico. I remember, very distinctly, the first time I heard it: my face contorted – first a disbelieving frown, then the highest of eyebrows. It seemed outrageous and far ahead of its time for 1994. Their approach to *Winter* sounded properly cold; they weren't afraid to sacrifice beauty of tone in the pursuit of theatre. These Italian musicians pushed tempos to their limits and played with extremes of dynamics, but then continued to create effects through extended string techniques such as using the wood of their bows rather than the hairs (*col legno*), and playing with overtones and harmonics to evoke the different formations of ice.

Theirs is now far from the most extreme version. Electronics and extra-musical sound effects have also found their way into many interpretations of these violin concertos, but these run the risk of sounding gimmicky if not underpinned by convincing *musical* interpretations. When it works, it's startling. The Norwegian Chamber Orchestra and violinist Terje Tønnesen infuse their interpretation with tape-loops and samples of the modern world – traffic noise and crowds, birds, ringtones and percussion. It's an intoxicating mix, in which Vivaldi's score is centre-stage despite some extreme departures from it.

The most persuasive special-effect interpretations present a multi-textured experience in which new characters, landscapes and scenes emerge, whether from sampled effects or the instruments themselves. Take the stylish French outfit Le Concert de la Loge, directed by soloist Julien Chauvin. The opening movement of *Spring* begins with such a swing that you are whisked away and feel as though you're flying through the trees amid birds, with the winds whistling through your hair. When the dog is heard in the second movement it's not just a sound that sticks through the textures, but really resembles a woof; there's no beautiful phrasing-off to make the music sing, it's a rasping, insistent bark.

With the whole piece clocking in at around forty-five minutes, it's rare to have an album that exclusively features *The Four Seasons*. It's a cue to contextualise. When Russian Baroque violinist and countertenor Dmitry Sinkovsky approaches *The Four Seasons*, he not only sings arias between concertos, but also plays his violin with inflections born of eighteenth-century vocal technique. As a result, the wild dreams of his drunken slumber in *Autumn* become a snapshot of Vivaldi's operatic stage, and the contrast of his ensuing fast and furious hunt has an immediate physical effect, leaving his listeners breathless.

Perhaps the ultimate heirs of Il Giardino Armonico in the shock-factor stakes are the Italian violinist Daniele

Orlando and his virtuosic group I Solisti Aquilani. Their *Winter* is so brutal, so harsh in the tearing sounds of hair across string, it brings tears to your eyes. But the brutality is more stark because there is beauty in there too, a fragile beauty threatened by the environment. Not only does their recording push the boundaries of sounds, making wild gestures to contrast with introvert moments, but it also offers two different acoustic mixes on the same album. They present a version with natural ambience, and a second, more contrasted, produced version. It's a heightened take, as if a camera drone moves around the stage and projects the music from myriad perspectives.

—

Categorising recordings can be useful, but has its limits. Your listening preferences may evolve with the changing seasons, and there's certainly more that unites these Vivaldi versions than divides them. It's a universal truth that a recording may live on in your memory for an effect it has on you at a particular point in time, but may not have the same impact when you return to it later. This is all the motivation I need to continue exploring a wide range of recordings, to find the elements that best bring these concertos alive in my own imagination.

PART FOUR
Winter

I: Allegro non molto

Winter scratches stiffly at the soul.
It stings with ice
and shivers through the crystal air.
Feet may try to stamp away its chill,
or teeth to rattle the lips to life,
but winter will not ease its grip.[1]

When Vivaldi evokes the brutality of the season in the first movement of his *Winter* concerto, it's certainly not from his imagination; it's a recent memory. On the morning of 17 January 1716, Antonio and his Venetian neighbours woke to a shocking view. Outside their windows, the world had frozen solid. Not just the city's narrow central waterways, the Grand Canal and the short stretches between islands, but the whole Venetian lagoon. Overnight, an extreme cold front had suddenly and dramatically blanketed western Europe in ice, and the floating city had come to a standstill.

This was no winter wonderland, and not a once-in-a-lifetime occurrence. Vivaldi would have experienced two earlier 'Great Winters', as they are technically known, in 1684 and 1709. The devastating effects of biting cold, days of snowfall and the lagoon turning into an inaccessible expanse of ice would live long in the memory of all Venetians. These harsh winters were traumatic for the city, resulting in the islands of the lagoon being cut off from the mainland, and leading in many cases to a fight for survival for their inhabitants.

Europe's Great Winter of 1709 was one of the most violent of the millennium, and the apex of what we now refer to as the Little Ice Age. 'The cold severity exceeded the thresholds established by the nature and the climate,' wrote the Venetian senator Pietro Garzoni.[2] The freeze coincided with the arrival of Frederick IV, King of Denmark, and although Vivaldi dedicated his second collection of printed concertos to him, popular legends tell of how the king was blamed for bringing the unusual snow and frost from the cold north. Garzoni confirmed that festivities were cancelled because all the internal canals and the lagoons were 'petrified by cold' and boats were locked deep into the ice.[3] He also reported that pick-axes were employed to attempt to cut out a route of sorts, in order to transport food and supplies. This was limited in success, however, and it was some time before the Venetians realised that the ice was strong enough both on the lagoon and the River Po to support horses and carriages to carry essentials over from the mainland. Without wood to burn, let alone enough food to eat, thousands of people died in frigid conditions. As the entire region was affected, supplies of basic provisions such as grain had to come from much further afield, with greater delays and expense. Prized historic vines that might just have survived the last great winter were no match for this one; they were decimated, along with olive, nut and citrus groves. There was little short of a famine in Venice, and disease, reaching epidemic proportions, followed in its wake.

As the situation was repeated in 1716, potentially mere months before Vivaldi put pen to paper on *The Four Seasons*, the full force of winter's brutality would have been at the forefront of his mind. There is little surprise, therefore, that this concerto begins with nature at her most terrifying. There is no trace of a melody in the opening bars, as the music reflects a landscape drained of colour. The lagoon's plants would shrivel back to their roots every winter, and only their seeds would survive until spring; that absence of life is brought to the fore in the music as the increasing layers of repeated notes lock all life under their sonic ice. There's a total absence of wildlife in the bitter-cold stillness. There is no birdsong to be heard, the music is all about texture, jagged icy lines, dissonant biting chords, and cold spiky articulation as bows collide with strings.

When the first gusts of wind blow from the soloist, Vivaldi writes 'Orrido vento' (frightening wind) in their part, and three times they swirl as the rest of the ensemble cowers at ground level. It's as if the soloist's airborne lines whistle across the ice, rising and falling in the frozen air of this natural, resonant acoustic. There's a magnificence in the writing, a thrill in the chill of an imposing landscape. But we have not yet encountered human life, and the tension rises as more string players join the fray, increasing the volume with faster notes until the entire ensemble heralds the arrival of people and the catchiest music of the movement: a sequence of alternating repeated notes and wide leaps.

These are the people of Vivaldi's sonnet: running and stamping their feet from the cold. But before they can get far, the cruel winds blow again – at first high up in the soloist's part, and then in gusts from a different direction with all the players. They buffet the people, hampering their progress across the ice. They briefly drop, offering a moment of respite, but it seems that then the temperatures plummet too: bows tremble and shudder to depict the chattering of teeth, with the people manipulated like puppets, barely in control of bodies animated by the cold. The wind picks back up and the running music returns as Vivaldi's characters attempt to carry on, but ultimately to no avail. This is a movement entirely devoid of comfort, and the high drama of the music immortalises Vivaldi's first-hand experience of the stark realities of the season.

As if to reinforce the harshness and the horror-filled vision of a frozen winter, Vivaldi uses much of this music again in an aria from his opera *Farnace* of 1727. The dissonant opening attack motif is so strongly evoked and so specific to this moment in *The Four Seasons* that when you hear it in a different context you shiver with cold, knowing instantly that there's ice involved. Within the plot of *Farnace*, Vivaldi's feelings on ice and its association with death become even more intense. 'I feel my blood like ice coursing through every vein,' sings Farnace, the defeated King of Pontus, mistakenly believing that his wife Tamiri has followed his command to murder their son. It's a horrific junction in the opera and highlights the characterisation of the deadly qualities of ice in Vivaldi's music.

The agricultural damage and financial chaos in the wake of the 'Great Winters' of 1684, 1709 and 1716 were staggering, and the death count ran into tens of thousands. Chilling meteorological events in every sense of the word, they couldn't be explained at the time as anything other than as acts of God. There were very few obvious benefits to the harsh winters of the seventeenth and eighteenth centuries, except perhaps one contentious one. The string instruments that emerged from the nearby Cremona workshops of the Stradivari, Guarneri and Amati families between 1650 and 1750 are some of the best that the world has ever known. Their success remains a mystery. Did the families have closely guarded techniques unique to their trade, a special recipe for varnish, or fine-tuning that they never revealed? Or is it possible that the wood from which they crafted their violins, violas, cellos and basses grew and matured more slowly in Alpine forests during the Little Ice Age? Many have pondered whether that could be the secret to these instruments' rich, resonant sounds. The theory about the special sound of certain violins being caused by use of slow-grown wood is hard to prove, as there were plenty of other luthiers turning out perfectly average instruments at the same time, using wood that grew under the same conditions. With many violin makers in Venice, Vivaldi would likely have played a local instrument, and it's a beguiling thought that he might have benefitted as a player from the Little Ice Age. It's particularly poignant when you hear his violins sounding the resonant textures of winter in the tones of their frosted world.

—

Could the frigid winter scene evoked by Vivaldi happen again? The shallow waters around Mantua and the many narrow canals within Venice can and still do freeze, but even that is becoming a rare occurrence owing to our increasingly mild climate. It takes exceptionally cold temperatures for the Venetian lagoon to freeze since the Adriatic brings an influx of warmer water at each tidal cycle. If that does happen, ice slabs form – but to freeze over completely it needs a very particular weather front. Snow is the first necessary ingredient, along with a combination of arctic air to keep temperatures down and a strong bora wind from the north-east to evaporate any excess water from the surface.[4] These conditions tend to be decades apart and the last Great Winter was in 1929. Between January and March that year both canals and the lagoon froze, and at the peak in mid-February daily temperatures dropped to minus-thirteen degrees Celsius, creating thick ice slabs of up to twenty centimetres that could easily bear the weight of people and animals. That was the last time the lagoon froze over completely, but there was a partial freeze in 1956 and again in 1985, when some people could cross parts of it on the ice.[5] 2012 marked the last winter that was technically classified 'very severe' and still the lagoon was only partially frozen. The fear factor of our age is not the floating city freezing over, but rather its sinking into the lagoon – which makes mapping its *future* (as opposed to its past) especially pertinent.

As is my wont, I set out at first light from my hotel on the Grand Canal, winter 'scratching stiffly' at my soul as I huddle under my big coat. There are few tourists out at this hour, rather people going to work and delivery boats doing their rounds with the day's fresh produce. The tide is low, revealing scum lines on the palaces, a reminder of yesterday's water levels. Paint damage and colour change in the stone are other telltale signs of tides gone by.

A high tide that reaches over eighty centimetres above the normal water line is a phenomenon known as *acqua alta* (high water), and not a new problem for the lagoon's inhabitants. The first record of *acqua alta* submerging all the islands of the lagoon dates back to the eighth century. It is a natural occurrence in an unstable lagoon environment, in which daily tides and winds dictate the agenda.[6] It's something Venetians are adept at navigating; however, it's becoming increasingly intolerable and damaging. *Acqua alta* is traditionally a winter phenomenon, in which the water breaches parts of the city, flooding piazzas and streets. A warning system alerts its arrival: an air-raid siren and a series of high-pitched beeps that indicate how high the tide is expected to be. Locals emerge in galoshes or wellies to go about their business, shops brace for the swell with sandbags, and furniture is moved upstairs – hopefully before water flows into streets and buildings. In 1966 an especially high tide, three days of rain and a powerful easterly wind submerged parts of the city to shoulder-height for twenty-four hours. It was initially thought to be a one-off *acqua alta* of the century, but the events of that November are now considered a new dawn of peril for the city.

While the string instruments crafted in Vivaldi's day have matured over the centuries, the turning, changing world continues to bring extreme weather. The difference is that now there is little mystery in the causes of it: human actions are accountable for global warming and the rising sea levels it brings. Until the end of the twentieth century, *acqua alta* was still considered a rarity, and it would not have often troubled Vivaldi. Scientists can in fact extrapolate this by studying the green-brown algae line Canaletto painted on his scenes of the Grand Canal in the early eighteenth century, markings considered accurate as he made early use of the camera obscura.

Rather than being an occasional threat of long-off climate change, the exceptionally high tides are now the norm. At worst, they reach more than 135 centimetres, and of the twenty-five most extreme instances in the last 100 years, more than half have occurred since 2009. But of greater concern is the fact that, since 2019, the worst of the instances haven't been confined to winter.[7]

My destination this bright winter morning is in the north part of the Venetian lagoon: the island of Torcello. The birthplace of Venice, Torcello was the first island to be populated as people moved out from the mainland. Once a major trading hub, it's now home to fewer than fifteen residents, and takes around an hour and a half to reach from San Marco. Leaving the Grand Canal behind me, I roll off the vaporetto at Fondamente Nove and after negotiating my Venetian nemesis – an unexpected substantial stepped bridge – I board a more seafaring vessel and head out onto the open lagoon. We stop at the glass-making island of Murano, then steer north to Burano, famous for its lace, and finally Torcello itself. En route, the island landscapes change from tightly packed terracotta roofs to colourful waterside houses, and, eventually, shrubs and grasses. Birds replace people, and yet the confusing sight of swans on the sea is a reminder of this very particular ecosystem, where salt and fresh water combine. Except for the planes making for Marco Polo Airport and fishermen zipping past on motorboats, it's quiet on the dock at Torcello, and I follow the sign for the vantage point of the bell tower at the isolated Cathedral of Santa Maria Assunta. With some trepidation, and plenty of time on my hands, I leave my wheelchair at the base, and inch my way up the stairs and ramps. Nearly an hour later, covered in dust and dirt, I make it to the top and count my lucky stars that it's not raining, let alone snowing or blowing a gale. Under the brightest of Venetian blue skies, the breathtaking panorama across the lagoon takes in the marshes, the islands, all the way back to La Serenissima herself. However, from up here I have a new perspective on the scale of Vivaldi's winter experience; the idea of this huge body of water freezing solid is terrifying. The islands represent just 8 per cent of the 550 square kilometres of the lagoon, and in Torcello you are miles away from anywhere. If the lagoon were frozen for months at a time, any inhabitants out here would be completely cut off from civilisation.

The fear embedded in Vivaldi's music is still an environmental terror, but instead of the peril of freezing over, Venice is now threatened by a combination of erosion, flooding and declining water quality. 'Climate risks are interconnected and do not occur in isolation,' says Silvia Torresan, co-director of the Risk Assessment and Adaptation Strategies Division at the Mediterranean Centre on Climate Change (the Centro Euro-Mediterraneo sui Cambiamenti Climatici). She goes on to counsel: 'if we don't employ a multi-risk approach [. . .]

Fig. 16: The Venetian lagoon from the Cathedral of
Santa Maria Assunta at Torcello

we could adopt measures that address one problem but generate or amplify others.'[8]

Perhaps the most significant and controversial project of recent times is the 'MOSE' project. Taking its name from the biblical figure of Moses, who parted the Red Sea, it is a system of some seventy-eight underwater barriers designed to seal off the entire lagoon from the high tides of the turbulent Adriatic Sea. It was more than thirty years in the making, a project beset by delays, scandals and a runaway budget exceeding six billion euros. Its barriers were activated for the first time on 3 October 2020, and despite a high tide, Venice was untouched by the excess waters. While the project appears to be working, the predictions for rising sea levels have changed since it began, as the UN science panel forecast ever higher global sea-rise averages.[9]

'Venice in the twenty-first century is an enchanted 1,500-year-old dream immersed in an apocalyptic contemporary nightmare,' says *National Geographic* journalist Frank Viviano.[10] Chiming with the words of the CMCC's Silvia Torresan about measures that address one problem but generate another, he describes his investigations of the fate of the salt marshes surrounding the lagoon. When Vivaldi was born, they spanned 100 square miles; now, thanks to human interventions and development of the land, they've shrunk to a mere sixteen square miles. This is a startling figure on its own with regards to the biodiversity of local ecosystems, but when you learn that one square kilometre of Venetian marshland annually removes 370 tonnes of carbon dioxide from the Earth's atmosphere – a rate fifty times greater than that of tropical rainforests – the magnitude of the situation becomes critical.[11] A huge over-simplification of a complex situation is that while the MOSE project may partially protect Venice, the more frequently the barriers are raised, the more they block the tides from replenishing the nutrients vital to pre-serving the flora and fauna of salt marshes. The more it's cut off from the sea, the faster the lagoon effectively becomes an artificial swamp, depleting the water's oxygen levels and preventing pollution from flowing back out again. 'All of its organic life risks decaying,' says architect and former city official Cristiano Gasparetto, and 'if the lagoon dies, Venice dies.'[12]

The physical destruction is alarming, but as Alberto Nardi, Chairman of the Associazione Piazza San Marco, points out, 'all this creates psychological damage', which is 'even more harmful and insidious than the obvious economic damage'.[13] This is similar to the fear that Vivaldi captures in this movement of *Winter*. It's not just the view of the ice and the shivering it causes, not just the threats in the music and the imagery of death; it's the psychology of the musical drama, the effect on the soul that leaves the lasting impact.

However, there are glimmers of hope. Vital, a subsid-iary group of the conservation organisation We Are Here

Venice, conducts research into the best ways of recolonising vegetation, and offers private investors the opportunity to offset their ecological, social and economic impact by contributing to work that supports the wellbeing of the lagoon.[14] They are seeing results, but it is a race against time. From my tower-top position on Torcello you can see the impact of human development in every direction.

The biting dissonance in the opening movement of *Winter* is a warning for any age that destruction is inevitable without positive action. For Vivaldi's audience, his winter concerto suggests that without Venetians taking precautions, without making provisions, nature could prove utterly terrifying. Preservation is the watchword here, whether that's the biodiversity of marshland, or a means of surviving the harshest of winters trapped amid snow and ice.

II: Largo

Yet, what a thing it is
to sit beside a blazing fire,
while the beating rain
is bent on drenching
every inch of world
and all who walk it.[1]

Winter, the fourth age of Vivaldi's *The Four Seasons*, is a time of dreaming by the fireside, and it's encapsulated in the middle movement of his fourth concerto.

The song of the solo violinist's part is wonderfully wistful, a melody that cries out for words as the musician sculpts the phrases, breathes through long lines, and leads us along Vivaldi's trademark sequences and patterns to expected – and a few unexpected – places. You can imagine it as the aftermath of a late-night walk through Mantua in the pouring rain – an all-too-familiar experience on my visit, and one, no doubt, fresh in Vivaldi's mind on arriving home and installing himself by the fire after being out in the city during winter. There is contentment, perhaps, but relief too, at being dry and toasting your toes while others, not so lucky, are outside getting drenched. The music sweeps along with a familiar sweetness, but also a lingering air of unease; after all, this is winter, and no comfort is here to stay.

This exquisite violin aria is locked between two ice-bound outer movements, just as eighteenth-century Mantua was by water. Frozen or not, the lakes surrounding the city formed a defensive moat, and the ancient turrets still rise up from the pearly mist just as they did when Vivaldi first crossed the Ponte di San Giorgio in 1718. There's something of that timelessness in this slow movement, whose lyrical phrases were potentially inspired by the rain-drenched city. The phrases arch like the porticos of the Piazza delle Erbe (the old marketplace), their smooth, curling melodies run like water off the white marble of Mantua's cathedral, the Cattedrale di San Pietro Apostolo, and the rich expansiveness in the harmonies is worthy of the labyrinthine Palazzo Ducale itself.

Vivaldi's music evokes the low winter light that casts long shadows through the leaf-stripped trees lining the edges of Mantua's watery defences. He also depicts the contrasting glow from the hearth and the fire's flickering flames through melody imbued with a luminosity pre-cious at this time of year. It's the same radiance as candles lit for Mass, bonfires for warmth outside or lanterns illuminating the faces of carol singers. This music brings a temporary contentment and a glimmering moment of calm – a softness to cherish, if not quite to trust. We know that before long the harsh conditions will return, but there is repose and comfort here in the dark warm tones of a key not heard in *The Four Seasons* until this point: E flat major. This contrast in atmosphere reflects the difference in the weather outside. Precipitation-wise rain falls here rather than the snow and ice of the first and last movements, and even though rain has the power to soak to the skin, it can be more forgiving.

—

By the warmth of the fire, we picture Vivaldi in the fourth and final season of his life: as an old man.

There is no happy end to Vivaldi's story. By the long harsh winter of 1739, his reception in Venice had also turned somewhat cold. The operatic dreams he'd chased throughout his life faded in his dotage. Advancing musical taste was moving faster than he was – as with many composers of his age – and, finding himself out of favour, he faced financial hardship.

In the late 1730s Vivaldi had three unsuccessful experiences staging operas in the city of Ferrara. In 1737, disputes arose about the choice of operas, payment and a singer's contract. In 1738, Cardinal Tommaso Ruffo forbade the composer to enter the city on the grounds both of his refusal to say Mass (on medical grounds) and of his 'friendship' with the singer Anna Girò, whom we encountered in *Summer*. Vivaldi indignantly protested his innocence, and local musicians deputised for him, but with little success. In 1739, the composer was again absent from Ferrara, supervising another production in Venice; his first opera for the city, *Siroe*, was much criticised, with the result that the authorities refused to stage the second opera, *Farnace*, and Vivaldi had to pay off the musicians, dancers and set and costume designers to the princely sum of 6,000 ducats. With few options left available to him, Antonio had one last card to play, not in Ferrara or Venice, but in Vienna.

Back in 1728, Vivaldi had been called upon by the Venetian Republic to join the diplomatic delegation attempting to dispute Emperor Charles VI's plans to develop the rival port of Trieste. It's a moment in history that begs questions about Vivaldi's political role in society, but during the proceedings he and the emperor, who was a similar age, seemingly talked about music. Charles VI was a musical man, and it's reported that in that one meeting he talked more to Vivaldi than he had to any of his ministers over the previous two years. Another member of the delegation, Antonio Conti, reported that Vivaldi was honoured with the title of knight (which seems unlikely as he never used it), and gifted 'a great deal of money and a gold chain'.[2] In return, he wrote the Concerto in C major RV 171 'per Sua Maestà Cesarea e Cattolica' ('for his Caesarean and Catholic Royal Majesty'), and also dedicated to him his prestigious op. 9 concertos, a collection called *La Cetra* (which means both 'the sceptre' and 'the lyre' – the emblem of the Holy Roman emperors). Vivaldi didn't take up any invitation to move to Vienna at that point, but he visited the Austrian capital with his ageing father two years later after a tour to Prague with his opera *Farnace* – the one with the aria borrowed from the first movement of this *Winter* concerto.

The problems of Vivaldi's final years took root in 1736, when his father Giovanni Battista died. This was a huge blow to Antonio. Vivaldi Sr. had been his ultimate champion and a very practical supporter who, alongside serving as a violinist at St Mark's, had assisted his son by working as a musical copyist, acting as joint impresario for their operatic ventures at the Teatro Sant'Angelo, and generally managing Vivaldi's finances. Without him, Vivaldi's life changed immeasurably and, from 1740, deteriorated rapidly.

In what appears to have been a bit of a panic, Vivaldi chose to sell off a number of manuscripts in order to fund a move to Vienna – or at least a visit to the Austrian capital en route elsewhere.[3] The sixty-two-year-old Antonio seems to have counted on rekindling the emperor's attention and establishing himself as a composer in the imperial court. When he'd raised enough money, Vivaldi took his leave of Venice, possibly incognito, and set his sights on mounting an opera at Vienna's Kärntnertortheater at the earliest opportunity. It was not to be. In October 1740, the wettest and coldest October in memory, the emperor died and, as a result, all the opera houses, including the Kärntnertortheater, closed for the season of Carnevale. Vivaldi maintained some hope that his new connections at court might support him until the theatres reopened, and fell back on the shaky business of selling concertos to the nobility, but any success was short-lived.

In 1741, Vivaldi became gravely ill. He couldn't afford to return to Venice, and in July he died in his apartment next door to the Kärntnertortheater. He'd been *that* close to his final dream, yet it was out of reach. Vivaldi's funeral record states that he died of 'Innerl[ichem] brand' (internal burning or inflammation) which, given his life-long, complex medical profile could mean pretty much anything from an infection to pulmonary congestion.[4] Unconventional to the end, the Red Priest, the fiery violinist and famous composer of Venice, died a poor man and was buried with little ceremony in an ordinary grave at Vienna's hospital burial ground.

—

We don't know the topics of conversation that had consumed Vivaldi and the Holy Roman Emperor Charles VI back in 1728, but at the time *The Four Seasons* was enjoying the height of its eighteenth-century popularity. You can imagine Charles wanting to show off his knowledge of artistic representations of the seasons, telling Vivaldi that one of his predecessors, Maximilian II, was given the great Milanese artist Giuseppe Arcimboldo's set of paintings *The Four Seasons*.[5] My fantasy is that Vivaldi made a point of seeing them in Vienna in the last months of his life.

Arcimboldo was famed for his portraits of human heads made up of vegetables, fruits, foliage and tree roots, items loaded with riddles and puzzles that catered to the Renaissance tastes for the bizarre. He completed *The Four Seasons*, a series of such heads, at least three times, and the set he offered to Maximilian in the 1560s was accompanied by a poem by Giovanni Battista Fonteo that explained their allegorical meaning. This mirrors Vivaldi's publication of poetry with his *Four Seasons*, giving weight to the idea that the concertos had been a talking point for him and the emperor.[6]

The pictorial depictions within Vivaldi's *The Four Seasons* have long invited speculation that they must have had some artistic visual inspiration, and painter Marco Ricci's name was once the bookies' favourite. The two men were both in Venice around 1716, but with no surviving paintings the evidence is lacking, and the idea has largely been debunked. (That being said, Ricci initiated a new style of Venetian landscape painting, a parallel to Vivaldi's approach in music.) What is certain is that the notion of depicting the seasons in art was increasingly in vogue, and another of Vivaldi's contemporaries who shared some of his ideals and principles caught my eye: Rosalba Carriera.

—

'Wrap up warm, there's rain forecast and it's freezing cold,' says my friend John Chu, Senior Curator of Paintings and Sculpture at the National Trust, as we arrange to meet one February night outside London's Royal Academy of Arts. He's not wrong. Even my oversized fake-fur scarf does little to guard against the chill, but it's worth it to chat about Vivaldi before the doors open for the preview we're attending. John is my regular platonic art date; I bring music, he brings paintings, and tonight I want to know his thoughts on Rosalba.

Carriera was five years older than Vivaldi – and outlived him by sixteen. Famed for her miniatures on ivory and credited with inventing the pastel portrait, she was born in Venice to parents who practised law and lacemaking, and found financial independence through her art. By 1700 she'd captured the fashionable market for decorated snuff boxes, and three years later progressed to portraiture. Her real success came with capturing the market of visitors to Venice on the Grand Tour. Commissioning a Venetian oil portrait would take some considerable time, but these delicate pastels were relatively quickly done – and easily portable for the journey onwards, or home. Were Vivaldi and Carriera aware of each other? I've no proof. Might *The Four Seasons* – a topic certainly in the Venetian air at the time – be a key to connecting them? In 1713, Carriera was living by the Grand Canal when she was visited by a young prince enjoying the Grand Tour, who would later become Augustus III, Elector of Saxony and King of Poland. He commissioned a portrait – in oil – and a series of allegorical works in pastel, among which are *The Four Seasons*.

By 1726, just a year after Vivaldi published his concertos, Carriera noted in her diary that she had packaged up her set of *The Four Seasons* to dispatch to London to a certain Sig. Smith. Its destination was the spot in which I'm now sitting, my fingers freezing in the bitterly cold courtyard of the Royal Academy. John opens a bag of popcorn, and I eat more than my fair share as he explains that the usual iconography of *The Four Seasons* in the early modern period is focused on control. 'Think of the Gardens of Versailles or the formal expressions of landscapes,' he says, 'it's usually saying that a monarch or a pope can control the world through the elements.' While we search up some of Rosalba's female portraits of *The Four Seasons* on my phone he continues: 'With Carriera we see a woman who knew the paintings of Antoine Watteau – but who has gone her own way, representing the seasons sensually.'[7] You don't want to look away from them, I say. 'Yes, that's the point,' John agrees, 'the fact that she used pastel is key to the way your eye is drawn in. It's like our conversation now,' he says, looking me in the eye, 'as I focus on your face, the background behind you is blurred, irrelevant, and in Carriera's hands that's what the pastel does so well, letting her shift between high focus and suggestion.' There are definite parallels here with Vivaldi and his soloist, times in which the focus is entirely on the virtuosic feats, while the surrounding musical details are merely suggested, and others where they are very specific and the whole ensemble presents the minutiae of the scene. The similarities are even more compelling when you think that both composer and artist were working with female subjects – if you imagine that possible performance of Vivaldi's *Four Seasons* at the Pietà that we encountered in spring.

You could conclude that the flowers, fruits and furs of these paintings are symbolic clichés of the seasons, but Carriera's pastels have the same human experience and degree of stark realism that I recognise in Vivaldi's concertos. For him, it's in the notes to musicians instructing very particular effects, such as shivering limbs, or smooth ice – the warts-and-all of humanity, rather than a romanticised view of winter. For her, it's in the realism in the faces of her nymph-like women: they look like people you might know, admittedly particularly beautiful ones. Her modern style brought a new honesty to portraiture, which becomes even more evident in her numerous self-portraits, many of which also place her within the seasons. Her most famous is part of the collection of self-portraits in the Uffizi Gallery in Florence. It epitomises the way she veered away from the customary ideals of a woman, instead celebrating her own unfashionable thin lips, large nose and the deep dimple in her chin. Rosalba lived through the harshest of Venetian winters, and this is reflected in her winter self-portrait, from the furs she wears to the lines on her face. She is an old woman in the fourth age of her life, exuding confidence as the light catches her pearl earrings, illuminates her wrinkled skin and brings a glint to mismatched eyes plagued with macular degeneration.

John looks through the windows of the Royal Academy, willing the gallery to open for the preview (of works by another great female artist, Angelica Kauffman) we're attending this frosty February night. Right on cue the doors swing out, throwing light across the courtyard and releasing a seductive smell of food. No wonder smell is the sense historically associated with this season. With the glow of the gallery imitating the allure of the blazing fire in the middle movement of Vivaldi's *Winter*, this is a very welcome invitation out of the cold and first spots of rain. We don't hang around.

—

Ultimately the most striking element of this middle movement is the care Vivaldi puts into the exquisite layers of the music – it is the most thickly textured movement in *The Four Seasons*. The idea of depicting falling rain in music wasn't new to him – as recently as October 1717 he'd worked on a *dramma per musica* (literally, a 'play for music') called *Tieteberga*, staged in Venice. Among its arias – nine of which are by other composers – Vivaldi had created one for alto castrato called 'Sento in seno ch'in pioggia di lagrime' (I feel in my breast a rain of tears). He'd used plucked strings to represent the droplets as the singer spins a plaintive tale, and the effect was so magical that he used it again in his 1724 opera *Il Giustino*. But the effect of the rain in either of those arias isn't a patch on the richness of sound he creates in this middle movement of *Winter*. Building on the idea of falling tears, Vivaldi layers up different water effects: from the pizzicato precipitation of the upper strings to the fat droplets landing in the cello, and between them, a single note from the sustained viola line, as if depicting a lone figure gazing out of the window. Meanwhile, the violin soloist spins decorative ornaments into a song of nostalgia, and you, the listener, choose the extent to which you experience this moment as one of repose, or of warning. It's certainly a melody that wouldn't survive long on the ice, but it could also be a big blanket of comfort by the fire as the rain hammers the windowpanes and pools on the sills.

III: Allegro

Winter's path is hard.
We must tread upon the ice
with such slow steps
so's not to slip.
For to rush would be to skid
and fall, but in that falling
should we crack
the river's skin of ice,
well, then we must be swift.

Winter's wind blows quick and true
through walls and floors
and bolted doors.
It is a boisterous battle-song of air,
for winter is a thing alive,
who brings
not only risk and strife,
but also joy.[1]

I own an elegant pair of white leather ice-skates. Broken in by a short line of skaters before me, they have names written in biro onto the back of each tongue, and crossed out with each new owner. They're the sort of objects that warrant short stories of their own. Once upon a time they gleamed pristine on a birthday or Christmas morning, and ensuing scuffs and marks proved signs of adventure in tentative beginner lessons and skating parties. The next biro-ed name perhaps saw a new round of whacking into the sides of the rink, and maybe even the bright lights of a school competition. Over the years, the back of the wardrobe has clearly been their main arena, except perhaps for a dusting down and a nervous lace-up for a first date. Now they're in the unlikely possession of a woman who uses a wheelchair.

Although I can't walk more than a few decent steps, I can skate. Not for long, and not very quickly but certainly longer and faster than I can walk. Maybe I have a distant muscle memory from a winter weekend finding my skating feet on the ice rink outside Vienna's Rathaus, where the glow of newly discovered glühwein and the help of not-unhandsome skating assistants fuelled my resolve for independence on the ice. The push and glide is a very different action to walking, sparing some impact on my hip, and so for a short spell it's possible – yet high risk. If I fell, the downsides of dislocating limbs would be pretty catastrophic, but for a few moments, that freedom is everything . . . And that's what's going on in the last movement of *Winter*. Vivaldi takes risks.

The single bass note in the opening bars portrays the smooth ice itself and, way above it, the soloist creates the perfect crystalline arches of the frozen liquid, with its mineral tone winding left and right as if checking the musical depth of the ice shelf. The other musicians join, one by one, testing their way, pushing off together, slowly and fearfully. It echoes the realisation Venetians had in 1709 that the ice was thick enough to transport people and goods over it rather than cracking up beneath them. Repeated phrases signal a cautious exploration, and if anxiety is high, it's easily explained by the challenge of finding new balance, and the perpetual fear of falling over – or even through – this false floor to the watery depths.

That fear is not unfounded: before long, the string players start to lose their footing; six times we hear a falling motif from the violins as if arms are flailing in circles to keep balance; before all the musical lines fall to the frozen ground in a unison descending scale. The soloist is the first to regain her equanimity. Picking herself up and, instructed by Vivaldi to 'Correr forte' (run strongly), she takes off across the frozen expanse, gaining confidence, progress and movement. The jeopardy lies in how long this can last. Harmonically, we're going nowhere quickly, so suspense is high. Then the music fractures. All the players are involved again – because what happens next is going to affect them all: with three sharp, isolated gestures, the ice breaks. The solo part echoes the effect, like the ricochet of a stone glancing off the surface of a frozen pond and bouncing away into the distance.

It's a traumatic moment. We don't know if anyone falls through – Vivaldi makes no poetic reference to it – but for a few moments, the music changes entirely. The bass line disappears, and the upper parts lift the texture high above the ground. Vivaldi notes in the parts that this is the warm Sirocco wind – unexpectedly blowing in a new feeling, a softness, a musical reference to the way *Summer* began. This evokes memories far from the reality of this winter scene. Free from malice, there is a halting comfort in Sirocco's song. The string lines rock gently together with such ease that you know it can't last. And it doesn't. This sub-zero landscape is anything but predictable, and with a gust of the cold north wind Boreas, the soloist takes off with racing notes, goading all the players into assuming the roles of a full cast of winds that join her until the end.

This is Vivaldi's 'boisterous battle-song', sweeping you, his listener, along with the winds, and possibly the skaters too, as they fly about the frozen lagoon with infectious abandon. This winter is about volatile reconciliation rather than brutality, the vitality and excitement in the music paying homage to a season that brings 'not only risk and strife, but also joy'.

—

It may come right at the end of the sonnet, but that joy is evident amid the brutality inherent in this movement's music. It's in the moments of exhilaration out in the cold, just as winter festivals like Christmas or Venice's

Carnevale bring inner joy – and warmth. The way in which Vivaldi creates a sense of motion, whether in the winds or the movement of the people, begs the question: did he ever skate? Considering his health condition, it's highly unlikely that Antonio took to the ice himself, but it would seem that those around him did, and he'd have watched, as they transported essential supplies, or tried their luck making shapes out on the ice.

Skating is a centuries-old winter sport, thought to have been started by the Finns, and early surviving examples of skates from Scandinavia are made from bone and copper. Vivaldi's fellow Venetians probably had iron blades that they strapped onto a wooden-block sole around their outdoor shoes – a Dutch invention from 1250 that made the skating experience much more stable. Not that stability is the feeling in this finale to *Winter*. Nor was it the experience even of the patron saint of skating, St Lidwina, who had incomplete success on the stability front. The famous 1498 woodcut of the saint by Johannes Brugman is entitled *Lidwina's Fall on the Ice*, demonstrating, as with the final movement of Vivaldi's concerto, that even the best of skaters hit the decks at some point. (In fact, according to the legend, Lidwina's fall was an 'act of God', to save her from an unwanted marriage.)

Northern Europeans had enjoyed skating for generations, especially as winters throughout the Little Ice Age were consistently cold, and rivers, lakes, and canals froze over annually. Ice skaters propelling themselves with poles were a common sight, and while the metal blades were the preserve of those who could afford them, the old medieval design of bone skates stayed in use across rural areas of Europe well into the twentieth century. Paintings and first-hand accounts from countries such as the Netherlands show that skating was embraced by people of all ages and classes – it certainly wasn't the preserve of the elite. Depictions of skaters in the Netherlands abound in sixteenth-century paintings such as Pieter Bruegel the Elder's *Winter Landscape with Skaters and a Bird Trap*, Adam van Breen's *Skating on the Frozen Amstel River* or Hendrick Avercamp's *Winter Landscape with Skaters*. They appear to show a romanticised view of winter, the ice providing a frozen playground where tumbles seem harmless, but deathly details (including an ominous icy fog, a beggar pleading for bread, or crows feasting on a horse's carcass) lurk round the edges, revealing the stark reality we've now come to expect in Vivaldi's concertos. The extreme effects of the Little Ice Age were felt in agriculture, social stability, and particularly health, as changing weather patterns altered the range of disease-carrying insects. In the freezing winters of the seventeenth century, epidemics of plague were rife, and despite the cold conditions, malaria persisted too. Prolonged harsh winters were nothing short of deadly, something not lost on Vivaldi, which is perhaps why the joy of the season is reserved for the very end of the concerto.[2]

A skating culture was to be expected in northern Europe, but not in the southern parts of the Mediterranean. The shock blast of 1709 in Vivaldi's Venice became legendary, and the frozen Venetian lagoon was depicted in two contemporary copperplate etchings by the Italian cartographer and globe-maker Vincenzo Coronelli. The first is titled (referencing the Venetian calendar): *The iced Lagoon facing Mestre [in the hinterland] in the year MDCCVIII.*[3] This view of the frozen lagoon looking across to the mainland would inspire many future paintings of great winters from artists such as Francesco Battaglioli, Francesco Guardi and Giacomo Guardi. Coronelli's depiction of the 1709 freeze is a serious affair, showing people trying their best to transport animals and supplies across the ice. Its partner etching, however, spins 180 degrees to offer another view: *The iced Lagoon facing Murano [island] in the year MDCCVIII* gives us the first visual account from 1709 of people having fun on the ice. A lady rides a mini-chariot while around her others glide about, race and fall, holding their arms in the air for balance and the pure joy of movement. Through the stark lines of this etching, you can sense both the frigid conditions and the delight that skating brings.

These scenes are fascinating, but not for their realistic documentation of events – there's nothing of the suffering, death and destruction here, let alone an accurate representation of the dense urban population of Venice (*c.*138,000), with only around twenty people present in this view. What Coronelli does is capture a feeling, a memory – or at least what he's chosen to remember. Documents and reports of the Great Winter of 1709 were preserved to inform, but Coronelli and Vivaldi, who were representing harsh winters such as this more generally, were working in a different dimension. They preserved human reactions and sensations in creations of time and place that spoke from the heart, something that was ultimately both memorable, and marketable.

———

At the heart of the Northern Italian winter of Vivaldi's lifetime was the pre-Lent celebration of Carnevale (carnival). According to Venetian tradition, it had begun when the town had gathered in St Mark's Square in 1162 to celebrate the republic's victory over its enemy – the Patriarch of Aquileia. By the time Vivaldi was born it was a centuries-old, full-scale festival, a winter escapade of up to eight weeks from Boxing Day to Shrove Tuesday that saw citizens, nobles and visitors alike allowed to act beyond their customary codes of class, rank and identity. From street parties to lavish banquets, Carnevale cultivated a culture of hidden and intentionally mistaken identity behind masks. It was the ultimate escape from the trudge of reality, a chance to get together and be raucous in the coldest winter months – and was so popular with tourists that the population of the city doubled during the festivities. The huge party was also ostensibly designed for eating up all the rich food and drink preserved since harvest, before the forty days of Lent began. That's where the name Carnevale came from – the Latin *carne* and *vale* – farewell to meat.

From the mid-sixteenth century, Venice's popular *commedia dell'arte* theatres (theatres specialising in stylised comic dramas) threw open their doors to the ever-growing swarms of visitors and quickly became magnets for outrageously daring activity. The Catholic Church was not happy with this situation, and sought to close these sinks of iniquity, but the ruling families had grown accustomed to finding ways of diversifying to keep the economy going, and they came up with a new idea. The opera scene that had begun at home during their grand banquets would go public, and with it a flurry of development – theatres, hotels and casinos that made Venice the playground of wealthy Europeans. The Tron family, the oldest of the Venetian noble dynasties, were the first to change the game in 1637 by opening their Teatro San Cassiano – the first purpose-built public opera house for a paying audience. With its first production, of Francesco Manelli's *L'Andromeda*, opera moved from the realms of private spectacle to the imagination of anyone who could buy a ticket. The following year the powerful Grimani family did the same with the Teatro Santi Giovanni e Paolo, and in 1639 the brothers Carlo and Vincenzo Grimani mounted the opera *La Delia* – with a libretto by Giulio Strozzi and music again by

Manelli – to begin the Carnevale season. These families set the stage for the creation of operas by the likes of Claudio Monteverdi, Francesco Cavalli and Carlo Pallavicino, and for an economically volatile world of entertainment that in the following century would beguile Antonio Vivaldi.

The fateful day in 1709 when the lagoon froze over coincided with the start of Carnevale. The opera houses were anticipating the opening of the season, but there was no chance of that. The intense cold didn't ease up and stretched well into March, leaving Venice with no profit from its prime tourism season that year. The doge was forced to cancel all official state activities, theatres remained closed, and Venice fell silent. The downturn in finances affected everyone, and by February Vivaldi was out of a job at the Pietà too. The following year the Grimani family enticed George Frideric Handel back to Venice. He'd swiftly found acclaim within key Italian circles so, catching the moment, Vincenzo Grimani commissioned a new opera, *Agrippina*, to headline at the Teatro San Giovanni Grisostomo for Carnevale in 1709–10 (new year fell mid-season). It was a simultaneous bid to rescue the theatre's flailing finances and – as Vincenzo himself furnished Handel with the satirical libretto – a chance to insert thinly-veiled criticisms of his nemesis Pope Clement XI. The opera was a runaway success, but the ticket-paying nobility who had battled the weather and frozen waterways to get there must surely have wondered about the messages of power and grand plans slipping away. Less than five years later, the economic reality was pretty grave, and the first of the Grimani theatres, the Teatro Santi Giovanni e Paolo, went bust. Venetian fortunes were waning – but this was the exact moment that Vivaldi seized his chance and began his tenure as composer at the small, quirky Teatro Sant'Angelo, where tickets were half the price of those at bigger theatres such as the Teatro Santi Giovanni e Paolo. In his own theatre, Vivaldi could realise his dream to oversee all aspects of operatic production, beginning with his *Orlando finto pazzo* (Orlando the Fake Madman).

Carnevale would be a constant mark in the calendar for Vivaldi, the operatic focal point of the year, when audiences arrived in their droves to hear the latest creations. Just after he likely wrote *The Four Seasons*, Antonio could be found back at the Teatro Sant'Angelo for the 1720 Carnevale, opening the season with his latest opera *La verità in cimento* (Truth in Trial). Like *Orlando finto pazzo*, this opera was a commercial flop at the time, however its comic plot of mistaken identity gives us an insight into the intrigue of this masked festival. In the course of the action, lead character Rosane is pursued by two suitors and sings a flirtatious aria, 'Solo quella guancia bella' describing how her mask reveals 'Just that pretty cheek'. It's the quintessential image of Carnevale, and of the vibrant disguises that women wore to the opera and casinos.

Carnevale itself would fall into decline over the course of the eighteenth century, and ended abruptly when Napoleon Bonaparte conquered Venice in 1797. He abolished the festivities and banned wearing masks outside; any masquerade balls had to be a private affair. It continued that way throughout the nineteenth century and the first half of the twentieth, save for a one-off celebration in 1867 and another organised by the fascist National Recreation Club in 1933, before Benito Mussolini banned the frivolous celebrations altogether. Yet, like the rolling year, the rolling centuries bring back age-old traditions. After some attempts to reignite the passion for Carnevale in the 1960s and '70s, a group of determined Venetian artisans revived it in 1979 and didn't stop until they had established a season that included a rowing competition, outdoor theatre, a grand ball in St Mark's Square and the burning of an effigy of the Venetian *commedia dell'arte* character Pantalone.[4]

Just like the Grimani family's old schemes, the modern artistic endeavours tap into tourism, and it's worked. Today La Serenissima draws around three million visitors every year for *Carnevale moderno*. Nearly three weeks of masked pageantry, revelry and sacred spectacle begin with the lavish water parade on the main Rio de Cannaregio and end with the drama of the silent Regatta, in which electricity is switched off along the Grand Canal and boats glide down it lit only by candles.

Carnevale marked the end of Vivaldi's winter, just as joy is made explicit at the end of this concerto. It also ushered in Lent, the ultimate preparation for spring. That is the nature and essence of the rolling year. However harsh, even the Little Ice Age frosts thawed; and with thaws come February's snowdrops, winter's cheer and the promise of warmer days. By the middle of the month, Valentine's Day signals the traditional date on which birds choose a mate, proving that Vivaldi's 'merry spring' is just around the corner and the rolling year will turn round again.

The Life Cycle of *The Four Seasons* – Scattering New Seeds

Re-imaginings

The final age in the life cycle of *The Four Seasons*, winter, is a time of reseeding. It is the promise of renewal that sees the next generation of musical interpretations take form and generate the momentum in a rolling year. It is fitting, perhaps, that in a world where the seasons have altered due to our impact on the climate, reworkings and re-imaginings of Vivaldi's *Four Seasons* should take on so many different forms. I remember as a teenager setting the melody of the slow movement of *Winter* to the Lord's Prayer. It *almost* works. But if a fourteen-year-old can make such a quick re-working, little surprise *The Four Seasons* has inspired a plethora of different perspectives that go far beyond varied approaches to the work's original concerto form. In the 1980s, *The Four Seasons* was the subject of a ballet by Roland Petit, and lent its name to a film starring Alan Alda – which was adapted for the 2025 Netflix series by Tina Fey, Lang Fisher and Tracey Wigfield. The concertos appear on myriad soundtracks from *The Sopranos* to *The Crown*, and in video games such as *Pump It Up*, *The Simpsons: Hit & Run* and *Frets on Fire*. They are cemented in the subconscious well enough to be recognised wherever they turn up, whether in their original string versions, or the techno remixes inspired by Thomas Wilbrandt's 1980s adaptation, which now proliferate memes and scenes on social media sites. The dreams of *The Four Seasons* appear limitless, as each generation of musicians takes up Vivaldi's idea of the trial or contest of harmony and invention. Reworkings vary in how much they preserve, alter or completely change the fabric of the original score, but most seek to be true to the essence of these concertos: Vivaldi's portrayal of the four seasons and all their natural phenomena.

In 2014, Karl Aage Rasmussen was composer-in-residence with the period instrument ensemble Concerto Copenhagen and wrote *The Four Seasons After Vivaldi*. His starting point was the idea that classical music is almost alone in its philosophy of the inviolability of the text, and so he set out to present these concertos in a way that modern ears might hear them with 'similar amazement to that which Vivaldi's audience must have felt'.[1] In doing so he didn't actually change the notes in terms of pitch or order, but drastically altered rhythms and stresses. The result plays with your perceptions and with the idea of predictability, confounding your expectations of knowing what Vivaldi wrote. Rasmussen's idea of a contemporary reading is an effect akin to changing stage lighting – and there's no doubting the shock factor, as you can't help but be drawn into what could happen next. Was that the eighteenth-century experience? We'll never know.

Rasmussen's rationale for these thoughts takes the form of a line from Giuseppe Tomasi di Lampedusa's novel *The Leopard*: 'If we want everything to remain as it is, everything must change.'[2] Everything, I wonder, or just enough?

Approaches such as Rasmussen's are naturally going to divide a room, and if you're up for doing that, you don't get many more extreme reworkings of *The Four Seasons* than *Recomposed* by Max Richter. It burst onto the musical map in 2012, and has become almost as popular as the originals themselves, featuring not only in concerts and festivals but also finding new fame in the score for the film *Arrival* (2016), in the series *Bridgerton* (2020–), and in recent Dior, Valentino and Fendi runway shows.

Recomposed is quite literally a re-composition, in which some movements remain true to the original almost note-for-note, while others take only the germ of an idea and distort the lines, looping musical patterns, blending and melding with electronic elements to create, or recreate, what is now probably the most famous electro-Baroque masterpiece. Richter described his process as 'throwing molecules of the original Vivaldi into a test tube with a bunch of other things, and waiting for an explosion', and the explosion certainly came, in both reactions and record sales.[3] If it annoyed some, then their views were largely summed up by one reviewer who concluded that 'in all cases Vivaldi's carefully designed forms and schemes of colour and contrast, as well as his programmatic intentions, are pretty much destroyed'.[4] But Richter says he had set out to take a 'new path through a well-known landscape', a project that countered the fact that the music is everywhere and that means that we 'stop being able to hear it'.[5] He never claimed that his version was definitive, rather that his aim was to fall in love with the original again – which he confirmed he did.

The popularity of *Recomposed* begs the question: whose music is this now? Is it Vivaldi's, or Richter's? And does it matter? Daniel Hope made the first recording of Richter's re-composition with the Britten Sinfonia, musicians who had played the originals for decades. The new score confounded expectations and Hope singled out the slow movement of *Winter* as a prime example, saying that 'it's as if an alien has picked it up and pulled it through a time warp'. 'It's really eerie,' he goes on, 'Max has kept Vivaldi's melody, but it's pulled apart by the ethereal harmonics underneath it.'[6]

My Radio 3 colleague Tom Service described *Recomposed* as a 'spring-clean' of *The Four Seasons,* but a decade later Richter himself spring-cleaned his own reworking.[7] In a new rendering, he engaged the majority Black and ethnically diverse Chineke! Orchestra and soloist Elena Urioste, challenging the young team with a twist of using period instruments. Describing it as a 'new trip through this text using Vivaldi's own colours', Richter said his aim was to have 'different eras talking to one another', and, talking like a true period performer, added: 'there's a romance about that, as if a layer of dust has been blown off.'[8] Elena tells me this was her first time dipping her toe into the period-instrument world, necessitating borrowing a period bow, having gut strings put on her instrument and so on. She describes simply 'trying to figure out how to honour, respect and enjoy the differences in touch and nuance required to make the strings and bow speak'. I put it to Elena that Richter could have booked a period band to record this, but chose not to. It turns out he had done exactly that in developing this version, and sent her the concert recording, but she realised that what he was after was what she describes as 'gritty and punk rock' sounds rather than refinement. 'He wanted a bit of crunch to it,' Elena says, and I suspect this was the essence, the freshness of finding particular sounds with a group new to the historical tools they were using. Not that it lacked integrity: after all, Chineke! Orchestra's founder Chi-chi Nwanoku CBE is an internationally renowned period double bass player. Richter himself joined the musicians with his own historically informed instrument: a vintage 1970s Moog, a first-generation synthesiser he chose for its wild and unpredictable side – a personality to match his re-imagined string characters of the eighteenth century.

Richter may have been among the first, but is certainly not the last to combine electronics with classical instruments in re-imagining *The Four Seasons*. Sampled electronic versions abound and are the soundtracks behind the aforementioned social media posts and film scores. And another notable composer to put their mark on the piece's performance history is Anna Meredith. Her 2016 *Anno* again deconstructs the original, but goes further than either Rasmussen or Richter in omitting some movements to make space for Anna's original writing and immersive visuals for the audience.. She retains Vivaldi's original strings but amplifies them, and adds electronics and sampled sound effects.

—

The ambition to see how a dialogue with the past can be created in the modern world has certainly made Vivaldi a household name. That's not only due to Nigel Kennedy as we saw in *Autumn* with his recordings of originals and also with his rock-and-roll *New Four Seasons*, or to Richter, but to others too – such as the Singaporean-born British violinist Vanessa-Mae. She was the wealthiest entertainer under thirty in the United Kingdom in 2006 on the strength of her album sales, central to which was her 1997 techno take on *Summer*'s Presto – renamed *Storm*. It reached No. 4 in the Austrian charts, and peaked at No. 27 in the UK; her electric violin improvisation amid violently distorted guitars and a driving beat brought Vivaldi to countless people who'd never heard his music before, and especially so when she performed *Storm* during the opening ceremony of the 2002 Winter Paralympics.

Improvisation, the art of spontaneous creativity, remains at the heart of the concertos. It's always been the way in which performers make their mark on them, whether in the eighteenth or the twenty-first century, as they realise and enrich the harmonies of the bassline or embellish the melodies. It's the heart of any potential contest between harmony and invention, and it's the soul of re-interpretation. Like Vanessa-Mae, the German quartet Salut Salon also took the Presto from *Summer*, and in playing on the rivalry of harmony and invention, made it into a visual stage *contest*. It's genuinely laugh-out-loud funny – and if you watch their filmed performances online, it's just as compelling to hear the live audience hoot and gasp as they witness this ingenious arrangement. The musicians play each other's instruments (in various combinations), crowd round for three to play the same violin, turn instruments upside down and play behind their backs, while throwing in references from James Bond to Bach. Silly perhaps, especially if you're thinking about the original, but improvisation of all kinds remains a way of keeping the concertos fresh, relevant and personal.

It's what Jacques Loussier would have told you. The French jazz pianist's career skyrocketed in 1959 when he combined his twin loves of jazz and classical music in re-interpreting Bach, and in 1997 his trio looked to Vivaldi and *The Four Seasons*. The themes are preserved, they're instantly identifiable despite being swung, but they are connected by the trio's distinctive, accessible jazz sound world, undoubtedly charting new territory for the eighteenth century. You're left in no doubt as to Loussier's respect for Vivaldi, spoken in his own language, the fusion of classical and jazz known as 'Third Stream'. Without his trio's work it's unlikely we'd have interpretations by the likes of the Alliage Quintett, who bring their own jazz flavours to each season, or jazz saxophonist Tim Garland, whose hypnotic interpretation plays with your senses of proportion and anticipation.

Extended improvisation is entirely in keeping with the approach to performance in Vivaldi's time – and wholly embraced by violinist and director Pekka Kuusisto and the Deutsche Kammerphilharmonie Bremen. They brought such a re-imagining to the 2023 BBC Proms when they were joined onstage by Nordic cittern player Ale Carr, and also presented improvisations inspired by other classical composers from Beethoven to Vaughan Williams, alongside a multiplicity of folk improvisations on traditional Finnish and Swedish folk songs. Presenting the Prom for Radio 3 that night, I chatted to Pekka backstage, and he told me that he thinks of his interpretation of *The Four Seasons* in the same way as he thinks about the fourth plinth in Trafalgar Square. Just as the rotating modern works of art give a slightly different resonance to the entire square, each re-imagining of the concertos can do the same. In the course of our conversation about Vivaldi's sense of seasonality and how it might differ from our own, Pekka also told me about a version of *The Four Seasons* created by his late brother Jaakko.

Välivuodenajat (Between Seasons) is both a stand-alone three-movement work designed to be a companion to *The Four Seasons*, and a series of pieces that can appear between Vivaldi's concertos themselves. Dubbed *The Seven Seasons*, commissioned by the Jyväskylä Summer Festival and premiered by the City Orchestra in 1996, the series retains the textures of a string ensemble and harpsichord, but there's no solo part, so each piece intentionally functions as a moment of repose for the violinist. The work's first movement 'Kevätkesä' (May Day) comes between *Spring* and *Summer*; 'Syyskesä' (Wind and Water) before *Autumn*; and 'Syystalvi' (First Snow) before *Winter*. Only the last one quotes Vivaldi, anticipating the opening of his final icy concerto, and all three evoke Kuusisto's inner feelings rather than external reactions or poetic inspirations for the rolling year. Whereas the first and last themes appear where you might expect, 'Wind and Water' – the elements associated with spring and winter – are placed in high summer to remind us that our seasons are becoming less predictable.

—

Few modern-day arrangers stick closely to Vivaldi's original published version of *The Four Seasons* as they rework them for their time and hemisphere. In the twentieth century, tango king Astor Piazzolla's *Las cuatro estaciones porteñas* (known in English as *The Four Seasons of Buenos Aires*), are tangos for cabaret band written individually between 1965 and 1970. He didn't originally set out to write the full set and beyond the title didn't exactly borrow from Vivaldi. It took another layer of imagination to do that. In the late 1990s Leonid Desyatnikov compiled the tangos in a suite – and that's the version more familiar to us today than Piazzolla's original. The original band had comprised violin, piano, electric guitar, double bass and bandoneon, but Desyatnikov's arrangement is for string orchestra and violin soloist, with the four individual pieces becoming movements in a more traditional concerto. He also added a few quotes from Vivaldi's score but, as he cleverly recognised that Piazzolla and Vivaldi lived in different hemispheres, Piazzolla's *Summer* includes excerpts from Vivaldi's *Winter*, and so on.

Violinist Elena Urioste has played the Piazzolla *Seasons* many times, and recalls four consecutive performances in San Diego in 2022 in which she presented both them and the originals, alternating between the two. 'I started with Vivaldi's *Spring*,' she tells me 'then Piazzolla's *Summer*, Vivaldi's *Summer* and so on, until ending with Piazzolla's *Spring* because it creates a moment of rebirth and a better place to end.' I wondered if, aside from Desyatnikov's added quotes, there were any resonances between the two, in spite of their being worlds and hemispheres apart. 'I'd love to say yes, but they are just four tangos,' she laughs. She adds that it fires up the imagination though: 'With the Piazzolla you have to plant yourself in the southern hemisphere, imagine the heat, the rain, in smoky-bar sexy-lady mode.' Then switching between the two? 'Well, you get to play two very different characters – or eight really – that make wildly different technical demands. The Vivaldi is extremely tiring to play, and alternating it with the passionate tangos is a bit of bodily reprieve.' This is a view of the rolling year that brings intangible resonances for the listener in echoes and images of the seasons across the world, whether implied or explicit.

Sometimes these things can be much harder to discern, however deliberate the association with Vivaldi. Take Philip Glass and his *American Four Seasons*, also known as his Violin Concerto No. 2. It was composed for the violinist Robert McDuffie and explicitly intended to be a companion piece to Vivaldi's concertos. The piece consists of four movements rather than concertos, each of which is preceded by a prelude or song for solo violin, resonating with the improvisation around Vivaldi's original. However, in reality the work is not derived from Vivaldi's music, nor the sonnets. Glass writes no instructions for the audience, no clues as to where spring, summer, autumn or winter even appear within the concerto, famously noting that it's an 'interesting, though not worrisome, problem for the listener'.[9] Which is why it is up to you to decide – apparently Glass and McDuffie aren't even in complete agreement themselves, and admit that any interpretation is welcomed. There's no doubting the motivation – Glass has been dubbed the 'American Vivaldi', and his violin focus and loaded title of *The*

American Four Seasons back this up – but from a sonic perspective this re-imagining of Vivaldi's work is our most extreme swerve to date.

A figure to rival this might well be British composer Roxanna Panufnik. Her *Four World Seasons* was commissioned by and for violinist Tasmin Little and her Stratford-upon-Avon festival Spring Sounds. Tasmin had been exploring Piazzolla's *Seasons* and was seeking a new companion piece to Vivaldi's originals. Panufnik writes that it was the global concern about climate change and seismic shifts in international political landscapes that prompted her initial thoughts. Then her mind went to the countries that have become culturally associated with each. There is, therefore, a programmatic element to the *Four World Seasons*, whether it is the snow in Tibet, the birdsong and budding of new life in Japan or the rustic dances in Albania, but the work is rooted in folksongs and dances rather than being based on poetry. 'I didn't want another version, a recreation, a re-identification of Vivaldi,' says Tasmin, 'these new seasons were to sit alongside, as a companion of contrast.' Panufnik's *Four World Seasons* appeared individually over the years, but Tasmin became clear on the order in which they should finally settle. 'I didn't want her to begin with spring,' she says. 'I wanted her to begin with autumn, an energetic start, and end up in summer – so that it would conclude in a blaze of colour.' Although she has performed them in alternation with Vivaldi's originals (as many do with

Piazzolla), Tasmin finds that the *Four World Seasons*
works better in its own half of a concert. Never a woman
to do things by halves though, she has played Vivaldi's,
Piazzolla's *and* Panufnik's *Seasons* all in one concert.

In an unforeseen twist, the most striking element of
Tasmin's commission was the resulting recording, which,
as intended, paired the *Four World Seasons* with Vivaldi's
original set. Perhaps surprisingly, this was her first time
in the studio with the originals. Tasmin is quite candid
about the reason; back in the 1990s she'd felt the market
was overflowing with recordings from famous violinists
and period-instrument outfits. 'I never wanted to make a
recording of something until such time as I felt I
really had something personal, something distinctive to
express,' she confesses, and working with Panufnik did
exactly that – as attested by the rave reviews.

If Roxanna Panufnik's *Four World Seasons* introduced the
idea of global concerns about the changing seasons, a
re-imagining that takes it even further is *The [uncertain]
Four Seasons*. Premiered in 2019 by the NDR Elbphilharmonie
Orchestra, it was a concept developed by Jung von Matt,
who used climate change data gathered from 1725 to 2019
to create an algorithm in order to re-score Vivaldi's four
violin concertos. Using geospatial climate predictions for
2050 – data from the Coupled Model Intercomparison
Project – composers, musicians and climate and computer
scientists created a musical commentary on climate change –
specifically predicting what will happen if our society does

not take significant action to reduce greenhouse gas emissions. As they say: 'in some regions, Vivaldi's storms have grown fiercer, in others, songbirds have fallen silent.' At the start of Youth and Public Empowerment Day at COP26 (Glasgow) on 5 November 2021, fourteen orchestras across six continents – half of which were youth orchestras – performed local variations on *The [uncertain] Four Seasons.* The music is identifiable as Vivaldi's work to begin with, but then changes in each region according to the environmental disruption. The effects are deeply disturbing, as the lines and harmonies deviate from where you want them to go, creating warped versions of the original. You can still experience it online, clicking around the globe to hear the different performances.[10] In *Winter,* for example, the performance from São Paulo references modelling on relative soil moisture content, and so beats are dropped from the score to create a feeling of irregularity and insecurity. This contrasts with the sounds of Seoul, where the rising temperatures are expected to distort the distribution of cold-adapted species such as pine trees; here, reduced regional rainfall is indicated in the music by changing speeds and tonality. The motivation behind this re-imagining was to elevate the voices of young people in the movement for climate action, the music joining their voices in placing pressure on world leaders to sign the Leaders' Pledge for Nature, a commitment to reversing biodiversity loss by 2030.

—

Young people taking ownership of Vivaldi's *Four Seasons* and recreating them to honour a new time and place was at the heart of *Four Seasons of the Caribbean*, premiered in Leeds in 2023. Four composers – Philip Herbert, Cassie Kinoshi, Renell Shaw and Ayanna Witter-Johnson – were each invited to take Vivaldi's string-based meteorological seasons as a starting point, then extend them with an additional steel pan soloist to offer a wider view of Caribbean culture, heritage and music. As a woman of Caribbean heritage, whose grandparents emigrated to the UK in the late 1950s as part of the Windrush Generation, Ayanna tells me she felt compelled to take part. 'It felt like a legacy project in celebration of my family's role in British history,' she said as she took on the *Winter* concerto. One late February morning we sat down to reflect on the process.

Black Star March, her new piece, is inspired by the Black Star Line, a steamship corporation established in 1919 by Pan-Africanist Marcus Garvey, and her three-movement piece charts a resilient journey from self-defence to freedom. Garvey's ocean routes linked the millions-strong African diaspora back to Africa; and one result of his legacy was Ayanna's family, who hail from the Caribbean island of Jamaica.

Her creative starting point for the sounds of a Caribbean winter is the festivity known as Jonkonnu. During 400 years of slavery across the English-speaking Caribbean, enslaved Africans were only given three days of holiday – Christmas Day, Boxing Day and New Year's Day – and on those days, they would revel in their spiritual roots. Ayanna explains that those participating in Jonkonnu would dress in masks and multicoloured costumes, form a parade line, and travel from house to house clapping, singing and dancing. They would perform until the homeowners, usually the performers' enslavers, came outside and paid them in coins. It's the essence of the Carnival that we know today. Jonkonnu is experiencing a revival in Jamaica at the moment, but Ayanna says there's an intensity to this festivity that also lends itself to the elements of a European winter – due to the contentious colonial aspect of the celebration. And so, her final inspiration for *Black Star March* came from the work of the Guyanese-British contemporary sculptor and visual artist Hew Locke, whose references to the slave trade synthesised with the essence of carnival and rebellion to give Ayanna a visual palette.

I was curious not only about the result, but also about how Vivaldi could fit into such a score. Ayanna said it was his musical choices that influenced her the most. 'I spent weeks noting his suggestions of nature in his orchestration,' she says, 'the tremolo strings, dissonant harmonies and repetitive rhythmic patterns depicting the howling winds and relentlessness of the cold, but also the winter melancholy reflected in the use of minor keys and sudden changes in dynamics that may portray the contrast between furious wintery storms and tranquil snowy landscapes.' From there it was the sense of pulsating energy and tempo choices in each movement that inspired *Black Star March*, rather than the European winter climate.

The first movement is a dance-hall inspired march with virtuosic strings and steel pan parts weaving in and out of the driving rhythms. 'I considered both violin and steel pan soloists a symbol of cultural collaboration,' says Ayanna. This combination is admittedly a rare sighting in classical music, but the soloists' conversation continues throughout all three movements. As with Vivaldi's model, the second movement is more reflective in nature, 'the tranquillity embodying a desire to unify as a community,' Ayanna says, before the final movement lifts the spirits by evoking the Jamaican folk music tradition through melodies passing between the parts in call-and-answer patterns.

It's a new narrative, not influenced by poetry in the same way as Vivaldi, but Ayanna similarly wrote instructions into the score such as 'With gusto! Strum back and forth rhythmically', 'Boldly. The stage is yours', and 'mechanically lyrical'. The premiere in November 2023 was a multi-sensory evening featuring music, food and costume, held at the Northern School of Contemporary Dance in Chapeltown, Leeds, an area of the city which is home to a large Caribbean community and one of the longest-running West Indian carnivals in Europe. How did the four pieces work together, I asked her? 'Well, we'd composed our concertos without conferring,' Ayanna confirms, 'but side by side, they were surprisingly complementary – the sonic line that joined them was Vivaldi's music.'

———

The Four Seasons are now so recognisable that they can crop up in any context and suggest a seasonal flavour, but a handful more examples bring me back to my teenage attempts at word setting, and extend Michael Morpurgo's desire to re-imagine the sonnet texts too.

Roxanna Panufnik took a literary approach when she embarked on a second seasonal cycle, her 2019 *Four Choral Seasons*, premiered by the Bach Choir at the Royal Festival Hall. In it, she portrayed an English year, beginning in summer, setting Christina Rossetti's 'A Summer Wish', before Laurence Binyon's 'Now is the time for the burning of leaves' for autumn, William Shakespeare's 'Blow, blow, thou winter wind', and finally Gerard Manley Hopkins's 'Spring'. The work's poetic bent aligned it more closely with Vivaldi's *Four Seasons* than her *Four World Seasons* had done, but in theme rather than any musical borrowing from his scores.

Placing new works between the originals is an increasingly popular option, as groups look to innovate, personalise, and show Vivaldi in a new light. The possibilities are endless and lead to projects such as that of the Zapico brothers and their Baroque ensemble Forma Antiqva, who commissioned Theo Bleckmann and Uri Caine to compose new sonnets sung between the concertos. The result was not only atmospheric music, but also a film in which Bleckmann and Caine acted as narrators, and eight new drawings by the Dutch painter and concept artist Marcel van Eeden, inspired by the work's sounds.

In 2015, British composer Oliver Davis set Vivaldi's original Italian poetry (rather than his music) in *Anno* for orchestra and solo soprano, but the idea of vocalising the musical score of *The Four Seasons* initially came to Ward Swingle. His 1972 album *The Joy of Singing* with the Swingle Singers included the complete *Spring* concerto note-for-note. They certainly don't cut corners in the filigree passagework, and the middle movement is an atmospheric turn, even if the dog seems to be sleeping rather than barking.

It's an idea that was picked up in another *Four Seasons* project in the southern hemisphere. Australia's premier vocal ensemble, The Song Company, and their Artistic Director, British composer Antony Pitts, collaborated with indigenous dance group Karul Projects to create a fusion of Vivaldi's landscape with an Aboriginal interpretation of Australia's diverse and changing seasons. The original concertos remained at the heart of programmes, that then included new music to reflect the festivals of Australian First Nations people. The Song Company initially vocalised Vivaldi's string parts, memorising them so that singers were free to move around the stage, before fragmenting them around the new pieces. In a further twist that embraced the nature of the rolling year, the date of any given performance determined the starting point in their cyclical programme; therefore the concert could present the seasons from summer through to spring or winter through to autumn.

These new versions leave the lasting impression that the ultimate aim in reworking *The Four Seasons* is to reach as large an audience as possible and to be accessible to people who aren't string players or for whom the European seasons are not the norm. The instrument we all possess is a voice, and prompted by the 300-year anniversary of the concertos' publication, British composer Joanna Forbes L'Estrange hit on the idea of a choral re-imagining. When we speak on the phone, she is midway through composing *A Season to Sing*. All the texts are chosen and the process of reworking the music in full swing. 'I love the process of making music singable by every kind of choir,' she says, and so I ask her about the prospect of choirs singing Vivaldi's famously virtuosic violin concertos. Joanna's knowing laughter is infectious as she reveals that, very sensibly, there is an organ part to play solo lines at strategic points — an organic extension of the idea that these concertos are ensemble pieces. Save for a prologue and epilogue setting the Bible passage 'for everything there is a season' to her own music, the forty-minute work comprises all four of Vivaldi's concertos, re-scored but with the full shape and scope of the originals. All becomes clear when she gives me a sneak preview of *Winter*.

The opening movement, 'Winter Freeze', features the choir half-singing, half-whispering each Italian syllable of Vivaldi's sonnet. 'It's as if they're so cold that they can't sing,' Joanna explains, 'but the vocal effects result in a simulation of teeth chattering against the cruel winds.'

When it comes to the middle movement 'Cosy Indoors (while outside it pours)', Joanna draws on her own history as both a soprano and Musical Director of the Swingle Singers, and resists that urge I felt as a teenager to set this timeless tune to text. 'Pale imitations result in various dooby-dooby-doo approaches to vocalising instrumental lines,' she admits, but Joanna knows the very specific scats that make a 'Swingle sound'. Here in deep midwinter, the choir has its first a cappella movement, with the melody, arpeggiated droplets and bass line all vocalised, arranged in homage to Ward Swingle, Joanna's mentor and close friend. 'The Swingles started out by singing Bach,' Joanna points out, 'and Baroque music lends itself so well to jazz interpretation; there are so many parallels, but essentially they are both a tune, chords and a bass line.' I can't help but smile, reckoning that there are more than a few people out there who would fancy a go at being a Swingle for a day.

The final movement, 'While Earth Remaineth', brings a different sort of challenge, a finality, as the last movement inspired by Vivaldi. 'I've settled on a biblical passage from Genesis 8:22,' Joanna says: '"While the earth remaineth, seedtime and harvest, and cold and heat, and

summer and winter, and day and night shall not cease."
It's a reminder that we need to look after the Earth,' she
counsels 'so that the seasons will always continue round
and round.' As she sings a little down the phone I hear
how the *Four Seasons* have seamlessly put on the winter
coat of an oratorio.

This is the essence of reworking Vivaldi's *Seasons*,
dreaming in days of calm and contentment by the
blazing fire of the ways in which Vivaldi's music might
speak to new audiences. These re-imaginings invite in
new players – and singers – and take nothing away from
the original, which waits around the corner to be heard
afresh as a result.

The Legacy of *The Four Seasons*

Separating fact from fiction is not easy in picturing Vivaldi's life, and it doesn't stop with the legacy of *The Four Seasons*. A final major myth surrounds the composer's 1741 funeral. Some say Vivaldi received a pauper's service, while others that it was a major event at Vienna's St Stephen's Cathedral, with the young choirboy Joseph Haydn among the ranks of singers. Neither is true. Vivaldi received an ordinary and simple burial – still a shocking end for a man who might well have been considered rich in his prime, before the expenses of care in advancing years and not-so-successful operatic ventures drained his finances. It is true that Haydn was a choirboy at the cathedral at that time; he may well have known of the composer, heard mention of his name in a service, but that was all. There was no singing at Vivaldi's funeral. It's a figment of *my* imagination that the ten-year-old Haydn might have overheard a snippet of a conversation about Vivaldi, a mention of his fame for *The Four Seasons* – and that this could have planted a seed in his musical mind. Some sixty years later Haydn would begin a new century with his own work: the secular oratorio *The Seasons*.

Before then, there were inevitably copycat versions of *The Four Seasons*. Vivaldi's fellow Italian Giovanni Antonio

Guido may well have taken the concertos as a model for his own inventive *Scherzi armonici sopra le quattro stagioni* (Harmonic Scherzos on the Four Seasons), which he based on the anonymous poems *Les Caractères des saisons* (Seasonal Characters) and published in Paris *c*.1728. It's tempting to imagine them being played by Paris's premier ensemble, resident at the recently inaugurated Concert Spirituel, as Guido was a leading violinist in the city during the reign of Louis XV. His *Seasons* are suites rather than concertos, an homage to each quarter of the year in courtly French-style numbers, but between the formal dances and rustic charm there's drama – especially towards the end of the year, with a terrified autumnal stag, and icy winter winds. Although the dates suggest Guido took inspiration from Vivaldi's virtuosic depictions, he may have written these scherzos earlier, inspired perhaps by his patron Pierre Crozat, whose dining-room walls were decorated with Antoine Watteau's depictions of the four seasons.

It's an evergreen muse. Over in eighteenth-century London, Frederick Louis, Prince of Wales, and his wife Augusta cultivated a collection of exotic plants at Kew Palace, the original site of Kew Gardens, which may have been the inspiration for visiting Scottish composer James Oswald's *Airs for the Seasons*: floral suites published between 1755 and 1761. These and other examples are not directly modelled on Vivaldi, but have resonances with his original idea. In 1731 Benedetto Marcello, Vivaldi's frenemy in Venice and author of the pamphlet that had satirised Antonio, was happy to ride on the success of the seasonal theme. He took up the idea for an oratorio titled *Il pianto e il riso delle quattro stagioni* (Lamentation and Joy of the Four Seasons). Written for the Jesuit church of San Giovanni in Macerata, and thereafter performed in Venice, the oratorio tells the tale of Winter returning from the mountains to meet his siblings, Spring, Summer and Autumn, who reveal that the Virgin Mary has died; the four subsequently celebrate her assumption into heaven. The work contains rich writing for each of the vocal soloists as personifications of the seasons, with added layers of chorus, orchestra and religious fervour.

Two years later at the court of Hesse-Darmstadt, Christoph Graupner personally engraved and printed his Four Partitas for harpsichord: *Die vier Jahreszeiten.* Was this link created by Vivaldi's employer in Mantua, Prince Philip of Hesse-Darmstadt? Once again, we don't know. It was certainly the last set of harpsichord pieces published by the fifty-year-old Graupner, and sadly only *Winter* has survived the centuries. Meanwhile in 1747, Naples-born composer Francesco Durante brought out another set of harpsichord sonatas: *Le quattro stagioni dell'anno* (The Four Seasons of the Year). Despite the change of medium from violin concertos to harpsichord sonatas, these do have an affinity with Vivaldi's approach. They make significant technical demands on the player, and Durante's labels on the score similarly include evocative headings for each section – general comments such as 'the heat grows', and specific effects of thunder and lightning, falling leaves or blustering wind.

But what of Haydn and his oratorio? Could there be any possible resonance with Vivaldi? This necessitates a trip back to the 1720s when the Scottish poet James Thomson began writing his epic poem *The Seasons* while living in Barnet, near (and now in) London. He published *Winter* in 1726, just a year after Vivaldi's *Four Seasons* appeared in print, and then proceeded to write and publish each season individually. They appeared in a refreshingly haphazard order: *Summer* in 1727, *Spring* in 1728, and then the completed set, including *Autumn*, in a collected edition in 1730. I've carried the epic around in my handbag while writing this book. The tiny font of my travel-sized second edition from 1822 has necessitated a natty pair of reading glasses, but the content is simultaneously dense and knotty, rich and rewarding. Whipping it out while sitting on a favourite bench on Hampstead Heath has certainly made me slow down, think, observe, *feel* the seasons.

The poem was five years in the making, so there's little wonder Thomson also saw fit to conclude the finished epic with a hymn. In the opening lines of what is *very* substantial, reverential praise of the Almighty Father, Thomson acknowledges (and inspires my title as he does so) that 'the rolling year is full of Thee'. A tiny recap of each season ensues, outlining God's presence in each quarter. 'Thy beauty walks, thy tenderness, and love' in *Spring*, and 'thy glory in Summer months with light and heart refulgent', despite the fact that 'oft thy voice in dreadful thunder speaks'. 'Thy bounty shines in Autumn unconfined', he goes on, and although *Winter* begins: 'awful thou' in relation to clouds and storms, he ends in with awe of a different nature as 'on the whirlwind's wing, riding sublime, thou bidd'st the world adore, and humblest nature with thy northern blast.'[1]

Thomson's blank verse was criticised by contemporaries for being pompous and contorted, but *The Seasons* was also hugely influential. Widely read and referenced, the poetry was translated and published in French and German, and inspired paintings by Joshua Reynolds, Thomas Gainsborough and Johann Sebastian Bach – grandson and namesake of the composer. It was embedded in the psyche of the eighteenth century, and provides further proof that seasonality was very much in vogue in the 1720s.

In 1740 the German composer Johann Christoph Schmidt set excerpts of Thomson's epic in his oratorio *The Seasons*. He was living in London at the time, as John Christopher Smith, Handel's assistant. His representations of nature, from spring birdsong to brutal winter storms, prove his mettle as a composer with a vivid imagination. If there were new elements of the *Empfindsamer Stil* (sensitive style) in his approach, they came thick and fast in a setting in 1788 by Thomson's fellow Scot, the composer Robert Barber. He condensed the poetry of the concluding hymn into a twenty-part cantata for soloists, chorus and large orchestra. It is likely that Haydn was at a London performance, and it made a strong enough impression on him to partially inspire his second oratorio, *Die Jahreszeiten* (The Seasons). Not only is the theme of Barber's duet 'Bleat out afresh' identical to that of Haydn's chorus 'Come, gentle spring' but, knowing how Thomson's seasonal poetry resonated with British audiences, Haydn's librettist Baron Gottfried van Swieten used it to construct the text of the oratorio.[2]

Premiered in Vienna in 1801, *The Seasons* is a lengthy and worthy partner to Haydn's *The Creation*, calling for a large orchestra and chorus alongside named solo roles for the countryfolk Hanne (soprano), Lukas (tenor) and Simon (bass). 'Spring' is a paean to nature and rebirth, and 'Summer' outlines a day from sunrise through the debilitating heat of the midday to an afternoon storm. 'Autumn' spells harvest thanksgiving, the hunt and drinking songs, before Winter's lost wanderer finds comfort by a village fire. These are themes that are strikingly familiar from Vivaldi's concertos.

Condensing and selecting highlights from more than 4,300 lines of Thomson's seasonal poetry and offering alternative librettos in German and English was no mean feat for Baron van Swieten, who focused on moments of descriptive detail in order to give Haydn as much imaginative free rein as possible. However, the ageing composer was not convinced. Nor were the punters. Whilst they generally praised the music, and Haydn's powers of expression depicting nature 'in all its guises', they had reservations about the text, and especially the composer's attempts to set explicit effects.[3] One critic summed up the general consensus among the dissenters, concluding: 'He should describe them, not as they are – their absolute appearance as physical nature – but only through the impression they make on us.'[4] However, time has proved favourable for this oratorio; these days lively performances, such as the one given by the London Symphony Orchestra and Chorus with Simon Rattle on the Chorus's fiftieth birthday in 2016, provoke sensational reviews of both music and text effects alike.

If Vivaldi's *The Four Seasons* had planted the seeds of programmatic music in Haydn's mind the reaction to his own *The Seasons* showed that the nineteenth century would take a different perspective. The Viennese audiences would only have to wait seven years for the dancing peasants, thunderstorms and birdsong of Beethoven's 'Pastoral' Symphony.

Conclusion

While Vivaldi's *Four Seasons* perennially revels in the spotlight, Antonio himself tends to shilly-shally in the shadows. Yes, he has a very public reputation as a dazzling virtuoso, a notorious boaster and a bit of a wheezy whiner, but scratch that surface and you open up . . . a void. When you spend time researching a musician, there's usually a point at which you feel as though you could second-guess their reactions – the shrug of a shoulder, a double-take or smirk – but Vivaldi has made me work for this acquaintance. Through the changing light of a year writing about *The Four Seasons*, this mysterious man has slowly emerged – and he's nothing like the character I always assumed him to be. The fragments of his biography and letters release a chaotic energy, but through my breathing the Mantuan air, seeing the Venetian sights and hearing the sounds of his musical calendar, an ambitious and creative yet sometimes disabled and frustrated man has appeared. He's a figure I've found I relate to far more than I ever thought I would, and I now view him from a completely new perspective.

I see a baby fighting for his life, then a boy realising he could play the violin even if he couldn't play outside, and that a considerable musical talent was the key to communicating with the wider world. I envisage a young man whose imagination ran wild to places his legs might never carry him. A man whose fiery heart was deeply touched by true artistry and by people who showed commitment and dedication to music, and who was always on the hustle for the next opportunity.

I empathise with a person battling an unpredictable and changeable disability, something not obvious to a stranger's eye – an invisible curse that, at times, took a huge toll on his physical and mental wellbeing. He was someone who would have periods of good health, but who equally experienced times in which he needed to carefully calculate the energy required for a great performance, and potentially hide the physical effects of it over subsequent days. I imagine a furrowed brow as he watched the weather, worrying about being trapped by ice or suffocated by heat, and perhaps dreamt of the clear Alpine air he'd experienced while touring operas far from the Venetian lagoon or Mantuan swamp.

I recognise an ambitious character, refusing to conform to the norm, and going twice the distance at double the speed to prove he was capable of greatness. A man who would sidestep to Mantua in order to move up the Venetian career ladder, and along the way realise he had networking skills and opportunities to reinvent himself musically and socially.

I imagine his desk at home – the place where he did his best work – revealing evidence of both his character and day-to-day practicalities: resin for his bow, a cushion for his carriage, ink splodged across manuscripts. His sanctuary, in which piles of books sat alongside a glass of wine, or the latest remedy to help soothe a tight chest. I admire the fascinating mind that animates the famous portrait of the baby-faced, bewigged redhead with violin in hand. He was an astute character who could envisage diplomatic resolution, speak to authority and hold an audience captive, whether in a one-to-one interview with the emperor or in a packed-out theatre. I feel the frustration of a soul who craved independence, but couldn't manage without a highly functioning network of family and supporters. I sigh for the old soul who paid the highest price for that independence with a death alone and penniless, far from home in Vienna.

—

Since my kitchen calendar of seasonal British produce prompted me to start thinking about seasonal listening, I can't claim to have listened *exclusively* to seasonal music in each quarter. But I've had a good go, both with Vivaldi and with his contemporary Baroque composers who wrote seasonal pieces, or simply sacred and secular works for specific moments of the year. J. S. Bach's Passions, for example, infused my spring while Handel's ceremonial music for royal cruises up the Thames are summer essentials; Telemann's music for feasting celebrates autumn, and Corelli's *Christmas Concerto* evokes the chill and cheer of winter. (You can find out more about these pieces, and others, in the 'More Seasonal Listening' appendix.) Just like attempting to eat seasonally and observing the changing world around me, consciously listening to music intended for specific times of year has had an intensely grounding effect on my life. It's taken a little more time and effort, but I have genuinely felt more in tune with the turning months, finding moments of meaning amid the bustle of modern society. I'm learning not to underestimate these sensations as global seasonality changes and we're forced to adapt, or to actively make an effort to preserve old ways. Admittedly change happens slowly, but you only need to think back to your childhood, or traditions kept by parents and grandparents, to realise the extent to which we're becoming disengaged from the gears of the year. In an age where we can eat whatever we want, and, if we choose to, wear the same clothes year-round – courtesy of central heating and air conditioning – it can be hard to hear the rhythm of the seasons.

I have a kindred seasonal spirit in food writer and cook Angela Clutton, author of *Seasoning – How to Cook and Celebrate the Seasons*. When we meet at London's Borough Market, autumn's pumpkins are sitting proudly centre-stage alongside the first root vegetables, and, um, strawberries. 'What are they doing here?' Angela asks, 'and where are the game birds that used to hang up around Borough not that many years ago?' Naturally the answer to that is caught up in consumerism; market sellers aim to meet the demands of their customers who don't want the faff of plucking pheasants, and do want to take advantage of deliveries from across the world. 'I think there are three reasons to eat seasonally,' Angela says:

> First, the environment, because produce with the lowest greenhouse gas emissions is local and seasonal. Second, the soul, because coming together to eat at certain times of the year creates anticipation and generates memories. And finally, the taste – because food is just better when in season, sweet summer berries are only really tasty in summer when they've ripened under the sun, and winter frosts bring out the sugars in parsnips.

In an age of recording and streaming, there's no real environmental issue with listening to music in or out of season, but I bet you look forward to live performances at particular times of the year – weddings, summer festivals, Proms, Christmas concerts. It's that sense of community, of experiencing live music *together*, and some sounds, especially at Christmas, still stir in us timeless feelings of family and place. However, not only have feasts such as Michaelmas been lost to the cultural calendar and our musical map of the year, but the produce that grew then and was an integral part of the feast's identity is also changing. If the feast of Michaelmas was a warning that 29 September was the last day on which you were supposed to eat blackberries, there's no danger of that now. In fact, you'd be hard pressed to still find them on the brambles that late in the year. 'Blackberries were once a key autumn fruit,' Angela explains. 'Their tartness is a great partner with rich game meats, but the commercial ones we buy now are far sweeter and marketed for desserts. Admittedly they [wild blackberries] freeze well and so you can easily enjoy them in autumn,' she continues, 'but for a lot of savoury recipes I sit them for twenty minutes in some red wine vinegar with bay leaves and juniper – a quick pickle gives them their tartness back.' There is a delight in stopping to observe, preserve and savour the year this way, and the same goes for music. It's in the simple joy of stopping to mark a moment. The combination of preserving musical heritage and permitting myself the time to do it has helped me hear the music with more perception and changed my sense of the season after the music ends.

I can't believe there'll be another year of my life when I spend so much time immersed in Vivaldi's *Four Seasons*, but looking back, I realise that I've rarely listened to them all in one go – as the complete set. My focus has been on each individual season, and I've liked that, but with live performances in my diary, it's time to put them back together and hear the whole year in an evening. It brings my thoughts back to the 'Four Seasons' pizza, and some new-found and somewhat conflicted feelings about it.

Neapolitans are historically the Italian pizza masters, and back in the seventeenth century they hit on the idea of quartering their universal foodstuffs by season. There was plentiful seafood to be had in the port of Naples, but today the *Quattro stagioni* has been standardised: artichokes represent the green shoots of spring; tomatoes and basil the bounty of summer; mushrooms the earthiness of autumn; and finally ham or olives illustrate the supplies in winter's larder.

Do I actually want the whole year on a plate, I ask Angela: hasn't the point of this book and year of listening been to experience the flavours in their own time? 'Whenever you order this pizza, you're eating unseasonal produce,' she agrees, 'but see it another way, the whole lot could be preserved.' It's true: you could bottle and preserve the artichoke in oil, you could use tinned or sun-dried tomatoes, dried basil or mushrooms, aged cheese, and the olives and prosciutto that were already in the larder. 'It's actually a clever way of enjoying the tastes of the seasons at any time,' Angela concedes, 'another way to savour the joy of the year, especially if you stop and notice the fresh element in each quarter.'

Vivaldi's *Four Seasons* are metaphorically bottled, preserved and pickled in time, and we taste them afresh through the various seasons of our listening lives. Fashions may come and go in the way the work is re-interpreted, but one thing is clear: these seasonal concertos are rejuvenated with every new performance and have the power to lead curious listeners into a world of seasonal listening.

Postlude

There is one last place at the Ducal Palace in Mantua that I've not yet told you about. It changes everything – and maybe nothing.

It is about the furthest point you can visit in the vast palace complex, a route that for me necessitated negotiating multiple stairlifts, ramps and tight doorways. Eventually we emerged onto a walkway high above ground level: the Cavallerizza Corridor. On one side: a grassed courtyard where Gonzagas and Habsburgs alike exhibited their horses, and on the other: the open water of the Mantuan lakes, the swamps and arable land beyond. Ahead of us was what is now known as the Appartamento di Troia (Apartment of Troy), a particularly impressive suite of rooms with bold, larger-than-life frescoes by Giulio Romano depicting tales from the Trojan War. Completed by 1540, this was once Federico Gonzaga's official apartment, but by the time Vivaldi worked here for Prince Philip it's very unlikely that anyone lived in this part of the palace. Instead, it was an area for entertaining, with unmissable artwork for any nobleman's Grand Tour visit. A long, thin hall abuts the Apartment of Troy, one that had originally been built by Romano as an open loggia, but was bricked up and decorated in the sixteenth century, with windows that look out onto the Cavallerizza courtyard. A place for entertaining and chamber music, it's called the Sala dei Mesi (Hall of Months), and among the allegories of time that festoon the walls, twelve alcoves contain depictions of each month, and stuccos show the hours of the day.

This beautiful hall was designed to show off these treasures, and is known to have been a venue for musical performances in the early eighteenth century. Its generous acoustics would have packed a sonic punch, and its situation would have brought Vivaldi close to nature without him actually having to leave the palace walls. As I wheel through the space, things start falling into place, and especially so when I reach the door back towards the Cavallerizza Corridor. It opens onto a wide porch, called Eleonora's Loggia, which affords spectacular views out across the lake. Unsurprisingly *that's* the attraction for modern visitors, who take selfies against the glorious backdrop before hurrying inside to see the wonders within. If they were to turn around and look at the palace walls, they'd just see the yellowed surface of the building, smooth, and worn clean of any decoration by the weather. However, if they looked up . . . they'd see that under the arches of the loggia are frescoes, one for each of the four seasons.

They appear in order, from *Spring*, on the far left, to *Winter*, far right, and are all framed portraits. The central figure of each season appears to have a different ethnicity, and, crucially, the figures age with the passing year. Outside the frame, each is flanked by cherubic types who offer symbols of the season and decorative details reflecting the passing of time, and who also age from *Spring* to *Winter*.

Spring is the most damaged by the elements, with patches of the fresco worn away, but still clearly shows a young white woman reclining in a fenced garden of flowers and foliage. Either side of her, young naked figures offer plates of blooms and a bird's nest.

Fig. 17: *Le Quattro Stagioni: La primavera (Spring)* (fresco possibly by Lamberti) in the Loggia di Eleonora at the Ducal Palace in Mantua.

Summer is an older male figure, possibly of Asian heritage, lying among ears of corn, and the young acolytes that flank the framed portrait carry great urns of produce: the said corn, but also fruits and vegetables.

Autumn portrays a reclining black man looking over his shoulder to hold our gaze. He reaches for a bunch of

Fig. 18: *Le Quattro Stagioni: L'estate (Summer)*
(fresco possibly by Lamberti) in the Loggia di Eleonora
at the Ducal Palace in Mantua.

grapes at his knee and rests on vines, with a crown of vine leaves atop his head. One of the two figures beside him raises a glass of wine – a fluted glass suggesting the Lambrusco of the region – while the second carries bunches of grapes, and appears to be beckoning companions to join them in their revelling.

Fig. 19: *Le Quattro Stagioni: L'autunno (Autumn)*
(fresco possibly by Lamberti) in the Loggia di Eleonora
at the Ducal Palace in Mantua.

Finally, almost tucked into the corner, *Winter* is the best preserved and gives a hint as to the boldness of the colours that the others once enjoyed. An old man in a turban, fully and generously clothed in bright flowing robes, warms his hands by a fire. Behind him, the trees are bare of leaves. The cherubs either side of his portrait are now fully grown: a manly one carries extra firewood away from the scene, and the last is an old man dressed in red with green boots and bells around his arms and legs, perhaps a Carnevale character jeering at this vision of old age.

Fig. 20: *Le Quattro Stagioni: L'inverno (Winter)* (fresco possibly by Lamberti) in the Loggia di Eleonora at the Ducal Palace in Mantua.

There are certainly mysterious elements among the classical symbols of each season, which continue up into the ceiling decoration, but we know that these frescoes were completed by 1612, possibly by Orazio Lamberti, and certainly by an artist close to the celebrated Antonio Maria Viani, court painter to Duke Vincenzo I Gonzaga. They were therefore more than a century old even by the time Vivaldi walked these corridors and, having now faced more than 400 years of weather, they're unsurprisingly not in peak condition.

My heart beats faster. A concert space reflecting the passing of time, entered through a loggia devoted to the four seasons at the meeting point of nature and high art. Could Count Morzin have visited Romano's frescoes of Troy and happened upon Vivaldi performing right here? Could this have been a venue proposed for Prince Philip's wedding celebrations that never happened? These frescoes have little to do with Vivaldi's sonnets – those would come later – but they could point to inspiration for the prototype concertos that Vivaldi hints at in his dedication to Morzin in the 1725 publication.

The next day I set out before sunrise for some morning air. As I cross the Ponte di San Giorgio over Mantua's Lago Inferiore, I'm momentarily enveloped in a rosy glow before the watery, winter dawn light breaks through the clouds. I turn at the other side of the lake to look back on the city. The Ducal Palace is 'neither beautiful nor regular', Maximilien Misson observed at the time the

Habsburgs took over the city, 'the houses are generally unequal and almost all very indifferent.'[1] He's right in a way, but there's a rustic magnificence to this higgledy-piggledy, ageless place, and at the forefront of any postcard view of the 'sleeping beauty' are the four arches of Eleonora's Loggia. I saw them the day I arrived, they're visible on every tourist's snap of this panorama, and yet until this trip I've thought little of them. Now I see them in a completely new light, knowing the seasonal secrets they hold. Yes, you have to know they are there, and get close for them to be revealed, but those frescoes are hiding in plain sight.

This is not a definitive answer to the questions of where, when or why Vivaldi wrote *The Four Seasons*, but as I sit among the reeds in the early-morning light, the music playing on my headphones, I suddenly feel as though they've arrived home.

Fig. 21: Mantua from the reedbeds.

More Seasonal Listening

From Jean-Baptiste Lully in the second half of the seventeenth century to Joseph Haydn in the first light of the nineteenth, this timeline represents a selection of the composers who were inspired by the theme of the four seasons. Their ballets, operas, and instrumental works were discussed in the chapters on the inspiration and legacy of Vivaldi's *The Four Seasons*, but I've added to them the brilliant suites by Antonio de Literes, Michel-Richard Delalande and André Cardinal Destouches, which take the close cousins of *The Elements* as their muse.

1661: Jean-Baptiste Lully, *Ballet des saisons*
1668: Christopher Simpson, Fantasia Suites for viol consort
1671: Robert Cambert, *Pomone*
1692: Henry Purcell, 'Masque of the Seasons' from Act IV of *The Fairy Queen*
1695: Pascal Collasse, *Ballet des saisons*
1702: Reinhard Keiser, *Pomona*
c.1718: Antonio de Literes, *Los elementos*
1718–20 (pub. 1725): Antonio Vivaldi, *Le quattro stagioni*
1721: Michel-Richard Delalande and André Cardinal Destouches, *Les Élémens*

c.1728 (pub.): Giovanni Guido, *Scherzi armonici sopra le quattro stagioni dell'anno* op. 3

1733: Christoph Graupner, *Die vier Jahreszeiten*

1737–8: Jean-Féry Rebel, *Les Élémens*

1740: Johann Christoph Schmidt [John Christopher Smith], *The Seasons*

1747: Francesco Durante, *Le quattro stagioni dell'anno*

1785: Robert Barber, *Thomson's Hymn to the Seasons*

1801: Joseph Haydn, *The Seasons*

In addition to prompting us to explore music on the theme of the turning year, Vivaldi's *The Four Seasons* pave the way for a calendar of seasonal Baroque music. It's something I've alluded to throughout the book and I offer here a mere starting point, in case you are tempted to join me in listening in a more actively seasonal way. This is a sample of the many season-specific works that punctuate my own listening year and that create similar feelings of being grounded or connected to old traditions, as I expressed with Johann Sebastian Bach's *Christmas Oratorio* in the introduction.

Spring

The season of air, of new sounds and fresh beginnings, prompts a springtime playlist headed up by Johann Sebastian Bach. The autograph score for the six inventive concertos for various instruments that we now know as the *Brandenburg Concertos* is dated 24 March 1721.

The spring equinox saw Bach send them off to the Margrave of Brandenburg in the hope of new employment. The exuberant second concerto of the set – for the unlikely solo line-up of violin, oboe, recorder and trumpet – may well have had further fresh starts at its heart. Bach had a new wife, the soprano Anna Magdalena Wilcke, and therefore a new father-in-law to impress in the form of Johann Caspar Wilcke, who was himself a trumpeter.

Rewind nearly sixty years and May 1664 signalled beginnings and a brand-new era at the French court of Versailles. King Louis XIV hosted the first of his great celebrations in the palace and grounds – a multi-day festival of entertainment called *Les Plaisirs de l'île enchantée* (The Pleasures of the Enchanted Island). When night fell on the opening evening, the gardens glowed with a thousand lights for a magnificent feast and ballet on the theme of none other than the four seasons. Squads of instrumentalists arrived – lutenists, viol players, the famous royal violin band and wind players, all dressed in elaborate costumes – accompanied by dancers and acrobats, dromedaries and elephants. Servants wore masks and carried platters piled high with exotic foods to serve to some six hundred guests. This was unprecedented merriment, with no expense spared in making a first impression, and a suite of Jean-Baptiste Lully's seasonal music – also called *Les Plaisirs de l'île enchantée* – survives to give a flavour of the sounds that filled the evening.

In the minds of both Antonio Vivaldi's audiences and of eighteenth-century physicians, the warm, wet nature of spring corresponded with the energy and flow of blood and with the body's principal organ: the heart. The ancient thinkers didn't know that blood carries air (technically oxygen) through the body, but their idea about it bringing breath and life was spot on. Inspiring more seasonal Baroque music, the idea of blood coursing through spring is a reminder of Vivaldi's early vocation as a violin-playing priest – offering the blood of Christ in the Mass – at the Pietà in Venice, and leads us to Easter. Around fifty sacred works by Vivaldi have survived, about half of them with some connection to the Pietà, and one for Easter chimes especially with the ideas of spring. The title of the piece, *Filiae maestre Jerusalem* (Mournful Daughters of Jerusalem), is no doubt a veiled reference to the women of the Pietà. The work is scored for strings, organ and a mezzo-soprano or countertenor soloist who implores the 'daughters of Jerusalem' to look on Christ as he carries the cross to his death. There is just one central aria and it's here that we encounter the air and breezes. 'Let the winds be hushed,' the soloist begins, and as fields freeze, the river dies and even the Sun and Moon darken, the shocking event of Jesus's sacrifice upsets the balance of seasons and nature.

Part of the Catholic musical experience of Easter, François Couperin's sensuous and deeply serious *Leçons de ténèbres* were published between 1713 and 1717. They were intended for the Abbaye Royale de Longchamp, one of the great convents in the Paris region, where the nuns liked to invite opera singers to perform at their Holy Week services. (The singers were only too happy to oblige, as opera houses were closed for Lent.) Couperin writes astonishing dissonances and decorated melodies to portray the emotions of the Prophet Jeremiah, who asks if there is any sorrow like his sorrow. *Leçons de ténèbres* translate as 'lessons of darkness', and traditionally began at midnight. They were an emotive and dramatic part of Tenebrae, the service of shadows: it was customary to place a candelabra holding fifteen burning candles in front of the altar, and to snuff them one by one, until the congregation heard the final prayers in almost total darkness.

The Protestant side of Baroque music for Easter leads us back to the Lutheran Johann Sebastian Bach. He is said to have set the Passion five times in his lifetime; the *St John Passion* and *St Matthew Passion* survive, and we have a libretto for the *St Mark Passion*. Bach's surviving Passions are among the greatest works of musical art, the most sublime settings for Passiontide. A tenor evangelist vividly tells the story of the Crucifixion, with a choir joining in the action in multi-part choruses; soloists reflecting on it in emotionally potent arias; and chorales (again for choir) highlighting the Passion's relevance to its listeners. Seek these works out; each annual listen will offer new surprises and resonances with our own world and experiences, ones that you won't be able to believe you haven't spotted before.

Bach's music also concludes this airy, windy spring-time of redemptive blood and new beginnings with the joyful fulfilment of the Easter story: the *Ascension Oratorio*. If you want to listen to it on the appropriate day, mark your diary on the sixth Thursday after Easter. The first part sees Jesus post-resurrection bidding farewell to his disciples, and the second lifts our gaze to the angels prophesying his return. Between the two is the Ascension itself – it really takes place during the sermon, but the preceding chorale confirms what's going on. Jesus is caught up in the air, and since air was considered the element between fire and water – between judgement and redemption – this is a critical moment. It marks a new beginning, a true spring thanks to blood shed for the world, and a lifting of the soul. In the chorale that ends Part One, the whole church of believers sing about the four building blocks of the Earth – the elements – coming together in this magnificent event:

Now all lies beneath you, apart only from yourself;
the angels must for ever and ever come to wait on you.
Princes also stand by the road and
are willingly subject to you;
air, water, fire and earth must all be at your service.[1]

Summer

The ferocity of Vivaldi's summer may have been shocking, but his audiences knew very well that this season signified hot and dry conditions, and had ancient associations with fire – and explosive temperaments. Where senses and their associations with the seasons came into play, spring was all about sound, autumn will be about touch and winter – smell. But here in summer sight is the corresponding sense and so this seasonal sojourn of Baroque music begins with the spectacle of a royal extravaganza . . .

The first British monarch of the House of Hanover was not a party animal. King George I found pageantry tiresome and avoided public appearances. However, in June 1717 he was persuaded to head a river party on the Thames, to the accompaniment of music by George Frideric Handel. The trip had to be carefully timed, not only for the weather but also because the old medieval London Bridge was the only way to cross the Thames, and its narrow arches were the only sluice gates that held the pressures of the tide at bay. The festivities had to coincide with the flow of the tide, which meant they had to be held late at night. The weather held and the royal party departed Whitehall accompanied by a large City Company barge transporting the musicians. For his *Water Music*, Handel used not only string and woodwind players but also one of the great sonic sensations and spectacles of the moment, a pair of majestic horns.

To add to the music's fashionable flamboyance, his musicians — very likely Bohemians — would have played with these horns raised in the air and with the bells open. The musicians played on and on, not only during the river cruise, but also indoors over a midnight midsummer supper.

Sensibly moving the music indoors was a tactic taken a decade earlier in summer 1707 by Elisabeth-Claude Jacquet de la Guerre as she presented her latest creations to King Louis XIV. The first French woman to compose an opera and to publish a book of harpsichord pieces, Elisabeth was ranked equal to court composers such as Marin Marais and second only to Jean-Baptiste Lully. The king consistently showered her with praise and she dedicated publications to him including, in July 1707, a set of six innovative sonatas for violin. These are not regular sonatas with a straightforward accompaniment of viola da gamba and harpsichord; rather, the virtuosic keyboard part reveals Elizabeth as an equal partner to the violin. Two members of the string-playing Marchand family joined her in a private performance of the full set for Louis. He sat at a table facing a long window in his chambers, enjoying the summer sun streaming through the glass, the music, and a *petit couvert*: a summer lunch of soups, salads, pastries, cold meats, and fresh and candied fruits.

Summer events indoors offered better acoustics and the option of a harpsichord, and removed the potential element of bad weather. However, some royal events were not so flexible or easily relocated – for example, the much-anticipated wedding of the Swedish king Adolf Frederick to Louisa Ulrika, a sister of the Prussian king, Frederick the Great. The nuptials took place on 17 August 1744 to much fanfare and a soundtrack provided by the Swedish composer Johan Helmich Roman. His *Drottningholmsmusiken* is a sparkling collection of twenty-five instrumental pieces, intended to be suitable for various situations throughout the festivities. This was summer music set in and around the ultimate wedding gift – the lavish Palace of Drottningholm itself – with the final hymn accompanied by blasts from a ship's cannon.

With his sister installed in Drottningholm and set to be Queen of Sweden, Frederick the Great turned his attention to other political allies, and colluded with Empress Elizabeth of Russia to strengthen the relationship between the Franco-Prussian axis and Russia by organising a marriage between Princess Sophie Auguste Friederike von Anhalt-Zerbst and Elizabeth's heir, Grand Duke Peter. They became engaged in the summer of 1744 (Sophie having converted to the Russian Orthodox Church and taken the new name of Catherine) and married a year later, their nuptials celebrated in an outdoor display of fireworks and music by Johann Friedrich Fasch. The *concerto grosso* for three choirs each containing three trumpets, three oboes, bassoon and timpani became known as Fasch's *Music for the Royal Fireworks* after the outdoor display in celebration of the newlyweds. On her husband's death in 1762, Catherine ascended the throne, becoming Catherine the Great of Russia.

In historical-medical realms, the humour corresponding with summer was yellow bile, a substance now thought to be cholesterol, and associated with choleric temperaments. An imbalance of yellow bile was said to cause hot tempers and irrational behaviour, which we find in abundance at the hotly debated opera competition held in London in the high summer of 1701 – incidentally one of the warmest summers of the age on record. The task at hand was a one-act opera to a new libretto by leading dramatist William Congreve, which piled contest upon contest to create a perfect storm. In the libretto for *The Judgement of Paris*, the shepherd (in reality a Trojan prince) Paris is commanded by Mercury to judge which of the goddesses is the most beautiful: Venus, Pallas (Athene) or Juno. After carefully reviewing their various charms – and shameless bribes – he plumps for Venus and awards her the golden apple. The other hot-headed goddesses are unimpressed – as were the four entrants by the competition's judging process. In fourth place, Gottfried Finger won just thirty guineas, accused the organisers of partiality, and took off back to the continent. Daniel Purcell, in third place, had been the favourite to win; he received forty guineas and went on to surprise everyone by publishing his score at even greater expense. Perhaps as a yellow-bile-fuelled final dig at the competition organisers, he wrote in the dedication: 'this age is so far sunk that the nearer a man approaches mastery, the farther he is generally from meeting with due encouragement.'[2] Second place went to John Eccles, and the winner was John Weldon – a young whippersnapper who'd generated a big crowd for the tactical audience vote. You know he means business from the outset, as trumpets, recorders and timpani announce the action before declamatory messages from the gods, seductive arias from the persuasive goddesses and balmy instrumental interludes infuse the score. But it's perhaps the choruses that contain the most blazing emotion, and none more so than the central number: 'Let Ambition Fire Thy Mind'.

The Judgement of Paris certainly epitomised both eighteenth-century summer entertainment and hot yellow-biled tempers at their finest.

Autumn

The harvest, drunken naps and early-morning hunt of Vivaldi's *Autumn* concerto would have conjured in his listeners' ears and imaginations the quintessential sounds, tastes and textures of the season. Classified as cold and dry, this quarter of the year was perfect for storing the bounty of harvest. It's a time for celebrating the riches of the earth with music to match, such as Georg Philipp Telemann's *Tafelmusik*. Originally titled

Musique de Table, this substantial collection comprises around four-and-a-half hours of music, organised into three parts or 'productions', each containing a suite, a quartet, a concerto, a trio, a sonata and a conclusion. The style is, in one word: fashionable. Telemann had the knack of keeping up with the latest musical trends, and in this case re-labelled the classic dances with emotive descriptions such as Dolce, Cantabile, Affetuoso and Furioso. Within them, he experiments with effects such as swiftly alternating major and minor, having a short slow section within a fast movement, writing for unexpected solo instruments such as the horn, or quoting on-trend melodies that people would have heard elsewhere. Telemann is said to have declared that the work would make him famous one day, and these suites are certainly among the last and best collections referred to as courtly table music, designed specifically for feasts and banquets.

In the early eighteenth century, the autumnal feast of Michaelmas was still a crucial date – one of the quarter days that launched the four periods of the financial, judicial and academic year. Michaelmas was a time to mark the end of the productive season and the beginning of the farming year, a time to re-hire workers, and the period in which bailiffs would work on the accounts for the year. The fairs at Michaelmas weren't just an opportunity to sell the best of the harvest, but also a time when debts were settled and workers found new employment.

Michaelmas, once the third most important feast day of the year, is now lost to our modern-day calendars since the celebrations associated with it were abolished in the late eighteenth century. Telemann, Vivaldi and their contemporaries were well acquainted with its significance in commemorating the victory of Archangel Michael in his heavenly war against Lucifer. It was a feast day ripe for festive, dramatic music as trumpeters and drummers joined the musicians in the organ loft at church. Johann Sebastian Bach wrote at least four cantatas for Michaelmas, all of which make the most of this dramatic moment in the church's year. To start with, try Cantata BWV 130: *Herr Gott, dich loben alle wir* (Lord God, we all praise you). Just imagine that morning in 1724 at Leipzig's Thomaskirche, when the opening chorus burst out from the organ loft. The angels are on parade and the chorus sings a song of praise to God, thanking Him for creating them. There are reminders along the way that excess – such as the drunkenness we saw in this first movement of Vivaldi's *Autumn* or that Bach's congregation might have seen in the market outside – is not the seemliest way to give thanks for the harvest, but the overall tone captures the mood of the moment. Celestial martial arts, dance and combat meet in the cantata's arias and choruses, with a trio of trumpeters announcing both the angelic forces and the hellish dragon, complete with menacing kettle drum.

Autumn is also the season associated with true melancholy, from a Greek word that literally translates as 'black bile' – a bodily excess of which was thought to be the cause of depression and bodily complaints. Vivaldi and his contemporaries understood it not as a passing mood, but rather as a distinct disease with mental and physical symptoms that included sleeplessness, irritability, despondency and persistent fear; baroque composers especially found lyricism in lamentations and the melancholic associations of specific musical keys.

October days always remind me of a trip to Sanssouci, the summer palace of King Frederick the Great, just outside Berlin. The palace itself was famous for concerts, including a very special visit by J. S. Bach in 1747, so I wanted to hear the acoustics and see the space, but I hadn't researched the grounds. Amid falling leaves and fountains stopped for the cold weather, I came across a monument: a Temple of Friendship. It was built by Frederick for his sister Wilhelmine, who died on 14 October 1758. The king was a man who found emotional engagement challenging, especially in his advancing years, but there is no denying that he was devastated by her death. She never reached the winter of an old age, but died in her autumn after a rich life dedicated to building projects in her marital home at Bayreuth, diplomatic missions, memoir-writing and composition.

Most of Wilhelmine of Prussia's musical compositions, including an opera, *Argenore*, are lost. However, in the hunt for the remnants of her work, a Harpsichord Concerto in G minor has come to light. It shows clear admiration and knowledge of Johann Sebastian Bach's concertos in the way that she spins out phrases, and also reveals how rigorous her youthful musical training from the famous lutenist Sylvius Leopold Weiss must have been. Unusually, the third movement includes a solo part for flute, perhaps in homage to her brother's passion for the instrument, but more likely for her flute-playing husband.

While we're in a melancholic mood, G minor is a key historically associated with that disposition. The great Baroque thinker and writer on music, Johann Mattheson, described it as almost the most beautiful key, capable of expressing yearning as well as happiness. It's the key of Henry Purcell's lament 'When I am laid in earth' from *Dido and Aeneas*, of Antonio Vivaldi's darkly brooding flute concerto *La notte*, and of Johann Sebastian Bach's majestic and emotionally complex Great Fantasia and Fugue. In this season of mists and mellow fruitfulness, musicians and artists in general have a tendency to dolefully express any number of mournful life experiences, from bereavement to heartbreak, or even just passing sadness.

Winter

Winter is a season long associated with cold, wet conditions, with a phlegmatic constitution and with the sense of smell. Musically it invites the songs of London's ice fairs, Purcell's theatrical shivering in the cold in *King Arthur*, and watery tales of antiquity in pieces such as Michel-Richard Delalande and André-Cardinal Destouches's *Les Élémens*. Antonio Vivaldi's *Winter* may have evoked the weather of the season, but his name doesn't crop up often in music directly associated with Christmas – unless you happen upon a certain Violin Concerto in E major. RV 270 has a specific title, which Vivaldi wrote himself on the manuscript: *Il riposo, per il Santissimo Natale* (Rest, for Holy Christmas), referring to the baby in the manger resting on Christmas night. He's after a hushed quality and ethereal sound in this concerto, and so indicates that all the string players should use their mutes, and that the harpsichord player should sit this one out, although sometimes the piece works well with a lullabying lute.

The Holy Night (Christmas Eve) signifies the end of Advent and the beginning of Christmas. It's a curious aspect of our modern age that today the reverse feels true – that Christmas Day feels almost like the end of Christmas. Aided and abetted by the drive of commercialism, Advent itself has become the Christmas period, and I know people who are only too keen, even relieved, to take down the decorations, the tree and all the festive lights on Boxing Day. No wonder January feels as though it lasts three times longer than any other month as a result. If I had my way, we'd decorate the tree on Christmas Eve, and revert to the traditional calendar. The twelve days of Christmas begin on 25 December, so that's a start. Then there's the arrival of the Wise Men at Epiphany (6 January), and after that I'd be happy to lose the most 'Christmassy' of decorations and do the traditional thing of leaving up the lights until Candlemas on 2 February. That way the glow of the season sees you through the darkest days and longest nights of the year. And music to go with it? I'm not advocating 'O Come, All Ye Faithful' all the way to February, but there's so much Christmas music to explore, it's definitely worth giving more of it a go.

If losing the words helps you to prolong the festivities, then why not try the Christmas concertos by Arcangelo Corelli, Pietro Locatelli, Francesco Manfredini or Giuseppe Torelli? Or you could continue the pastoral themes with the *Concerto Pastorale* by Johann Christoph Pez (pronounced 'pets' like the domestic animals rather than 'pezz' like the sweets). It has the most incredible passacaglia, a feisty dance number that unfolds over a repeating bass line that's guaranteed to lift the spirit.

However, if you've bought into the idea of an extended Christmas, then go for vocal numbers! Marc-Antoine Charpentier's *Messe de minuit* (Midnight Mass) is a quint-essential sound of the season, but its first performance at Paris's Jesuit Église Saint-Louis, which probably took place in 1694, was something of a risk. The joy of Christ's birth always had special musical significance in France with a long tradition of including carols in Christmas services, whether in organ arrangements or vocal works. Against this backdrop, Charpentier included ten French carols in the actual music of the Mass itself. The Council of Trent had banned the use of secular melodies in Masses, but here the composer got away with it just because it was Christmas. This Midnight Mass is gloriously uplifting, and if you enjoy it, Charpentier also wrote a Christmas oratorio that you can seek out: *In nativitatem Domini canticum*.

Christmas cantatas explicitly telling the Christmas story abound; but let me point you especially in the direction of Alessandro Scarlatti's *Cantata pastorale per la natività di Nostro Signore Gesu Cristo*, or towards the wide variety of joyous ones that Johann Sebastian Bach wrote for Christmas Day services in Leipzig, such as BWV 110 from the year of *The Four Seasons'* publication, 1725: *Unser Mund sei voll Lachens* (May our mouth be full of laughter). And if you're up for exploring further afield, look to Mexico and Juan García de Zéspedes's *Convidando está la noche* (The Night is Inviting), which portrays the startling sounds of the lively Christmas celebrations in the cathedral at Puebla. These are the comforts of a Baroque Christmas, offering hope and joy from the harshest of conditions, whether in a stable or out on the Venetian ice.

Further Reading

Sources

Unless otherwise stated, all direct quotes attributed to the following are from interviews and correspondence with the author:

Tom McKinney, Rachel Podger, Hattie McCall Davies, Micky White, Andrew Bush, Michael Talbot, Daniel Pioro, Michael Morpurgo, Ron Merlino, Stefano L'Occaso, Adrian Chandler, Erik Bosgraaf, James Ehnes, Gloria Beggiato, Anna Maria Pentimalli Biscaretti di Ruffia, John Chu, Elena Urioste, Tasmin Little, Ayanna Witter-Johnson, Joanna Forbes L'Estrange, Angela Clutton.

Vivaldi Essentials

Everett, Paul, *Vivaldi: The Four Seasons and Other Concertos, Op. 8* (Cambridge: Cambridge University Press, 1996)

Getzinger, Donna, and Felsenfeld, Daniel *Antonio Vivaldi and the Baroque Tradition* (Greensboro, North Carolina: Morgan Reynolds Publishing, 2004)

Gullo, Giuseppe, 'Antonio Vivaldi's Chronic Illness: Shedding New Light on an Old Enigma', *Studi vivaldiani* No. 22 (Venice: 2022), pp. 3–55.

Heller, Karl, *Antonio Vivaldi: The Red Priest of Venice*, translated by David Marinelli (Portland, Oregon: Amadeus Press, 1997)

Hogwood, Christopher, 'Introduction' in the score to *Vivaldi: Le Quattro Stagioni* (London: Bärenreiter, 2000)

Kolneder, Walter, *Antonio Vivaldi, documents of his life and works* (New York: C.F. Peters, 1982)

Landon, H. C. Robbins, *Vivaldi: Voice of the Baroque* (London: Thames and Hudson, 1993)

—— and John Julius Norwich, *Five Centuries of Music in Venice* (London: Thames and Hudson, 1991)

Lockey, Nicholas, 'Antonio Vivaldi and the sublime seasons: sonority and texture as expressive devices in early eighteenth-century Italian music', in *Eighteenth-Century Music*, Vol. 14, Issue 2 (Cambridge: Cambridge University Press, 2017), pp. 265–83

Maunder, Richard (C. R. F.), *The Scoring of Baroque Concertos* (Woodbridge: Boydell Press, 2004)

Pincherle, Marc, *Vivaldi: Genius of the Baroque*, translated by Christopher Hatch (New York: W. W. Norton & Co., 1957)

Selfridge-Field, Eleanor, *Venetian Instrumental Music from Gabrieli to Vivaldi* (Oxford: Basil Blackwell, 1975)

Talbot, Michael, *Master Musicians: Vivaldi*, fourth (paperback) edition (Oxford: Oxford University Press, 2000; originally published London: J. M. Dent, 1978)

—— *Venetian Music in the Age of Vivaldi* (London: Routledge, 1999)

—— *The Vivaldi Compendium* (Woodbridge: Boydell
Press, 2011)
—— ed., *Vivaldi* (London: Routledge, 2017)
Vivaldi, Antonio, *Le quattro stagioni: da Il cimento
dell'armonia e dell'inventione op. VIII: per violino
principale, due violini, viola e basso*, edited by Paul
Everett and Michael Talbot (Milan: Ricordi, 1996)
White, Micky, *Antonio Vivaldi: A Life in Documents, Studi
de musica veneta, Quaderni vivaldiani* Vol. 17 (Florence:
Leo S. Olschki Editore, 2013)

Baroque Essentials

Arikha, Noga, *Passions and Tempers: A History of the
Humours* (New York: Harper Collins, 2007)
Butt, John, *Playing with History: The Historical Approach
to Musical Performance* (Cambridge: Cambridge
University Press, 2002)
Cyr, Mary, *Performing Baroque Music* (Portland, Oregon:
Amadeus Press, 1992)
Kenyon, Nicholas (ed.), *Authenticity and Early Music: A
Symposium* (Oxford: Oxford University Press, 1988)
Lawson, Colin, and Robin Stowell, *The Historical
Performance of Music: An Introduction* (Cambridge:
Cambridge University Press, 1999)
Philip, Robert, *Early Recordings and Musical Style:
Changing Tastes in Instrumental Performance
1900–1950* (Cambridge: Cambridge University
Press, 1992)

—— *Performing Music in the Age of Recording* (New Haven and London: Yale University Press, 2004)

Snodin, Michael, and Nigel Llewellyn (eds), *Baroque: Style in the Age of Magnificence, 1620–1800* (London: V&A Publishing, 2013)

Spitzer, John, and Neal Zaslaw, *The Birth of the Orchestra: History of an Institution, 1650–1815* (Oxford: Oxford University Press, 2005)

Taruskin, Richard, *Text and Act: Essays on Music and Performance* (New York: Oxford University Press, 1995)

—— *The Danger of Music: And Other Anti-Utopian Essays* (Berkeley and Los Angeles: University of California Press, 2009)

Toman, Rolf, *Baroque: Architecture, Sculpture, Painting* (Cologne: Könemann, 1998)

Wilson, Nick, *The Art of Re-Enchantment: Making Early Music in the Modern Age* (New York: Oxford University Press, 2013)

Seasonal Essentials

Adler, Shane, 'Seasons', in Vol. II of Roberts, Helen E. (ed.), *The Encyclopedia of Comparative Iconography: Themes Depicted in Works of Art* (Chicago: Fitzroy Dearborn, 1998), pp. 793–5

Blom, Philipp, *Nature's Mutiny: How the Little Ice Age Transformed the West and Shaped the Present* (London: Picador, 2019)

Clutton, Angela, *Seasoning: How to cook and celebrate the seasons* (London: Murdoch Books, 2024)

Degroot, Dagomar, *The Frigid Golden Age: Climate Change, the Little Ice Age, and the Dutch Republic, 1560–1720* (Cambridge: Cambridge University Press, 2018)

Fagan, Brian, *The Little Ice Age: How Climate Made History 1300–1850* (New York: Basic Books, 2000)

May, Katherine, *Wintering: The power of rest and retreat in difficult times* (London: Rider, 2020)

Norman, Russell, *Venice: Four Seasons of Home Cooking* (London: Fig Tree, 2018)

Steer, Rosie, *Slow Seasons: A Creative Guide to Reconnecting with Nature the Celtic Way* (London: Bloomsbury Publishing, 2023)

Acknowledgements

In my twelve months spent with Vivaldi, I was accompanied by many trusted companions. I was determined to write each season in real time, and am therefore enormously grateful to everyone who joined me through my rolling year.

My springtime thanks to Tom McKinney for our meeting of music and ornithology; violinist Rachel Podger for spilling the tea on the essence of period playing; Hattie McCall Davies who displayed heroic patience while I tried to play her bagpipes; Micky White for taking me backstage at the Pietà one spring more than a decade ago; and Carrie Churnside for detective work on Eleonora di Guastalla.

In summer, thanks to Andrew Bush for his open and historically imaginative medical mind; to Michael Morpurgo for sharing panna cotta at Hay, and for permission to include his summer sonnet here; to violinist Daniel Pioro for being so generous about his interpretation of the work; and to Nicholas Sternberg and Ros Edwards at Manchester Public Library for access to and permissions for publishing select pages from the surviving manuscripts held there.

Autumnal thanks to Ron Merlino, a modern-day impresario if ever there was one; to Stefano L'Occaso, the director of the Ducal Palace in Mantua for making me so welcome, and his team, especially Maria Ferlisi, Elena Montanari and Margherita Ruocco at the Ministry of Culture; and to violinists Adrian Chandler and James Ehnes and recorder player Erik Bosgraaf for their insights into being in Vivaldi's driving seat. My special thanks to new Venetian friends at the Hotel Metropole for having me to stay in their beautiful palazzo as their guest: to director Gloria Beggiato and her colleagues including Anna Meneghini and Claudia Malfitano, and to Giuliano Brogliato for making La Serenissima surprisingly accessible.

In winter, my thanks to architect Anna Maria Pentimalli Biscaretti di Ruffia; to Jane da Mosto at We Are Here Venice – a conservation group I'd urge anyone to seek out and support; and to Maria Spinelli for the magic of chance encounters. To art curator John Chu for helping me see Vivaldi through artists' eyes; and to composers and performers Elena Urioste, Tasmin Little, Ayanna Witter-Johnson, Pekka Kuusisto, Antony Pitts and Joanna Forbes L'Estrange for sharing their new visions of Vivaldi's turning year.

Perennial thanks to Kate Wakeling for her vivid translations of Vivaldi's sonnets; to the esteemed Vivaldi scholar Michael Talbot for his genuine enthusiasm and guidance; and to Angela Clutton for getting me back into the kitchen with renewed determination to cook seasonally.

Thanks to Sabhbh Curran at Curtis Brown for believing in this project from the get-go and to the stellar team at Faber for bringing it into being, with creativity and grace: Hannah Knowles, Joanna Harwood, Lauren Nicoll, Sophie Clarke, and Sara Cheraghlou; to Sophie Harris for the handsome artwork; and Kate Hopkins for making my voice and intentions clear.

Numerous BBC colleagues have supported me this project, including Sam Jackson, Olwen Fisher, Dominic Wells, Sara Mohr-Pietch, and above all David Fay and Les Pratt, experts in riding the waves of deadlines and broadcasts. My appreciation too to those who've encouraged me with musical conversation and reassurance along the way . . . particularly Delma Tomlin, Chris Butler and Ann Barkway, and Lars Henriksson; and grateful thanks to the eagle-eyed who proofread: Fr Robert Titley, Katie Bircher, Bernice Arthur and Ashley Solomon.

A book requires a village to carry the physical and mental load, especially when you have your hip reconstructed in the middle of it. For that specifically I thank Jonathan Hutt and Thomas Edwards at UCLH; and for the rest, in many different ways: Alexandra Notay, Michelle Reynolds, Emma Crosthwaite, Eva Forrester, Maria Pico, George Eely, Anna Yap, Becky Wildish, Katie Murphy, Fr Stephen Hearne, Fr Stephen Evans and my mum Janice Riddell. Most of all my heartfelt thanks to Paul and Thomasina, for fuelling my resolve, putting up with my absences of mind and body, and never tiring of talking about seasonality and Vivaldi.

Image Credits

Fig. 1: 'De reliquarum volucrium vocibus' (On the voices of other birds) in Athanasius Kircher's *Musurgia Universalis*. Public domain

Fig. 2: Façade of Santa Maria della Pietà. Photograph © Hannah French

Fig. 3: Bust of Vivaldi in the Ospedale garden. Photograph © Hannah French

Fig. 4: Manuscript of the soloist's part of Vivaldi's *Summer*, Movement III. Permission for reproduction granted from the Henry Watson Music Library – courtesy of Manchester Libraries, Information and Archives, Manchester City Council

Fig. 5: Manuscript of the sonnet for Vivaldi's *Summer*. Permission for reproduction granted from the Henry Watson Music Library – courtesy of Manchester Libraries, Information and Archives, Manchester City Council

Fig. 6: Excerpt from the first movement of *Summer*, first edition. (Il cimento dell'armonia e dell'inventione, Op.8 (No.2) (Amsterdam: Michel-Charles Le Cène [1725]). Plate 520. Public domain

Fig. 7: Antonio Vivaldi (engraving by François Morellon de La Cave, from Michel-Charles Le

Cène's edition of Vivaldi's op. 8, Amsterdam, 1725)
Public domain

Fig. 8: Frontispiece for Il cimento dell'armonia e
dell'inventione. Public domain

Fig. 9: Giardino dei Semplici at the Ducal Palace in
Mantua. Photograph by permission of the Ministry
of Culture – Palazzo Ducale di Mantova

Fig. 10: The Church of Santa Maria della Salute across
the Grand Canal. Photograph © Hannah French

Fig. 11: Hotel Metropole on the original site of the
Ospedale della Pietà, alongside the Church of Santa
Maria della Pietà. Photograph © Hannah French

Fig. 12: Column from Santa Maria della Visitazione, the
original Pietà Church, now in the bar of the Hotel
Metropole. Photograph © Hannah French

Fig. 13: The Church of Santa Maria della Salute.
Photograph © Hannah French

Fig. 14: The floating votive bridge across the Grand
Canal by the Church of Santa Maria della Salute.
Photograph © Hannah French

Fig. 15: The *castradina* at Trattoria da Remigio.
Photograph © Hannah French

Fig. 16: Photograph of the Venetian lagoon at Torcello.
Photograph © Hannah French

Fig. 17: *Le Quattro Stagioni: La primavera (Spring)* (fresco
possibly by Lamberti) in the Loggia di Eleonora at the
Ducal Palace in Mantua. Photograph by permission of
the Ministry of Culture – Palazzo Ducale di Mantova

Fig. 18: *Le Quattro Stagioni: L'estate (Summer)* (fresco possibly by Lamberti) in the Loggia di Eleonora at the Ducal Palace in Mantua. Photograph by permission of the Ministry of Culture – Palazzo Ducale di Mantova.

Fig. 19: *Le Quattro Stagioni: L'autunno (Autumn)* (fresco possibly by Lamberti) in the Loggia di Eleonora at the Ducal Palace in Mantua. Photograph by permission of the Ministry of Culture – Palazzo Ducale di Mantova.

Fig. 20: *Le Quattro Stagioni: L'inverno (Winter)* (fresco possibly by Lamberti) in the Loggia di Eleonora at the Ducal Palace in Mantua. Photograph by permission of the Ministry of Culture – Palazzo Ducale di Mantova.

Fig. 21: Mantua from the reedbeds. Photograph © Hannah French

Notes

I: Prelude
1 Roger Scruton, 'Programme music', Grove Music Online
(published 2001) <https://doi.org/10.1093/gmo/9781561592630.
article.22394>, accessed 13 August 2024.
2 The key relationships are discussed at length in Joshua L.
Dissmore, 'Baroque Music and the Doctrine of Affections: Putting
the Affections into Effect', Cedarville University Research and
Scholarship Symposium, No. 18 (2017) <http://digitalcommons.
cedarville.edu/research_scholarship_symposium/2017/
podium_presentations/18>, accessed 16 September 2024. See also
Paul Everett, *Vivaldi: The Four Seasons and Other Concertos, Op. 8*
(Cambridge: Cambridge University Press, 1996), p. 45. Johann
Mattheson's words are captured in Hans Lenneberg and Johann
Mattheson, 'Johann Mattheson on Affect and Rhetoric in Music',
Journal of Music Theory Vol. 2, No. 2 (1958), p. 236.

PART ONE: SPRING
I: Allegro
1 The sonnets are produced here in a new English translation by
poet Kate Wakeling. The original Italian of the first sonnet reads:

> Giunt' è la Primavera e festosetti
> La Salutan gl' Augei con lieto canto,
> E i fonti allo spirar de' Zeffiretti
> Con dolce mormorio scorrono intanto:
> Vengon' coprendo l'aer di nero amanto
> E Lampi, e tuoni ad annuntiarla eletti
> Indi tacendo questi, gl'Augelletti;
> Tornan' di nuovo al lor canoro incanto

Original Italian texts taken from Paul Everett, *Vivaldi: The
Four Seasons and Other Concertos, Op. 8* (Cambridge: Cambridge
University Press, 1996), pp. 72–5.

2 You can view the whole of Athanasius Kircher's *Musurgia Universalis* online: <https://archive.org/details/chepfl-lipr-AXC19_01>

3 Bartolomeo Scappi, *The Opera of Bartolomeo Scappi (1570): L'arte e prudenza d'un maestro cuoco: The Art and Craft of a Master Cook*, translated with commentary by Terence Scully, The lorenzo Da Ponte Italian Library, General Editors: Luigi Ballerini and Massimo Ciavolella (Toronto: University of Toronto Press, 2008), p. 203.

II: Largo e pianissimo sempre
1 The original Italian text reads:

> E quindi sul fiorito ameno prato
> Al caro mormorio di fronde e piante
> Dorme 'l Caprar col fido can' à lato.

2 David Hume, *A Treatise of Human Nature*, ed. L. A. Selby Bigge, second edition rev. P. H. Nidditch (Oxford: Clarendon Press, 1978), p. 398.

3 Music had flourished at St Mark's since the mid-sixteenth century thanks to a long line of distinguished choral directors and organists, all of whom had been inspired by its spectacular acoustics. Composers Andrea and Giovanni Gabrieli and Claudio Monteverdi in particular had played with the spatial possibilities of the balconies, creating echo effects in lavish multi-choral and instrumental pieces. Such sonic extravaganzas had attracted congregations and tourists in droves, but by the end of Monteverdi's life (1643) the novelty was waning, and new musical attractions were on the rise in the city – namely, opera. As a result, the most recent directors of music at St Mark's in Vivaldi's youth had been organists who were not necessarily first-rate composers. However, Giovanni Legrenzi arrived with ideas aplenty, most notably reorganising and expanding the orchestra to an unprecedented thirty-four instrumentalists. Within the doors of St Mark's, Giovanni Battista Vivaldi – and potentially Antonio too – met many musicians who would go on to make their names both in Venice and elsewhere, such as the organist Carlo Francesco Pollarolo, the singer and organist (and later composer) Antonio Lotti and the cellist Antonio Caldara. In this light, St Mark's emerges as a meeting place for ambitious young talents and a sacred laboratory of musical ideas. It might have

provided a true spiritual home for Antonio Vivaldi in more ways than one; however, we only have confirmation of one performance he gave there – during the Christmas festivities of 1696. See Eleanor Selfridge-Field, *Venetian Instrumental Music from Gabrieli to Vivaldi* (Oxford: Basil Blackwell, 1975), pp. 3–25. Also see Karl Heller, *Antonio Vivaldi: The Red Priest of Venice*, trans. David Marinelli (Portland, Oregon: Amadeus Press, 1997), pp. 26–7, and the introduction to Michael Talbot, *Venetian Music in the Age of Vivaldi* (Abingdon: Taylor & Francis, 2024). Talbot information retrieved from <https://www.perlego.com/book/4574626/venetian-music-in-the-age-of-vivaldi-pdf>, accessed 2 April 2024.

4 Giovanni Battista's life is chronicled in Michael Talbot, *The Vivaldi Compendium* (Woodbridge: Boydell Press, 2011), pp. 195–6.

5 The dynamic between the various violinists is perfectly encapsulated on Chouchane Siranossian's album *Duello d'Archi a Venezia* (Alpha Classics, 2023) with the Venice Baroque Orchestra directed by Andrea Marcon, and in this recording's sleeve note, 'A Rite of Virtuosity' by Olivier Fourès.

6 Geoff Brown, 'Classical Review: Rachel Podger: Vivaldi; Les Siècles: Ravel', *The Times* (20 April 2018) <https://www.thetimes.com/culture/music/article/classical-review-rachel-podger-vivaldi-les-siecles-ravel-25jzhtznx>, accessed 26 April 2024.

7 Richard Fairman, 'Vivaldi: *Le quattro stagioni* – "high quality throughout"', *Financial Times* (6 April 2018) <https://www.ft.com/content/0c5307b2-3829-11e8-8eee-e06bde01c544>; Charlotte Gardner, 'VIVALDI *The Four Seasons* (Podger)', *Gramophone Magazine* (May 2018) <https://www.gramophone.co.uk/review/vivaldi-the-four-seasons-podger>; Geoff Brown, 'Classical Review: Rachel Podger: Vivaldi; Les Siècles: Ravel', *The Times* (20 April 2018), all accessed 26 April 2024.

III: Allegro pastorale

1 The original Italian text reads:

> Di pastoral Zampogna al suon festante
> Danzan Ninfe e Pastor nel tetto amato
> Di primavera all' apparir brillante.

2 I am grateful for information on the Pietà from direct correspondence with Vivaldi scholar Micky White. Also see Micky

White, *Antonio Vivaldi: A Life in Documents, Studi de musica veneta, Quaderni vivaldiani* Vol. 17 (Florence: Leo S. Olschki Editore, 2013).

IV: The Life Cycle of The Four Seasons – *Roots and Shoots*

1 Karl Heller makes this assertion in *Antonio Vivaldi: The Red Priest of Venice*, trans. David Marinelli (Portland, Oregon: Amadeus Press, 1997), p. 171.

2 Eleanora's court life continued in Florence, where she surrounded herself with a tight-knit circle of scholars and men of letters, including the bibliophile Antonio Magliabechi and the poet and dramatist Giovanni Battista Fagiuoli. See Irene Cotta's entry on Eleonora Gonzaga in the *Dizionario Biografico degli Italiani*, Vol. 57 (2001) <https://www.treccani.it/enciclopedia/eleonora-gonzaga_(Dizionario-Biografico)>, accessed 9 July 2024.

3 Stefano L'Occaso, 'Scenografie bibienesche per l'attività mantovana di Antonio Vivaldi (1718–1720), Qualche nuovo documento', in *Musica & Figura* (a magazine published with support from the Università degli Studi di Padova – Dipartimento dei Beni Culturali: archeologia, storia dell'arte, del cinema e della musica, and from the Ugo and Olga Levi Foundation for musical studies), Vol. 3 (Venice, 2015), pp. 91–110.

4 This is referenced in Vivaldi's preface to the 1725 publication of op. 8. See Part Four, *Summer*, Chapter IV: The Life Cycle of *The Four Seasons* – Branching Out, p. 146.

5 Michael Talbot, *The Vivaldi Compendium* (Woodbridge: Boydell Press, 2011), p. 124.

6 Ibid.

7 Johann Joachim Quantz, *On Playing the Flute* (1752), trans. Edward R. Reilly (London: Faber and Faber, 2001), p. 323. Quantz's treatise extends far beyond flute technique to notions of taste and opinions on contemporary composers.

8 Translation by Pamela Dellal, taken from <https://www.emmanuelmusic.org/bach-translations/bwv-27>

9 Paul Everett, *Vivaldi: The Four Seasons and Other Concertos, Op. 8* (Cambridge: Cambridge University Press, 1996), p. 3.

10 Charles de Brosses quoted in Laurence Dreyfus, *Bach and the Patterns of Invention*, third edition (Harvard: Harvard University Press, 2004), p. 44.

NOTES

PART TWO: SUMMER
I: *Allegro non molto*
1 The original Italian text reads:

> Sotto dura staggion dal sole accesa
> Langue l'huom, langue 'l gregge, ed arde il Pino;
> Scioglie il Cucco la Voce, e tosto intesa
> Canta la Tortorella e 'l gardelino.
> Zeffiro dolce Spira, mà contesa
> Muove Borea improviso al suo vicino;
> E piange il Pastorel, perche sospesa
> Teme fiera borasca, e 'l suo destino;

2 Leonardo da Vinci, 'The Love of Virtue', No. 1220 in *The Notebooks of Leonardo da Vinci – Complete*, trans. Jean Paul Richter (printed in the UK by Amazon, 2020), cccxvi.

II: *Adagio e piano – Presto e forte*
1 The original Italian text reads:

> Toglie alle membra lasse il suo riposo
> Il timore de' Lampi, e tuoni fieri
> E de mosche, e mosconi il stuol furioso!

2 The letters to Marchese Guido Bentivoglio are published in full and translated into English by David Marinelli in Karl Heller, *Antonio Vivaldi: The Red Priest of Venice*, trans. David Marinelli (Portland, Oregon: Amadeus Press, 1997), p. 287–9.
3 Andrew Bush MD FHEA FRCP FRCPCH FERS FAPSR ATSF is Professor of Paediatrics and Paediatric Respirology at the National Heart and Lung Institute and the Imperial Centre for Paediatrics and Child Health, Imperial College. He is also Consultant Paediatric Chest Physician, Royal Brompton & Harefield NHS Foundation Trust, and NIHR (National Institute for Health and Care Research) Senior Investigator Emeritus.
4 Letter to Marchese Guido Bentivoglio, reproduced in Heller, *Antonio Vivaldi: The Red Priest of Venice*, p. 288.
5 Ibid., p. 287.
6 Anecdotes in Michael Talbot, *Master Musicians: Vivaldi*, fourth (paperback) edition (Oxford: Oxford University Press, 2000), p. 2, and Heller, *Antonio Vivaldi: The Red Priest of Venice*, p. 43.

7 For more on the gap in Vivaldi's employment records see Giuseppe Gullo, 'Antonio Vivaldi's Chronic Illness: Shedding New Light on an Old Enigma', *Studi vivaldiani* No. 22 (Venice: 2022), p. 41.

8 For more information on John Floyer and his work, see Mark Jackson, *Asthma: The Biography* (Oxford: Oxford University Press, 2009), p. 58.

9 John Floyer, *A treatise of the asthma: Divided into four parts* (London: Richard Wilkin, 1698). Source: Wellcome Collection. You can view the complete work online at <https://wellcomecollection. org/works/bkj4pj6g>, accessed 12 March 2024.

10 From Baldassare Monteverdi's letter from Cremona to Duke Vincenzo Gonzaga, 9 November 1608, reproduced in Paolo Fabbri, *Monteverdi*, trans. Tim Carter (Cambridge: Cambridge University Press, 1994), pp. 101–2.

11 John Breval, *Remarks on Several Parts of Europe: Relating Chiefly to Their Antiquities and History. Collected upon the Spot in several Tours since the year 1723; and Illustrated by Upwards of Forty Copper-Plates from Original Drawings* (London, 1738). Sourced via <https:// archive.org/details/bim_eighteenth-century_remarks-on-several- parts_breval-john_1738_1>, accessed 1 October 2024.

12 Jackson, *Asthma: The Biography*, p. 68.

13 Floyer, *A treatise of the asthma*, pp. 67 and 120–5.

14 Any scarring or damage to the lungs after IRDS (Infantile Respiratory Distress Syndrome) is the result of modern interventions, which can create situations worse than leaving the baby alone, as was historically the case. Research shows that infants who survive the first three days of life will recover completely and by seven to ten days of life will have normal lungs radiographically. See W. H. Northway Jr, R. C. Rosan and D. Y. Porter, 'Pulmonary disease following respirator therapy of hyaline-membrane disease. Bronchopulmonary dysplasia', *New England Journal of Medicine*, No. 276, Issue 7 (16 February 1967), pp. 357–68, <doi: 10.1056/NEJM196702162760701>.

15 Giuseppe Gullo's article 'Antonio Vivaldi's Chronic Illness: Shedding New Light on an Old Enigma' is a detailed attempt to conduct a medical trial complete with clinical testing as far as is possible with historical data. Its findings are historically compelling but, according to Andrew's own findings, medically

contentious. The primary problem with Eisenmenger syndrome is usually an uncorrected congenital heart defect which allows some blood to bypass the heart (left-to-right shunt) and flood the lungs. In response, the lung blood vessels constrict, raising the resistance to this shunt flow, which eventually ceases. Then, as the resistance continues to rise, blood shunts the other way. The net result is that low-oxygenated blood is rejected by the lungs and goes straight back to the body, placing a massive strain on the right chamber of the heart, and ultimately causing heart failure and death.

16 The potential complications of Eisenmenger syndrome are wide-reaching. Gullo concedes that had any of these symptoms been understood, bloodletting would have been the likely treatment, which would have made things worse, adding dehydration into the mix.

17 Gullo goes into lots of detail regarding the effect of Eisenmenger syndrome on sexual function, rendering this unlikely relationship between Vivaldi and Girò also non-viable.

18 Marais' piece is referenced in Jackson, *Asthma: The Biography*, p. 68.

19 Jackson, *Asthma: The Biography*, p. 63.

III: Presto

1 The original Italian text reads:

> Ah, che pur troppo i suoi timor son veri
> Tuona e fulmina il Ciel e grandinoso
> Tronca il capo alle spiche e a' grani alteri.

2 Philipp Blom, *Nature's Mutiny: How the Little Ice Age Transformed the West and Shaped the Present* (London: Picador, 2019), pp. 13–18.

3 Ibid., pp. 18–19.

4 Nicholas Lockey, 'Antonio Vivaldi and the sublime seasons: sonority and texture as expressive devices in early eighteenth-century Italian music', in *Eighteenth-Century Music*, Vol. 14, Issue 2 (Cambridge: Cambridge University Press, 2017), p. 275.

5 Holdsworth's letter is reproduced in Michael Talbot, 'Vivaldi's "Manchester Sonatas"', *Proceedings of the Royal Musical Association*, Vol. 104 (1977–8), pp. 20–29, on p. 22 and footnote 9.

6 For more on this, see ibid., pp. 27–8.

7 Daniel's interests in early music have led to projects such as an all-day cycle of Heinrich Biber's *Rosary Sonatas* and his debut album,

Saint Boy (Platoon, 2023), in which ancient and contemporary worlds of sacred and secular music collide. He concluded his 2022/23 residency at London's Southbank Centre with a concert with the musicians of Manchester Camerata that paired Antonio Vivaldi's *Four Seasons* with Gérard Grisey's *Vortex Temporum*.

8 Giovanni Antonio Mauro could even have acted as an amanuensis. See Giuseppe Gullo, 'Antonio Vivaldi's Chronic Illness: Shedding New Light on an Old Enigma', p. 23 and footnote 34.

9 The arguments are outlined in Antonio Vivaldi, *Le quattro stagioni: da Il cimento dell'armonia e dell'inventione op. VIII: per violino principale, due violini, viola e basso*, ed. Paul Everett and Michael Talbot (Milan: Ricordi, 1996), pp. 149–50.

10 For more on this see Michael Talbot, *Master Musicians: Vivaldi*, fourth (paperback) edition (Oxford: Oxford University Press, 2000), pp. 130–1.

11 See Paul Everett, *Vivaldi: The Four Seasons and Other Concertos, Op. 8* (Cambridge: Cambridge University Press, 1996), p. 70.

12 Lockey, 'Antonio Vivaldi and the sublime seasons: sonority and texture as expressive devices in early eighteenth-century Italian music', p. 271.

13 Reproduced by kind permission of Sir Michael Morpurgo.

IV: The Life Cycle of The Four Seasons – *Branching Out*

1 For more information on Vivaldi's publication history up to this point, see Eleanor Selfridge-Field, *Venetian Instrumental Music from Gabrieli to Vivaldi* (Oxford: Basil Blackwell, 1975), pp. 220–1.

2 A review of Vivaldi's music for the wedding of Louis XV to the Polish princess Maria Leszczyńska in *Le Mercure de France*, quoted in Michael Talbot, *Master Musicians: Vivaldi*, fourth (paperback) edition (Oxford: Oxford University Press, 2000), p. 54.

3 Vivaldi's dedication can be read on the digitised parts (pdfs) available at IMSLP (International Music Score Library Project) <https://imslp.org/wiki/L%27estro_armonico,_Op.3_(Vivaldi,_Antonio)>, accessed 24 May 2025.

4 For more details see Samuel F. Pogue, rev. Rudolf A. Rasch, 'Roger, Estienne', Grove Music Online (published 2001). Accessed 29 Jan. 2025, from <https://www.oxfordmusiconline.com/

grovemusic/view/10.1093/gmo/9781561592630.001.0001/omo-
9781561592630-e-0000023665>.

5 All quotes from the dedication from Paul Everett, *Vivaldi: The
Four Seasons and Other Concertos, Op. 8* (Cambridge: Cambridge
University Press, 1996), p. 9.

6 Michael Talbot 'Wenzel von Morzin as a Patron of Antonio
Vivaldi', in Michael Talbot (ed.), *Vivaldi* (London: Routledge, 2017),
pp. 125–33. Substantial payments sent to Mantua from Morzin's
bankers, the firm of Franz Sigk and Del Curto, began in April
1719, and continued to be paid over the next decade, exchanged
into local currency when Vivaldi returned to Venice. Talbot
draws an even closer connection between this op. 8 Amsterdam
publication and Morzin's accounting, suggesting that part of the
extremely generous renumeration could have formed the *regalo* for
the collection. A *regalo* was the term for the subsidy that a dedicatee
was honour-bound to give an author for a publication. This could
either be cash, or a valuable object, such as a work of art.

7 Everett, *Vivaldi: The Four Seasons and Other Concertos, Op. 8*, p. 9.

PART THREE: AUTUMN
I: *Allegro*

1 The original Italian text reads:

> Celebra il Vilanel con balli e Canti
> Del felice raccolto il bel piacere
> E del liquor de Bacco accesi tanti
> Finiscono col sonno il lor godere.

2 Stefano suggests that Monteverdi's *Orfeo* was perhaps played on
the ground floor of Margherita Gonzaga d'Este's apartment, or the
'Camera Imperiale', there is no definitive location.

3 It's worth noting that Monteverdi's music room, a hexagonal
space watched over by frescoes of musical angels, still exists. It's an
area currently closed to the public and under reconstruction, both
to preserve it and to help people try to imagine how it might have
looked and sounded before a giant bricked-off staircase was built
through it in the eighteenth century, potentially ruling it out as a
place enjoyed by Vivaldi.

4 Quoted in Karl Heller, *Antonio Vivaldi: The Red Priest of Venice*
(Portland, Oregon: Amadeus Press, 1997), p. 56.

II: *Adagio molto*

1 The original Italian text reads:

> Fà ch' ogn'uno tralasci e balli e canti
> L' aria che temperata dà piacere,
> E la Staggion ch'invita tanti e tanti
> D'un dolcissimo Sonno al bel godere.

2 Paul Everett, *Vivaldi: The Four Seasons and Other Concertos, Op. 8* (Cambridge: Cambridge University Press, 1996), p. 5.

3 Karl Heller, *Antonio Vivaldi: The Red Priest of Venice* (Portland, Oregon: Amadeus Press, 1997), p. 13. See the first chapter in Heller's book for a detailed description of the various events surrounded the re-discovery of Vivaldi.

4 Ibid., pp. 14–15.

5 Arnold Schering, *Geschichte des Instrumentalkonzerts bis auf die Gegenwart* (Leipzig: Breitkopf & Härtel, 1905), p. 60, quoted in Heller, *Antonio Vivaldi: The Red Priest of Venice*, p. 15.

6 Wilhelm Altmann published the catalogue. See Michael Talbot, *Master Musicians: Vivaldi*, fourth (paperback) edition (Oxford: Oxford University Press, 2000), p. 5.

7 For the full story see Heller, *Antonio Vivaldi: The Red Priest of Venice*, pp. 17–18.

8 For a broader discussion of the Durazzo family inheritance and full details on Soranzo see Talbot, *Master Musicians: Vivaldi*, pp. 6–7.

III: *Allegro*

1 The original Italian text reads:

> I cacciator alla nov'alba à caccia
> Con corni, schioppi, e cani escono fuore
> Fugge la belva, e seguono la traccia;
> Già sbigottita, e lassa al gran rumore
> De' schioppi e cani, ferita minaccia
> Languida di fuggir, mà oppressa muore.

2 A solemn procession followed the service – the first of fifteen processions held on successive Saturdays, in which the clergy carried the republic's most venerated image of Mary, the Madonna Nicopeia, around St Mark's Square. See Andrew Hopkins, 'Plans and Planning for S. Maria della Salute, Venice', in *The Art Bulletin*,

Vol. 79, No. 3 (September 1997), p. 440. This article sets out the full details of the relationship of the building to the events of 1630. See also Andrew Hopkins, 'The Influence of Ducal Ceremony on Church Design in Venice', in *Architectural History*, Vol. 41 (1998), pp. 30–48.

3 See Rosie Razzall and Lucy Whitaker, *Canaletto & the Art of Venice* (London: Royal Collection Trust, 2017), pp. 174–7.

4 James H. Moore, '"Venezia favorita da Maria": Music for the Madonna Nicopeia and Santa Maria della Salute', in *Journal of the American Musicological Society*, Vol. 37, No. 2 (Summer 1984), p. 350.

5 Ibid., pp. 326–55, especially pp. 353–4.

6 Each Italian city has a public holiday in honour of its patron saint, but as St Mark's Day was already a holiday to mark the Second World War's Liberation Day, the Venetians added Santa Maria della Salute to their calendar in the late 1940s.

IV The Life Cycle of The Four Seasons – *Fruits and Flowers*

1 Louis Kaufman, *A Fiddler's Tale: How Hollywood and Vivaldi Discovered Me* (Madison: University of Wisconsin Press, 2003), p. 194.

2 Ibid.

3 However, Kaufman wasn't finished with Vivaldi: in the fading light of 1947 he'd read Alfred Einstein's programme notes for the recording, which explained that *The Four Seasons* were the first four concertos of op. 8. This set him on a quest to find the rest, one that ended in the Royal Conservatory of Brussels library and resulted not only in his 1950 recording being the first of Vivaldi's complete op. 8, but also in his becoming known as an exponent of eighteenth-century Italian Baroque music. He championed Vivaldi's op. 3 and op. 9, before seeking out more manuscripts by the likes of Benedetto Marcello, Arcangelo Corelli and Giuseppe Torelli, while maintaining his lifelong love for Bach and Handel. There is considerable detail of Kaufman's escapades on the trail of Vivaldi and his popularisation of the composer's works in *A Fiddler's Tale*: see pp. 188–95, 219–29, 245, 254, 298–312.

4 Paul Everett, *Vivaldi: The Four Seasons and Other Concertos, Op. 8* (Cambridge: Cambridge University Press, 1996), p. 1 and footnote 1. 'Nineteen per year' included arrangements and re-releases.

5 Nigel Kennedy, *Uncensored!* (Stroud: Fonthill Media, 2021).

6 Ibid., p. 54.

7 All quotes in this paragraph ibid., p. 56.

8 Ibid., p 57.

9 For more details on the recording process, you can listen to Nigel Kennedy talking to John Wilson for *Mastertapes*, series 5 (sourced via BBC Archives). The A-Side: <https://www.bbc.co.uk/sounds/play/b06ybnh5> and the B-Side <https://www.bbc.co.uk/sounds/play/b06ycr4s>, both accessed 4 November 2024.

10 Kennedy, *Uncensored!*, p. 57.

Part Four: Winter
I: *Allegro non molto*

1 The original Italian text reads:

> Agghiacciato tremar trà nevi algenti
> Al severo spirar d'orrido Vento,
> Correr battendo i piedi ogni momento;
> E pel soverchio gel batter i denti

2 Dario Camuffo, Chiara Bertolin, Alberto Craievich, Rossella Granziero and Silvia Enzi, 'When the Lagoon was frozen over in Venice from A.D. 604 to 2012: evidence from written documentary sources, visual arts and instrumental readings' (2017) <https://doi.org/10.4000/mediterranee.7983>, paragraph 108. Accessed 8 January 2014.

3 Ibid.

4 Ibid., paragraphs 50–6.

5 Ibid., paragraph 140.

6 Eleonora Sovrani and Jane da Mosto, *Acqua in piazza: Livelli d'acqua a Venezia. Tendenze e addattamenti* (Venice: Lineadacqua edizioni, 2016), p. 45.

7 See Frank Viviano, 'Saving Venice from flooding may destroy the ecosystem that sustains it', *National Geographic* (25 July 2022) <https://www.nationalgeographic.com/environment/article/saving-venice-from-flooding-may-destroy-the-ecosystem-that-sustains-it#:~:text=A%20system%20of%20moveable>, accessed 9 January 2024.

8 'A climate resilient Venice: how to meet the challenge', a study by the CMCC (the Centro Euro-Mediterraneo sui Cambiamenti Climatici (Mediterranean Centre on Climate Change)) Foundation and Ca'Foscari University Venice (27 May 2022) <https://www.

cmcc.it/article/a-climate-resilient-venice-how-to-meet-the-challenge>, accessed 9 January 2024.

9 A 2021 report published by the European Geosciences Union puts Venice's worse-case scenario for sea-level rise by the end of the century at a whopping 120 centimetres. For full details on the MOSE project see <https://www.mosevenezia.eu/project/?lang=en>, accessed 9 January 2024.

10 Viviano, 'Saving Venice from flooding may destroy the ecosystem that sustains it', *National Geographic* (25 July 2022).

11 Ibid.

12 Cristiano Gasparetto is widely quoted saying this, in the *New York Times*, *Smithsonian Magazine*, and various websites including <https://www.ecowatch.com/venice-flood-barrier-2648098487.html>, accessed 9 January 2024.

13 Alberto Nardi cited in Eleonora Sovrani and Jane da Mosto, *Acqua in piazza: Livelli d'acqua a Venezia. Tendenze e addattamenti*, p. 9.

14 The work of We Are Here Venice and the specific mission of Vital can be read about here: <https://www.v-i-t-a-l.org/en/about>, accessed 9 January 2024.

II: Largo

1 The original Italian text reads:

> Passar al foco i dì quieti e contenti
> Mentre la pioggia fuor bagna ben cento.

2 Karl Heller, *Antonio Vivaldi: The Red Priest of Venice* (Portland, Oregon: Amadeus Press, 1997), p. 157.

3 There is a record of the Pietà governors rejecting an offer to buy concertos from Vivaldi in April 1740, but also further evidence that they bought twenty a month later.

4 For more detail on Vivaldi's death see Giuseppe Gullo, 'Antonio Vivaldi's Chronic Illness: Shedding New Light on an Old Enigma', Studi vivaldiani No. 22 (Venice: 2022), p. 36.

5 Arcimboldo had been court portraitist to Ferdinand I at the Habsburg court in Vienna in 1562, and later court decorator and costume designer to Maximilian II and his son Rudolf II at the court in Prague.

6 Only *Summer* and *Winter* survive from the original set and hang in the Kunsthistorisches Museum in Vienna. Both figures look to

the right (*Spring* and *Autumn* looked left), and while *Summer* is an animated young woman with cherry lips, cucumber nose, aubergine ear and dress of straw, *Winter* is, as you might expect, the exact opposite. The male figure is composed of a single object, a tree – its twisted, gnarly, warty roots representing older, wrinkled, more fragile skin. He has something of a weary grimace, with a mushroom for a mouth and wispy whiskers. Winter ivy wraps around his head, which has only a little hair left, and the lemons at the nape of his neck represent the last fruits of the year, ripe to be preserved over the cold season.

7 Rosalba Carriera's seasonal pastels proved hugely popular, and she made several versions of the female allegorical figures. A set in the Royal Collection Trust gives a good sense of her universal approach throughout the 1720s–40s. *Spring* is personified as a young, blonde woman swathed loosely in yellow and white fabric; she has flowers in her hair and is receiving more bright blooms from a cherub. Come the portrait of *Summer*, blue is the dominant hue – both the colour of the paper itself, suggesting the sky behind blurred trees, and the shawl around a youthful brunette who reaches for a basket of fruit. *Autumn* also shows fruits, as a woman, naked from the waist up but surrounded by brown fabrics, ribbons and pearls, holds a basket of fruit from which a cherub has picked up a bunch of grapes. In *Winter*, a young woman gives a knowing look as she clasps an ermine-fur-trimmed wrap across her bare chest; the pastel pigments that have lived under the protection of the frame over the centuries reveal that there were once bright fuchsia notes to the fabrics she wears.

III: *Allegro*

1 The original Italian text reads:

> Caminar sopra 'l giaccio, e à passo lento
> Per timor di cader girsene intenti;
> Gir forte[,] sdruzziolar, cader à terra
> Di nuove ir sopra 'l giaccio e correr forte
> Sin ch' il giaccio si rompe, e si disserra;
> Sentir uscir dalle ferrate porte
> Sirocco[,] Borea, e tutti i Venti in guerra
> Quest' é 'l verno, mà tal, che gioia apporte.

2 For more on the climatic, social, and economic impact of the Little Ice Age see Philipp Blom, *Nature's Mutiny: How the Little Ice Age Transformed the West and Shaped the Present* (London: Picador, 2019); Dagomar Degroot, *The Frigid Golden Age: Climate Change, the Little Ice Age, and the Dutch Republic, 1560–1720* (Cambridge: Cambridge University Press, 2018) and Brian Fagan, *The Little Ice Age: How Climate Made History 1300–1850* (New York: Basic Books, 2000).

3 The year 1708 in both titles is no mistake. Until the fall of the Venetian Republic in 1797, the Venetians eschewed the Gregorian calendar that we use today, rather following the ancient Roman custom of the year beginning on 1 March, a system they called *More veneto*.

4 An old miser with a crooked nose dressed in red and black, he caricatured the city's merchants, and his name also referred to the phrase *pianta leone*: lion planting, the Venetian practice of erecting a tall pillar with a lion atop in all the main squares of the towns they annexed to the Republic.

IV: The Life Cycle of The Four Seasons *– Scattering New Seeds*

1 Karl Aage Rasmussen, 'After Vivaldi', trans. by John Irons: liner notes for *The Four Seasons After Vivaldi* (Copenhagen: Dacapo Records, 2019).

2 Ibid.

3 Tom Service, 'Max Richter spring-cleans Vivaldi's *The Four Seasons*', *Guardian* (Sunday 21 October 2012) <https://www.theguardian.com/music/2012/oct/21/max-richter-vivaldi-four-seasons>, accessed 6 February 2024.

4 Ibid.

5 Ibid.

6 Ibid.

7 Ibid.

8 Max Richter talking to Clemency Burton-Hill, from his website <https://www.maxrichter-fourseasons.com/uk/products/the-new-four-seasons-digipack-bookle---12-.html.>, accessed 6 February 2024.

9 Philip Glass in his liner notes to *Violin Concerto No.2 – The American Four Seasons* (Orange Mountain Music, 2010), also at <https://philipglass.com/recordings/american4seasons/>, accessed 13 February 2024.

10 You can explore more and listen here: <https://the-uncertain-four-seasons.info/experience>, accessed 13 February 2024.

Epilogue: The Legacy of The Four Seasons
1 James Thomson, 'Hymn', in *The Seasons* (originally published 1730, this edition London: Charles Whittingham, 1822), p. 155.
2 See David Johnson, 'Barber, Robert (ii)', Grove Music Online (published 2001) <https://www.oxfordmusiconline.com/grovemusic/view/10.1093/gmo/9781561592630.001.0001/omo-9781561592630-e-0000001993>, accessed 24 May 2025.
3 Newspaper report submitted to Moscow and St Petersburg, *Moskovskie vedomosti*, No. 40 (18 May 1801), quoted in H. C. Robbins Landon, *Haydn: the Late Years 1801–1809* (London: Thames and Hudson, 1977), p. 42.
4 An extensive criticism written in the widely read *Journal des Luxus und der Moden*, dated 10 June 1801, quoted in Landon, *Haydn: the Late Years 1801–1809*, p. 46.

Postlude
1 Maximilien Misson, *A New Voyage to Italy* (London, 1714), reproduced in Daniele Lucchini, *Rise and fall of a capital. The history of Mantua in the words of those who wrote about it* (Finisterrae, 2014; Kindle edition).

More Seasonal Listening
1 Translation by Francis Browne <https:/www.bachcantatas.com/Texts/BWV11-Eng3.htm>
2 Bruce Wood, 'Daniel Purcell: The Judgement of Paris', sleeve note to CD (Resonus Limited, 2014 RE10128)